The German language in a changing Europe

MICHAEL G. CLYNE
Monash University, Australia

CAMBRIDGE
UNIVERSITY PRESS

Published by the Press Syndicate of the University of Cambridge
The Pitt Building, Trumpington Street, Cambridge CB2 1RP
40 West 20th Street, New York, NY 10011-4211, USA
10 Stamford Road, Oakleigh, Melbourne 3166, Australia

The German language in a changing Europe succeeds and replaces *Language and
society in the German-speaking countries*, published by Cambridge University Press
in 1984 (hardback 0 521 25759 X; paperback 0 521 27697 7)

First published 1995

Printed in Great Britain at the University Press, Cambridge

A catalogue record for this book is available from the British Library

Library of Congress cataloguing in publication data

Clyne, Michael G., 1939–
    The German language in a changing Europe / Michael G. Clyne.
        p.   cm.
    Includes bibliographical references and index.
ISBN 0 521 46269 X (hardback). – ISBN 0 521 49970 4 (paperback)
        1. German language–Social aspects.   2. German language–Dialects.
    3. Sociolinguistics.   4. German language–Europe, German-speaking.
    I. Title.
    PF3073.C54   1995
    430–dc20   94-44585
                                                                        CIP

ISBN 0 521 46269 X hardback
ISBN 0 521 49970 4 paperback

SE

CONTENTS

Recent sociopolitical events have profoundly changed the status and functions of German and influenced its usage. In this study, Michael Clyne revises and expands his original analysis of the German language (in *Language and society in the German-speaking countries*) in the light of such changes as the end of the cold war, German unification, the redrawing of the map of Europe, increasing European integration, and the changing self-images of Austria, Switzerland and Luxembourg. His discussion includes the differences in the form, function and status of the various national varieties of German; the relation between standard and non-standard varieties; gender-related, generational and political variation; Anglo-American influence on German; and the convergence of East and West. The result is a wide-ranging exploration of language and society in the German-speaking countries, all of which have problems or dilemmas concerning nationhood or ethnicity which are language-related and/or language-marked.

The German language
in a changing Europe

MAPS AND TABLES

Maps

Tables

ACKNOWLEDGEMENTS

My thanks are due to all those who provided me with information for this monograph, including those colleagues who sent me publications and preprints and/or provided me with insights and ideas during stimulating conversations, the German and Austrian political parties, the Consulate-General of the Federal Republic of Germany in Melbourne, the Austrian ambassador in Australia, Stephan Toth, those in the German-language countries who answered my many questions, Lee Kersten, Klaus Mattheier and Gerhard Klein, who arranged for some interviews in Eisenach. I also wish to express my thanks to my research assistants, Theresa Wallner, who helped with data collection and analysis, and Melissa Rogerson, who assisted with the bibliography and the presentation of the manuscript, to Sue Fernandez for compiling the index, and to the Australian Research Council for a grant for the project The German Language in a Changing Europe. I am also indebted to Stephen Barbour, who read the manuscript and suggested numerous improvements, to those who read and commented on some sections – Leslie Bodi (Chapters 1–3), Heinz Kreutz (Chapter 3), Rudolf Muhr (the Austrian part of Chapter 2), Anne Pauwels (the gender part of Chapter 6), Horst-Dieter Schlosser (Chapter 3), Gerald Newton (the Luxembourg part of Chapter 2), Richard Watts (the Swiss part of Chapter 2) and an anonymous referee, and to those who made helpful comments on *Language and society in the German-speaking countries*, especially Ulrich Ammon, Werner Besch, Manfred Hellmann, Rudi Keller, Hermann Scheuringer and the late Broder Carstensen. The responsibility for the remaining shortcomings, of course, rests with me. I record my thanks to Langenscheidt for permission to reproduce Map 2 from the *Kleine Enzyklopädie deutsche Sprache*, to the Monash University Department of Geography for redrawing the maps, to the Institut für deutsche Sprache, Mannheim, for putting its library and other facilities at my disposal a number of times, and to colleagues at Cambridge University Press for their kind co-operation.

Map 1   Places mentioned in the text.

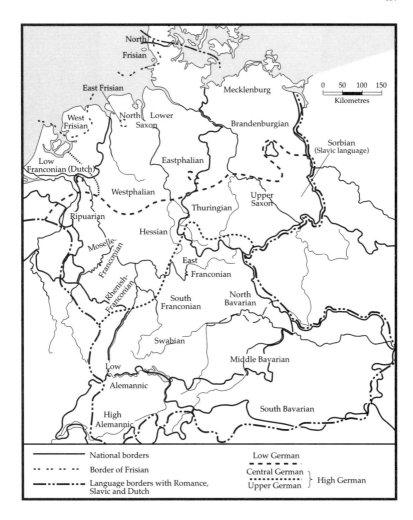

Map 2   German, Dutch and Frisian dialects, *c.* 1965 (H. Protze), based on Fleischer (1983: 411).

Introduction

This book is intended as an introduction to the sociolinguistic situation in those countries in which German has the status of a national language, with some consideration of those in which it has regional official status. Because a language is an index of the cultures and societies of its users, the monograph may be of value to German Studies and European Studies programmes as well as to students of sociolinguistics and to teachers and students of German. It supersedes *Language and society in the German-speaking countries* (1984). Momentous sociopolitical changes have taken place since the appearance of that monograph. I am referring not only to the end of the cold war and the unification of Germany, but also to changes in the self-images of Austria, Switzerland and Luxembourg expressed in language use and language planning, the 'redrawing of the map of Europe', influencing the use and status of German as an international language, and internal sociopolitical changes within the various countries, e.g. relating to the status of women.

The publication, in 1990, of Stephen Barbour's and Patrick Stevenson's *Variation in German* has given us a comprehensive and complementary text which is a critical and contrastive account, devoted specifically to variation, written from the context of Anglo-American sociolinguistic research. This abrogates the necessity to add such a perspective which was absent from my 1984 publication (Barbour 1985). The present monograph, like its predecessor, offers an interpretative synthesis of local studies of the relation between language and society in the German-language countries, complemented by some of my data, to present a coherent picture. The findings of much recent research have been incorporated into this book. The references in brackets (according to social science conventions) are meant to direct the reader to the source of the information. Translations are given for the benefit of those with limited German, and a glossary of some linguistic terminology employed is intended for Germanists and other readers with little training in linguistics. Some of

the studies used as a basis employ linguistic methods set in a social context while others employ sociological methods to research broader questions of language behaviour, policy and attitudes. The enormity of the subject matter renders it impossible to deal with every topic relating to each German-language country. Some areas have been investigated much less than others and can be treated only cursorily in this book. The recent speed of change means that some findings are only indicative, being based on very sketchy or preliminary data, and in some cases anecdotal and impressionistic. They are included here to stimulate discussion and research.

The study of the sociolinguistics of German is a rewarding one, for it offers the opportunity of comparing the same language in action in societies with different historical and cultural traditions. It also enables us to assess the effects on a language of political division and the attempts to eradicate these effects in a short period. Because of the diversity of German in Europe – international but not to the same extent as English, with a presence in both Eastern and Western Europe, pluricentric and in some areas competing with a rising L language and/or another H language (see below, 1.2) – there are many dimensions that may have more universal relevance.

To prevent the scope of this book from extending to unmanageable dimensions, I shall exclude from consideration minority languages of ethnic or migrant groups in German-language countries. For these topics, the reader is referred to the relevant sections of Barbour and Stevenson (1990).

1

The status of German in contemporary Europe

1.1   The contemporary language situation in Europe

The language situation in Europe today is driven by two seemingly contradictory tendencies – tendencies towards what Fishman (1971) terms 'massification' and 'diversification' – which are operating simultaneously. Examples of massification are open economic borders between member countries of the European Union (then European Community) as from January 1993 and the enlargement of the Union to include Austria, Sweden, Norway, and Finland in 1995, and the development of an expanded European Economic Region progressively to include former Soviet Bloc countries, all of which could have homogenizing effects on language and culture. On the other hand, diversification is exemplified in the resurgence of regions in Western Europe and the re-emergence of smaller, largely language-based, nation-states in Central and Eastern Europe to replace the multinational empire of the USSR and the multinational political entities of Yugoslavia and Czechoslovakia. The language-based nature of these nation-states brings to the fore longstanding ethnolinguistic tensions and disputes over minority rights which may result in new post-Communist nations of Central and Eastern Europe splitting up into more and more separate entities.

But alongside this diversification, we see the opening up of nations and groups which have been closed to half of Europe and much of the rest of the world for over forty years. This has brought the challenges of communicating with other peoples in a range of contexts.

Another aspect of diversification is the legal strengthening of regional and ethnic minority languages through the passing of the Charter of Regional and Minority Languages by the Council of Europe member states in 1993. This affords ethnic minorities and regional groups (but not migrant workers) the right that their language be used in administration,

education, the media, care of the aged, and communication across national boundaries.

In this chapter, we will discuss this in relation to the status and functions of German as a medium of inter-cultural communication (see below, 1.4.2 and 1.4.3). This needs to be considered with regard to four questions: the present status of German; the competition with other languages, notably English, the language situation in the European Union, and the future of multilingualism in Europe. But first let us survey the countries in which German has national or regional official status.

1.2   The German-language countries

German is the mother tongue of over 94 million people divided among a number of different countries. It has official (or quasi-official) status in five. In each of these it appears in a different form and has different functions. Each nation has its own variety of Standard German with which its people identify, as well as regional and local varieties, whose status and relation to Standard German will be discussed in later chapters.

The countries with German as an official (or *de facto* official) language are:

Germany   81 million users of whom 65.3 million live in the western states and 15.7 million live in the eastern states. Although the former GDR was incorporated into the Federal Republic of Germany in October 1990, the process of unification is not complete in practice, as we shall see in Chapter 3.

Austria   7.5 million users. The old centre of Central Europe, Austria has maintained cultural links with the surrounding newly independent non-German-language nations, even during the time when most of them belonged to the Soviet Bloc and Austria pursued a policy of active political neutrality (i.e. even-handed politics, rather than non-involvement, see also 6.3.2). It has undergone a separate development from Protestant North Germany since the Reformation and from the Prussian-dominated 'ethnically based' nation-state of Germany ('*Kleindeutschland*') in the nineteenth century. Since becoming an independent republic for the second time in 1955, Austria has developed into a highly industrialized welfare state and has derived self-esteem and a new national awareness from its economic prosperity (low unemployment and a relatively low inflation rate). In 1995, Austria became a member of the European Union.

Switzerland   A nation with official national multilingualism (German, French, Italian and, at the regional level, also Rhaeto-

Romansh), Switzerland has its languages distributed on a territorial principle, i.e. most cantons are monolingual, a few are bilingual, and one, Graubünden, is trilingual (in German, Italian, and Rhaeto-Romansh). According to Dürmüller (1991: 115), only 6.2% of the Swiss actually grow up multilingually, most of them not in the German-language area. However, almost all Swiss acquire some competence in one of the other languages of Switzerland at school (Dürmüller 1991: 126–7). The 4.2 million German users (about 74% of Swiss citizens and 65% of inhabitants of Switzerland) were thought to provide us with a classic example of what Ferguson (1959) terms 'diglossia' – a language situation in which two different languages or varieties are functionally complementary. In this case Standard German (the 'High' language, hereafter H) fulfils written and formal spoken functions, while the other, a dialect (the 'Low' language, hereafter L), is used for informal ones. But as we shall see in Chapter 2, L is intruding into some previous domains of H. This is having negative effects on relations between the language groups. German speakers are over-represented in the bureaucracy (Hauck 1993: 156) and draft legislation is available only in German and French. Public servants communicate by speaking their own language and understanding at least one other (Hauck 1993: 151).

Switzerland has enjoyed longstanding economic prosperity and political neutrality. It practises grassroots democracy deriving from the survival of feudal and early capitalist structures into the modern age, something that often appears parochial.

Luxembourg The population of 372,000 use Lëtzebuergesch, German and French in a functionally complementary relationship[1] (see 2.7). Through language planning, i.e. the development of a policy on the use and standardization of languages, the dialect of Luxembourg, Lëtzebuergesch (Luxembourgian) has been assigned some of the functions of a standard language. Luxembourg has maintained many traits of a nineteenth-century German duchy with a small bureaucracy and an inherent conservatism. But it has, for centuries, enjoyed an intermediate position between the French and German spheres of influence and now has a strong attachment to the European Union. It acts as host to its parliament and court and to several of its agencies. In 1993 it was the richest country (per capita) in the European Union.

Liechtenstein 15,000 users. Liechtenstein is a tiny principality of a predominantly rural character without an airport. It is sandwiched

---

[1] There are, among them, about 62,500 foreign-born, some of whom have great difficulty adapting to the complex situation.

between Austria and Switzerland and has assumed the function of a tax haven for many business companies. Liechtenstein has had a customs union with Switzerland since 1923 but, unlike Switzerland, voted in favour of membership of the European Economic Region in December 1992.

In addition, German now enjoys regional official status in some eastern parts of Belgium (130,000 German speakers) and South Tyrol (200,000 German speakers, part of Italy), and an emerging special status in Alsace-Lorraine (1.5 million, part of France). In Namibia (once German South West Africa), there are still some state schools employing German as a medium of instruction, but English is being developed as the only official language. Furthermore, German is spoken as an ethnic minority language in Hungary, Romania, parts of the Russian Federation, and in the US, Canada, Australia, Brazil, Colombia and other immigrant countries.

1.3   German in Eastern and Western Europe

The German language has undergone a marked decline in significance in Western Europe and the world. Part of this is due to the unparalleled popularity of English – seen variously as the language of the liberators from Fascism and of resistance to Communism, the language of technological and economic progress, and the language of protest, ecological renewal and youth solidarity. Conversely, part of the decline of German can be attributed to the atrocities committed by Nazi Germany, which were linked with the language not only subjectively in the eyes and ears of the oppressed, but objectively through the use of German by the occupation forces in the execution of oppression and genocide.

The situation in Eastern and Central Europe was somewhat different in so far as there had been a more recent occupying power or dominating force using another language, Russian, as an instrument of oppression and dominance. In this region, the antithesis was provided by German and English – in quite different ways – English as the language of *ultimate* hope (especially in the younger generation), for the liberation which occurred in 1989–90 was not anticipated, and German for more immediate and practical purposes. German, as the language of the GDR, was not sanctioned as an 'enemy (or suspect) language' in the Eastern Bloc as English was, but it did give access to the capitalist world, its scientific and technological developments, and, for the lucky few, a language for the place of escape, usually the Federal Republic, Austria or Switzerland.

It was popularly believed that, with the collapse and dissolution of the

Soviet Union, the vacuum created for a lingua franca to replace Russian, the compulsory language used officially but liked and mastered by few, would be replaced by German. This was because German had been the second language of the cultured and influential middle class in Central and Eastern Europe before the Second World War (and even more so before the First World War when many of the countries were part of the Austro-Hungarian Empire) and because the language did enjoy some continuing use and interest in the days of the communist régimes. Since the political upheavals there has been a renewal of the concept of 'Central Europe' (*Mitteleuropa*), which had been bypassed during the division of Europe into East and West. Banac (1990: 253) describes 'Central Europe' as a 'cultural network strongly connected with Vienna'. It has a mythology centring on tolerance and cultural pluralism but with German playing a link role. Central Europe is generally defined to include Austria, Croatia, the Czech Republic, Hungary, Poland, Slovakia, Slovenia and probably Northern Italy. It may also include Germany, and, since unification, Germany is clearly playing an important role in the link between East and West. The 'new world order' of the late 1980s was based largely on the notion of regional co-operation. This brought to the fore co-operative networks such as the Adria-Alpine consisting of Austria, Croatia, Hungary, Northern Italy, Slovenia and the then Czechoslovakia.

German did attract some increased use and favour as a school language, but the interest in English was not fully anticipated in Germany. It is particularly in multilingual and multicultural areas of Central and Eastern Europe that the position of German shows signs of revitalization. This includes Transylvania (in Romania), Galicia (Ukraine), parts of Slovakia, and East Prussia, a former German-speaking area from which Germans were forced to emigrate when it became part of Russia after the Second World War and which has now become geographically separated from Russia. (East Prussia is re-emerging as a free trading zone.)

1.4   The current status of German in Europe

1.4.1   Factors determining the status of German

In considering the actual situation of German today, let us discuss the factors that give a language an international status. Ammon (1991) makes the useful distinction between a lingua franca and an 'asymmetrically dominant' language. German is a lingua franca when Hungarians and Slovaks communicate with each other in it. It is an 'asymmetrically

dominant' language when Hungarians or Slovaks use it to communicate with German speakers and German speakers do not learn Hungarian or Slovak to communicate with speakers of those languages. As a generic term for both categories I will employ 'language of inter-cultural communication' (LICC). Ammon (1991) offers the beginnings of a quantitative method to assess this. Indicators include (i) the size of the 'mother tongue community' internationally and in the country concerned, (ii) the number of countries using the language officially, (iii) their economic strength, (iv) the size of the community employing the language as a foreign language, and (v) 'communicative events' in the language, including radio programmes, academic publications, and number of citations from academic publications in the language. Of a range of measurable and immeasurable factors discussed by Kloss (1974) as determining the international status of a language, Kloss places at the top the number of people who are learning or have learned it as foreign language speakers of other languages. This is followed by the use of the language in international conferences and organizations, and the number of books translated from it. Coulmas (1991, 1993) has given much attention to the economic value of a language, a question of great importance when it comes to status. He has singled out five factors of paramount importance in language status, whether for a national or an international language:

(i) communication radius
(ii) functional potential of the language
(iii) investment in the language
(iv) demand for the language as an economic commodity
(v) what the language can on balance achieve for the language community

The value of German can be gauged by the fact that about 19 million people throughout the world are learning the language, including 12 million in 'Eastern Europe', 6.2 million of them in Russia (Schirmer 1993, Kowar 1992, Domaschnew 1993a, Földes 1993). Kowar (1992) makes the point that Germany and Austria will be the two prime movers that Central and European countries will use to gain them entry into the European Union.

The case for German is strengthened by the number of speakers, economic argument and traditional cultural links, but this has to be offset against the perpetuating of negative stereotypes (Born 1993: 164ff.), a factor that is continually made by German researchers (see also Ammon 1991).

1.4.2   The actual position of German in various domains in Europe today

In terms of Ammon's and Coulmas's factors, the following points need to be made:

(i) Numbers   The 94 million native speakers of German in Europe put the language second in Europe after Russian (with 115 million) and well ahead of English with 58 million and French with 62 million native speakers in Europe. The communication radius which a knowledge of German reaches is, however, rather limited, compared with that of English (320 million native speakers throughout the world), French (90 million) and Spanish (300 million), all of which are spoken on several continents. There are five countries of Europe with German as a national official language and three others where it has regional official status (see 1.2). English has official status in only two European countries and French in five, of which one (Monaco) has recently declared its Italian variety (Monégasque) the official language (Magocsi 1993), making France the only European nation with French as its only language. German has sole official language status in three countries.

(ii) Functional potential   German has been developed to cope with almost every conceivable domain and field of knowledge. For example, German is used in the Engineering Faculty of the Technical University of Sofia (Bulgaria), and in a number of faculties of some Turkish universities. (But see 1.4.6 for a discussion of German's declining role as an international academic language.) It is in the area of computer technology that it has been left behind, with software and e-mail networks mainly in English.

Ammon's (1991) study of German as a language of academic publications suggests that virtually no one outside the German-language countries still publishes in German in the natural sciences. There is, however, substantial reception of German-language scientific publications, restricted to Europe and strongest in Central and Eastern Europe. German trails both English and French in many humanities and social sciences. Even in the universities of German-language countries, German has been overtaken by English in many such disciplines, still leading only in Law, Literature, Classics, History and Theology, and tying in Linguistics. 'Applied' sciences use more German than 'pure' sciences. At the time of Ammon's research, 1989–90, East German and Eastern European scholars used the most German, presumably because of the GDR's technical supremacy in the Eastern Bloc (Ammon 1991: 212–26).

German is not even recognized as an official language of the United

Nations and its organizations, and in comparison with French and particularly English, it plays a limited role as a conference and organizational language in the academic fields (Ammon 1991: 242–51, Skudlik 1990). Nevertheless, German is sometimes one of the conference languages of international conferences held in Germany, and East Germans are more likely than West Germans to read conference papers in German (Ammon 1991: 249).

   (iii) Economic aspects   The German-language countries are still economically very strong. Switzerland and Luxembourg are, per capita, the wealthiest countries of Europe (*Mannheimer Morgen*, 31 December 1993/1 January 1994, p.9). The German economy is, in spite of recession, the strongest in Europe, the one on which most other countries are dependent. German is, after English and Japanese, the language of the economically most powerful language community (Ammon 1991: 151). However, there is a tendency for German businesses to communicate with other countries in foreign languages, notably English and French (Ammon 1991: 170) and for the periodicals of German chambers of commerce in other countries to be partly or wholly in a language other than German (Ammon 1991: 174). However, within Europe, German emerges from Ammon's data as an asymmetrically dominant language. With the political changes, there was a dramatic rise in the number of Japanese business people learning German in Goethe Institutes (Alois Ilg, personal communication). Tourism, a major industry in Austria, Switzerland and parts of Germany (Ammon 1991: 333–7), and the need to provide for German tourists in other countries (Ammon 1991: 337–42) have promoted the German language. It should be noted, however, that the old Federal Republic had the most negative balance of trade in tourism of any European country (Ammon 1991: 337).

   (iv) Investment in the language   German is traditionally taught and studied as a foreign language in the schools and universities of many other countries (Ammon 1991: 423–41, 462–7). Germany is one of the main countries putting economic resources into the propagation of its language and culture through institutions such as the Goethe Institute and the Deutscher Akademischer Austauschdienst (DAAD, German Academic Exchange Service). The Goethe Institute promotes the learning and teaching of German as a foreign language as well as German culture through courses, lectures, exhibitions, teacher training and upgrading in co-operation with institutions in its centres in Germany and many other countries. The DAAD furthers academic exchange between Germany and other countries through scholarships and lecture tours as well as through the appointment of German lecturers at univer-

sities in other countries. Of 481 such lectureships, 281 are in Europe. Both bodies have recently been required by the German Government to reappraise their priorities and to transfer more resources to Eastern and Central Europe. It has been estimated (Germany 1992) that there was, in 1992, a shortfall of between 10,000 and 12,000 German teachers in Poland and 6,000 and 8,000 in the then Czechoslovakia. This is being redressed gradually by the sending out of teachers from German-language countries and by the Goethe Institute retraining programmes for teachers of Russian in Eastern Europe. Austria has also increased its involvement in exporting German language and the culture of the German language (see 2.2). *Language Problems and Language Planning* (1991: 109) reports that in the first eighteen months after the upheavals in Eastern Europe, the British Council (the equivalent of the Goethe Institute) had spent $US 6 million to support English in Eastern Europe so that it and not German is taught as the first foreign language in place of Russian. The Spanish Government is investing nearly $US 70 million a year to promote its language in the world (Coulmas 1991: 54). Germany spent $US 22 million in 1992 on the promotion of the German language in Central, Eastern and South-Eastern Europe alone, not including support for German-speaking minorities (*Deutscher Bundestag*, 12. Wahlperiode, p.7). Often the investment is offered in a less direct way, for example through the provision of German advisors in industrial development or reconstruction work in Latvia and Lithuania. The controversial question is how much Germany can push its language now that it has more political and economic supremacy in Europe if it wants to continue to regain goodwill lost through National Socialism. This sensitivity has been more strongly advocated by the SPD than by the CDU/CSU.

There are German, Austrian, Swiss or bilingual day schools run or sub-sidized by the home nation in a number of countries. Ammon (1991: 451–2) refers to 336 *Auslandsschulen* run by a German network in 1986 with a total enrolment of about 130,000 pupils and 16 Swiss schools in 1990 (mainly in Europe and Latin America), and there is an increasing number of Austrian schools (see below, 2.2) beyond the 3 mentioned by Ammon. These schools are either for expatriate nationals or intended for inter-cultural encounter. There are also a large number of Saturday schools in countries with German-speaking immigrants, and the European Schools tend to include German as one of the languages of their bilingual education. The state churches in Germany, both Catholic and Protestant (*Evangelisch*), also provide clergy for German-speaking congregations in many parts of the world.

(v) Minorities   Born and Dieckgießer (1989: 15) indicate the size of the German-speaking minorities in the following European countries (excluding those with German as a regional official language, see Chapter 2):

> Former Czechoslovakia: 62,000 (about 5,100 now in Slovakia)
> Denmark: 20,000–35,000 in North Schleswig
> Italy: 11,000 outside South Tyrol (see also Born and
>   Dieckgießer 1989: 105)
> Hungary: 62,000 (in 1980)
> Poland: *c.* 1.1 million
> Romania: about 200,000–220,000 (many of whom have since
>   migrated to Germany)
> Old Soviet Union: 1.9 million (1979, many of whom have
>   since migrated to Germany). Over 900,000 of them were in
>   Kazakhstan and over 790,000 in Russia.

1.4.3   The situation of German in Central Europe

In relation to Central Europe, Ammon (1991) pinpoints four areas as significant for the status of German:

(i) contact with German-language countries
(ii) consciousness of German-speaking minorities
(iii) curriculum of German as a foreign language
(iv) official language policies of German-language countries

The last of these factors is of considerable significance. The significance of the second is waning because of the language shift and migration to Germany from the Soviet Union, Poland and Romania in the late 1980s. German is stronger as an asymmetrically dominant language in Eastern and Central Europe than as a lingua franca, in which role it has been overtaken by English. Statistics provided by Ammon indicate the strong standing of German in Slovakia and the Hungarian-speaking parts of Romania. Even at the time of his book, Ammon was sceptical about the revival of German as the lingua franca of Central Europe because of the attraction of English, and, to a large extent, his position has been vindicated. The general picture in most of Eastern and Central Europe is as described by Csaba Földes for Hungary as a result of his research (personal communication): older people are more likely than younger people to use German for external communication because they will have learned it rather than English as a foreign language. Women are more

likely to use it than men in so far as their communication radius is more limited. For the same reasons, inhabitants of small places will use it more than those who live in big cities. This applies also to countries of the Commonwealth of Independent States, including Russia, Belarus, Latvia, Georgia and Kazakhstan (Földes 1992). Those on national borders use German more than those in the interior of a country. This will be due to the needs of border groups to communicate more extensively with other ethnolinguistic groups. It should also be remembered (Földes 1992) that the German border in Central Europe is Europe's longest border and the number of languages and countries in contact would increase if the Austrian borders were added to the German one. Those with right-wing political views tend to employ German as a lingua franca and those with left-wing views, English. The 'Russian era' has produced large numbers of people in Eastern and Central Europe who are functionally monolingual (Földes 1992). It also seems possible to make the generalization (see below) that primary schools and less academic secondary schools have more students taking German while those in the more academic secondary schools are more likely to study English. Eastern and Central European countries are experiencing an acute shortage of German (and English) teachers, which is being resolved largely through retraining of teachers of Russian. Before the political changes, there was a conspicuous presence of GDR tourists in Prague; now people are coming from all over the world (*Wochenpost*, 5 August 1993, pp. 36–7) and using English rather than German. Czechs and other Central Europeans are going much further for their holidays.

Hungarians are an important group for the propagation of German. Because they speak a non-Indo-European language which speakers of most European languages find difficult to learn, the onus is usually on them to speak another language for communication with other peoples. Hungarian speakers constitute a community of over 13 million speakers in Hungary and neighbouring areas – the Vojvodina (a former autonomous region of Yugoslavia now closely integrated into Serbia), the Transylvanian region of Romania, the Carpatho-Ukraine and Slovakia, with minorities also in the Austrian province of Burgenland (Heuberger and Suppan 1993: 314). They have strong cultural links with the German language from Imperial times. 40% of Hungary's trade and 70% of its tourist contact are with German-speaking countries (Földes 1993). There is a sizeable but shrinking German-speaking community in Hungary, and 14 newspapers and periodicals are published in German. Gal (1993: 355) notes some revaluation of German among ethnic Germans in Hungary, especially young adults. A small number of parents are speaking the

language to their children to keep future migration and work opportunities open and there is a high primary German enrolment in areas with German speakers (Gal 1993: 355). In the 8-year schools (Year 1 to Year 8), German is taken by one and a half times as many pupils as English (outside Budapest) while English is studied more in Years 9 to 12 in the secondary schools (Földes 1992). German is perceived by taxi-drivers, waiters, service-station operators as well as professionals as a language that is used increasingly in the professions (Bassola 1992). Foreign newspapers in news-stands tend to be in German, as does cable TV received in Hungary (Földes 1992).

In Slovakia and the Czech Republic, the urban–rural divide and the level-of-education divide are also important variables, with English being taken as a school subject more in Prague, and German in other places. According to Houssa (1993: 107), 54% of the pupils in the then combined state were taking German at primary school and 33% at secondary (grammar) school as opposed to 40% and 43% respectively doing English. The proportion of high-school pupils taking German is higher in Slovakia than in the Czech Republic (De Cillia and Anzengruber 1993, Bahlcke 1992), even though there is a much larger German minority in the latter. A German theatre has been (re-)established in Prague. The foreign language known by most Slovaks is German, but this is changing, as in other successor states to the former East Bloc countries. The foreign newspapers sold on the streets of Brattislava are German high-quality papers and the mass-circulation Viennese *Kronen Zeitung*. In the Baltic States, German learners represent about half the total number of pupils (LPLP 1991), while about 30% of secondary-school students in Poland study the language. The Baltic States are developing links with the Nordic Union through Estonia, which shares cultural ties and linguistic similarities with Finland. This is moving these states more into the English LICC area. Lithuania also has strong connections with North America through emigrant communities there. Latvia is the Baltic state which is maintaining its traditional links with the German language most, but mainly in the older and middle generations (alongside Russian). In Slovenia, people normally use German to communicate with Austrians, Germans and Hungarians. More generally, the 40–60-year-olds would employ German as their language of inter-cultural communication whereas the under-40s would tend to use English. 17% of school students take German as their first foreign language. Most of the others take English and 92% of these take up German as their second foreign language (Lustker Pristavec, personal communication).

Both German and English are providing lexical transfers for signs and

advertising in former East Bloc countries to create a more fashionable image. Jakob (1992) cites examples from Poland – e.g. *Wand und Boden* (wall and floor) and *anders wohnen* (different living) in a furniture store, and *K.-und-K.-Wasser* (Imperial water) for mineral water from the one-time Austrian province of Galicia (now in the Ukraine).

1.4.4   The European Union

Officially, each of the languages of the European Union, representing the member states, has equal status. With the admission of Austria, Finland and Sweden, there are now twelve languages, making for 144 combinations of languages for interpreting and translating purposes. The costs and difficulties of implementing the equal-status policy will rise with the eventual membership of smaller Central and Eastern European countries, all with different languages. While all documents and speeches are translated into all the Union languages, a principle that is inherent in the rationale for the European Union, the versions in the less commonly used languages generally take longer to become available than those in the three languages of inter-cultural communication, English, French and German. There were, in 1993, 1,200 translators, terminologists and revisors working for the Commission, 500 for the Council, 400 for the Parliament and 120 for the economic and social committees (Born and Schütte 1993). In addition, there were about 3,000 interpreters (Von Donat 1993). Some bodies function mainly in one language, e.g. the European Coal and Steel Community (in French). In effect, there are two predominant languages, English and French, and French is by far the more significant within the bureaucracy of the European Union. It is the French version that is generally the model for translation into other languages. Schloßmacher (forthcoming) surveyed 373 officials of the then European Community and Parliament and 119 of the 518 members of the European Parliament on their use of the then nine languages in various situations. There was a strong predominance of French as the oral working language, especially in communication with EC organs but also with EC member countries. English was used more only in communication with non-EC member countries, and German was hardly used at all.

Only 3% of communications by non-German speakers were stated to be in German – mainly by Dutch speakers. Schloßmacher points out that the proportion using English is constant, while French is increasing its use at the expense of German and other languages. This may change once Central and Eastern European countries are able to join the Union.

Parliamentarians are slightly more likely to use English than French,

Table 1 *Language use of EC staff (%)*

	French	English	German	Others
All uses	59	33	6	2
With EC organs	69	30	1	0.6
With EC countries	54	42	3	1
With non-EC countries	30	69	1	0.5

Source: based on Schloßmacher (forthcoming).

Table 2 *Language use of members of the European Parliament (%)*

	French	English	German	Others
All uses	38	46	8	8
With parliamentary admin.	46	44	6	4
With EC Commission	46	46	5	3

Source: based on Schloßmacher (forthcoming).

although French predominates marginally in communication with the parliamentary administration.

English is slightly more likely to be employed in these contexts by non-native speakers than is French. If you eliminate native speakers, the use of German becomes minimal (4% total, 0.5% with administration, 2% with Commission).

Because German is employed less than the two other LICCs, the German-language translators are the largest contingent and there has been a popular demand in Germany for an improvement in the status of the language in the European Union (Von Donat 1993).

The challenge of the European Union is to promote diversity within a structure that is very centralist. French speakers are very conscious of the 'threat' posed by the spread of the English language and have clearly been successful in protecting the position of French which predates the entry of Britain and Ireland into the European Community. The strength of French within the Union administration is clearly not reflected in many other European contexts (see other sections of this chapter), in which French has not only been exceeded by English but has also fallen behind German. Born (1992) and Angeli (1992) draw attention to the fact that there is no European language policy and to the need for one. The impediments are nationalism, economic considerations, and legal problems.

In internal EC communication, English and French are influencing the German of officials – in transfers, e.g. *Scotch* (< American English, for *Tesafilm*, sticky tape), *Chemise* (for *Aktendeckel*, folder), *Bic* (for *Kugelschreiber*, ballpoint), and in 'Euro-words', e.g. *Komitologie* (sorting out communication problems between committees) and *erweitertes Präsidium* (presidium plus representatives, based on French *bureau élargi*) (Born 1992). For a description of day-to-day translation problems in the EC, see Born 1993 and Von Donat 1993.

1.4.5   General competition with other languages, and pluralistic solutions

In the above discussion, we have often contrasted the situation of German with that of English. Ammon (1991) makes the point several times that, while the position of German may be improving in some ways, it is unreasonable to expect it to compete with English, which, as the language of high technology and pop music, has a particularly strong appeal to the younger generation. In fact, most of Central and Eastern Europe appreciates the value of both languages, especially in economic terms (Kowar 1992: 64) and is striving to educate young people who are competent in both – German as the specifically European LICC and English as the world language, the international language *par excellence*. Several Western European countries which have, in the recent years, concentrated their language teaching efforts on English, have expressed regret at the declining resources in other languages, including German. The Netherlands, for instance, is moving towards a return to the three large European languages (German and French as well as English) in the school curriculum (Nationaal Actie Programma). French had declined substantially in Dutch schools, and German was very much subordinated to English in spite of (or because of?) a very strong economic dependence on Germany and perhaps not entirely unrelated to lingering negative attitudes to Germans (*Mannheimer Morgen*, 4/5 September 1993, p.10). France is introducing German and Spanish as well as English into the primary schools, and Italy is introducing French and German as well as English. Some states of Germany itself are implementing a policy of regional language teaching with an emphasis on 'getting to know your neighbour' (French, Dutch, Danish). In Spain, German is catching up on French as a foreign language in schools because of the demands of trade and tourism and due to the contacts through Spanish migrant workers in Germany and the German-language part of Switzerland.

In a project in progress, Ammon and his colleagues have been studying the (self-rated) knowledge of English, German and French among

academics from France, Russia, Poland, the Netherlands and Hungary as well as the USA and Japan. The academics are distributed across the natural and social sciences and humanities. 91.3% of those surveyed had a knowledge of English, 65% of German, and 49.6% of French. While the incidence of a knowledge of English was almost identical among those under 45 (90.8%) and those 45 and older (91.7%), there was a significant difference in the incidence of German competence between the older (70.5%) and the younger (60%) sub-group. This would suggest that German would decline further as an academic language. The difference between the proportion of scholars claiming English and German competence was greater in Western countries (99.3% : 69.2%) than in Eastern European countries (82% : 60.2%). A further question, on which language(s) they would recommend young scholars in their field to learn, yielded a clear result in favour of English, followed by German, with French third. The highest results for German were received from Polish (79%) and Hungarian scholars (69%) and the lowest ones from Japanese (21%) and Russian scholars (26%). In a study conducted before the political changes in Eastern and Central Europe, Medgyes and Kaplan (1993) found that, in science and technology, English had already established a lead over all other languages. Of 330 scholars surveyed, 82.1% considered the international language of 'professional communication' to be solely English, 12.7% English and another language (usually German), and 5.2% another language (mainly German). 50.9% rated their English skills as adequate and 20.7% regarded their competence in the language as low or non-existent. Of those proficient in English, 71% had skills in English technical reading and only 36% in reading. Not being proficient in English was thought to be a disadvantage at an international conference. While English was the undisputed lingua franca of the natural sciences, its position in the humanities and social sciences was not quite so strong and German had a relatively substantial presence in these types of disciplines.

Another survey based on a search of job advertisements requiring languages conducted by Ammon and his team in 1991 confirmed the place of German between English and French. The survey covered newspapers from Britain, France, Hungary, Italy, Poland and Spain. Only in Hungary was German in the greatest demand. German came second to English in France and Poland, but the demand for it was exceeded by that for French in Britain, Italy and Spain.

A proposal to promote multilingualism which has received some attention is Posner's (1991) 'polyglot dialogue' whereby everyone has passive command of a number of languages (as well as active command of some). In this way, people can speak their own language but be understood by

many others. This mode of communication prevailed in large parts of the Austro-Hungarian Empire, is normal in the Swiss public service (Dürmüller 1993) and in bilingual families. In some ways, it builds on the semi-communication (Haugen 1967) among speakers of related Scandinavian and Slavic languages. In response, Ammon (1992) argues that this proposal would be unworkable for the amount of linguistic diversity that exists in Europe and would ultimately disadvantage the speakers of less commonly used languages who would need to acquire still more languages, at even greater cost. In any case, in the Europe of many cultures, it is likely that linguistic diversity will be increasingly propagated and German will continue to play a role, not only as a national and ethnic language but also as a language of inter-cultural communication.

1.5   Brief summary

In the 'redrawing of the map' of Central and Eastern Europe, Germany has given renewed attention to the international status of German. Since and as a result of the Second World War, German has declined in the face of the rise of English as the main international language. In the Eastern Bloc, the status of German was guaranteed by its being both an Eastern and Western European language. Since the political changes of 1989–90, it has redeveloped its position as a link language between East and West, an asymmetrically dominant language, and a regional lingua franca in some parts of Central Europe.

Its position is between that of English and French in Europe. It has certainly not been able to resist the appeal of English, used across continents as a lingua franca and especially among the young. As an academic language, German has given way to English in the natural sciences and, to a much lesser degree, in the humanities and social sciences. Within the organizations of the European Union, the position of German is overshadowed by both French and English. While there is competition between German and English in the Central European education systems, both are favoured languages. German is likely to continue to play an important role in the multilingual future of Europe.

1.6   Further reading

Ammon (1991) is a comprehensive study of this field but will be superseded by the results of his more recent project. Coulmas (1993) deals with the economic aspects of this question. Born and Stickel (1993) contains conference papers covering many aspects of the topic.

2

German as a pluricentric language

German, like English, French, Swahili, Spanish, Arabic, Bengali, Chinese and other languages, is an instance of what Kloss (1978: 66–7) terms a 'pluricentric' language, i.e. a language with several interacting centres, each providing a national variety with at least some of its own (codified) norms. Hans Moser (1989: 20) describes pluricentric languages as ones which, while uniform across regions in all substantial structural features, cannot be viewed from the perspective of a single centre. This chapter starts by examining the properties of pluricentric languages and then describes the form and function of Standard German in each of the German-language nations and those in which German has some kind of official or quasi-official status. At the end of the chapter, convergence between national varieties of German is discussed.

2.1   Pluricentric languages

None of the national varieties of Standard German has developed into a separate language. Kloss (1978: Ch. 1) gives two criteria for language status: *Abstand* (distance) and *Ausbau* (elaboration). Some languages are guaranteed recognition as such, merely because of their distance from other languages (e.g. Frisian as distinct from Dutch and English). Some, on the other hand, could, historically speaking or in terms of linguistic distance, be regarded as varieties of the same language but are independent because they are assigned the same functions as all other (standard) languages, usually to stress political distinctiveness (e.g. Indonesian as distinct from Malay; Hindi as distinct from Urdu; Slovak as distinct from Czech). Sometimes such languages are written in different script. Following the dissolution of Yugoslavia and the Soviet Union, Croatian and Serbian have diverged increasingly, but Moldavian, which had been declared a separate language after the annexation of Moldavia by the

Soviet Union in 1941, has been redeveloping into a variety of Romanian.

National varieties of the standard language should not be confused with (regional or local) dialects in use or status, even though they may share linguistic features with them, e.g. Austrian Standard German shares some features with Bavarian dialects in Germany, and Swiss Standard German shares some with Alemannic dialects in Germany. The standard language may be defined as supraregional (within the nation concerned), institutionalized, subsuming all other subsystems, originally used by the more educated sections of society, and transmitted through the education system (Löffler, Pestalozzi and Stern 1979, Lewandowski 1980). As Muhr (1987a: 6) points out, such definitions have their limitations because of their monocentric nature.

The relationship between national varieties is usually a dynamic and interactive one because they are affecting one another and being affected by common influences. The *actual* differences between national varieties in terms of phonology, vocabulary and grammar may not be very great. Wardhaugh (1986: 31) projects the difference as one of 'flavor' rather than 'substance'. It is this difference that becomes a marker of national identity. At national borders, regional variation is insignificant but different national varieties are employed on either side. For instance, Scheuringer (1990) demonstrates this in a study of the language use of Braunau (Bavaria) and Simbach (Austria), which are on the Austro-German border. Seidelmann (1989) found some divergence of the dialects of the twin town of Laufenburg on the German–Swiss border, influenced by the national variety of the standard language, with the national border creating a new dialect boundary.

The national varieties of pluricentric languages do not necessarily enjoy equal status either internationally or in the individual countries, i.e. pluricentricity *may* be symmetrical but is usually asymmetrical. Traditionally, the national varieties of the more dominant nations, for example British (actually English), and American English, have been afforded a higher status than, say, Australian, Canadian or New Zealand English, let alone the indigenized English varieties of Singapore or India. The status of national varieties is determined by the relative population size of the nations, their economic and political power, historical factors (e.g. the 'original heartland' of the language), whether the language is the dominant language of the nation, and whether the language is native (as English in England) or nativized (as English in Singapore). Elsewhere (Clyne 1992a: 459–60), on the basis of studies of a range of pluricentric languages, I have differentiated between the position of D(ominant) and O(ther) varieties:

(i)   The D nations have difficulty in understanding the 'flavor rather than substance' notion of pluricentricity, dismissing national variation as trivial.

(ii) The D nations tend to confuse 'national variation' with 'regional variation' on the strength of overlapping linguistic indices without understanding the function, status and symbolic character of the 'national varieties' and their indices.

(iii) The D nations generally regard their national variety as the standard and themselves as the custodians of standard norms. They tend to consider national varieties of O nations as deviant, nonstandard and exotic, cute, charming and somewhat archaic.

(iv) Cultural élites in the O nations tend to defer to norms from the D nation(s). This is related to the fact that the more distinctive forms of national varieties are dialectally and sociolectally marked. It is also the result of conservative and unrealistic norms.

(v)   Norms are not believed to be as rigid in O nations as in D nations.

(vi) Convergence is generally in the direction of D varieties when speakers of different national varieties communicate (e.g. in international work teams, conferences, migration, tourist encounters in third countries).

(vii) D nations have better resources than O nations to export their varieties through foreign-language teaching programmes.

(viii) D nations also have the better means of codifying the language as the publishers of grammars and dictionaries tend to be located in such countries.

(ix) There is a belief, especially in the D nations, that diversity exists only in the spoken norm.

(x)   In some cases, members of D nations are not even familiar with (or do not understand) O national varieties.

A model of codification devised by Ammon (1989: 86–97) distinguishes between national varieties that form their own norms ('endonormativity') and those that import their norms from other nations ('exonormativity'). Ammon's model also differentiates between national varieties which have their own codex (defining dictionaries, spelling and pronunciation guides, grammars) and those that simply have models (e.g. model speakers and texts, model writers and written texts). This makes it possible to develop a scale from 'full centres', through 'nearly full centres', and 'semi–centres' to 'rudimentary centres' of a language. For instance, the

US and England are 'full centres' of English, while Australia, with a dictionary and pronunciation guides but no codified grammatical norms is a 'nearly full centre'. Canada and New Zealand ('semi-centres') have not developed codices to the same extent but have models for their national norms.

The nation-state of the nineteenth century mould was constructed on the basis of language being the common factor, so clearly language was, and remains, the basic identity marker. (Hobsbawm 1990: 37). What we are dealing with in pluricentric languages is a cultural differentiation between 'unequal partners' (cf. Riekhoff and Neuhold 1993) being marked by a limited number of linguistic indices, which help define the community (cf. Anderson 1983).

2.2   The pluricentricity of German

The existence of autonomous German, Austrian and Swiss national varieties of Standard German is now widely accepted due to the longstanding independent Austrian and Swiss nations and because of specific linguistic features of the varieties. The relative status of the varieties, including the relation between national varieties and regional ones (dialects) has not been resolved. The question of an autonomous East German national variety in the recent past – perhaps continuing into the present – will be discussed in Chapter 3.

The issue of German pluricentricity has been the subject of much discussion for over a decade (e.g. Reiffenstein *et al.* 1983, Clyne 1984, Muhr 1987a, 1987b, 1989, Hans Moser 1990, von Polenz 1988, Sieber and Sitta 1988: 20, Hellmann 1989a, Besch 1990, Pollak 1992). As in other languages (Clyne 1992a), there has been increased tolerance towards other national varieties.

The relation between the German and the other national varieties of German is determined by the factors mentioned under 2.1. There have been a number of aspects of the issue where the attitudes of the past have not been fully overcome.

The first is a semantic confusion between *deutsch*/'German' pertaining to Germany, and *deutsch*/'German' pertaining to the pluricentric language. This is due to the fact that the states which unified under Prussia in 1871 chose the name *Deutschland* although there were some German-language areas outside the new nation-state. In the Austro-Hungarian Empire, the word 'German' or 'German-Austrian' was used to distinguish German speakers from the other ethnolinguistic groups. This is compounded by a widespread acceptance, by Germans, of the superiority of their variety. For

German are widely regarded, in Germany (especially the old Federal Republic), as regional norms rather than national ones on a par with that of Germany (cf. e.g. Hugo Moser 1985, von Polenz 1988). 'Richtiges Österreichisch ist anders als richtiges Deutsch' (correct Austrian is different from correct German), says H. Weigel in *O du mein Österreich* (1968). The authoritative Mannheim *Duden-Rechtschreibung* (spelling) dictionary lists not only words that are specifically Austrian or Swiss, but also ones that are *regionally* distributed within Germany. As from 1974, the *Duden-Rechtschreibung* (spelling) dictionary and, since 1969, even the Siebs *Deutsche Aussprache*, traditionally the prescriptive handbook of German pronunciation, have made allowances for Austrian and Swiss Standard German. The *Duden-Aussprachewörterbuch* (dictionary of pronunciation) has refrained from listing such pronunciations as specific entries. Bister and Willemyns (1988) contrast the interest in the O varieties as manifested, for instance, in the existence of the Austrian and Swiss commissions (advisory committees) of the Duden, with the way in which pluricentricity as such is often ignored in German dictionaries and lexicographical treatises. Beersmans (1987: 426) makes the point that the German language is more tolerant of variation than is, say, Dutch.

It will be shown (2.4, 2.5) that the Austrian and Swiss national varieties do employ in everyday usage words which are regarded as 'archaic' in GSG or which are considered part of a formal or bureaucratic register in that variety. It will be demonstrated (3.1.1) that, at least during the period of division, some items used in West Germany were regarded as archaic in East Germany and vice versa. The term 'archaic' is therefore relative and biased. What is old-fashioned, outdated or decadent for some, may be seen by others as normal and representative of continuity. As the GDR's policy was to emphasize the 'cultural independence and separateness' of the two German states, many scholars in the GDR tended to accept that there were four *nationalsprachliche Varianten* of the German language – those of the GDR, the Federal Republic, Austria and Switzerland (e.g. Lerchner 1974 and various books in the *Sprache und Gesellschaft* series). But GDR linguists rarely turned their attention to any but the first two, although the Leipzig edition of the Duden recorded more Austrian Standard items than did the West German dictionary (Fenske 1973).

The convergence of the varieties from different German-speaking countries when speakers communicate will be discussed under 2.9. Emphasis is placed in this chapter on lexical, phonological and grammatical variation. The pragmatic and discourse dimensions are treated separately in Chapter 5 and the Anglo–American influence on the national varieties in Chapter 8.

2.3   Germany

GSG is the product of migration movements, political, economic and religious power conflicts, and the attraction of cultural and intellectual centres over many centuries. The development of GSG and its status are closely related to the notion and essence of German nationhood. As is the case with all languages, standardization has been a relatively recent process. While English and French were standardized on the basis of the dialect of the most powerful centres, London and Paris respectively, Standard German had its origins as a compromise variety (Blackall 1978). As is the case with Italian, German retained great dialectal diversity because of the late unification of a political entity. We shall return to these questions later in the section.

The main division of dialects in German-language countries is based on the High German Sound Shift, which began between the sixth and eighth centuries AD in the south of the German-language region, and gradually moved northward. It changed voiceless stops /p/, /t/, /k/ to voiceless fricatives /f/, /s/, /x/ ([ç] or [x]); and affricates /pf/, /ts/, /kx/ and voiced stops /b/, /d/, /g/ to voiceless stops /p/, /t/, /k/. Dialects (in the far South) which were wholly, or almost wholly affected by the sound shift are termed *oberdeutsch* (Upper German), those (in the Centre) partially affected are designated as *mitteldeutsch* (Central German), and those (in the North) unaffected are termed *niederdeutsch* (Low German). (See Map 2.) Compare the following pairs of words:

Low German *pad*, Upper German *Pfad* (English 'path')
Low German *dag*, Upper German *Tag* (English 'day')
Low German *ik*, Upper German *ich* (English 'I')
Low German *bōk*, Upper German *Buch* (English 'book')
Low German *skip*, Upper German *Schiff* (English 'ship')
Low German *heit*, Upper German *heiss* (English 'hot')
Low German, Central German *Kuh*, Swiss German *Chue*
    (English 'cow')
Low German *bāk*, Upper German (Bavarian) *Pach* (English
    'stream of water')
Low German *dör*, Upper German *Tür* (English 'door')
Low German *genuch*, Upper German (Bavarian) *kenug* (English
    'enough')

(For more details, see R.E. Keller 1978, Barbour and Stevenson 1990: 33–6.)

Until the seventeenth century, Low German had a separate existence as an important literary and commercial language; as the language of the

The proportion of the population accepting the notion of an Austrian nation (as opposed to state) is greater than ever. Comparisons of public polls taken four times between 1965 and 1992 (SWS Bildstatistiken) show that the proportion of the population believing that there is a separate Austrian nation has increased from half to nearly three-quarters of the sample during this period. Nevertheless, the dilemma of Austrian nationhood vs membership of a German nation is still under discussion in some circles (Bruckmüller 1984, K.D. Erdmann 1987). With the end of the cold war, Austria lost its role as a mediator between East and West Germany and, more generally, between Eastern/Central and Western Europe. The economic and political strength of, and dependence on, the 'big brother' Germany stands in contrast with a continuing cultural cringe in Austria (Muhr 1989, 1993b, Pollak 1992, Ratholb, Schmid and Heiß 1990). As the author Georg Schmid (1990: 32) argues, Austrian German has become foreign through the acceptance of an evaluation from outside. A manifestation of this is the pendulum swing between the planning of an autonomous national variety and an acceptance of German norms.

2.4.2   National variety

According to Wodak-Leodolter and Dressler (1978: 30), 'Standard High German', as described in Siebs (1969) and the Dudens, is 'not used in everyday speech at all and rarely in schools' in Vienna. The 'highest' variety employed in Austria is what Wodak-Leodolter and Dressler term 'Austrian Standard'. The German used by the highest ranking strata of Austrian society, whether in government, the public service, or the academic professions, is distinctively Austrian (Muhr 1987a). On radio – and, to a decreasing extent, on TV – announcers and newsreaders employ a pronunciation unlike that of any naturally interactive register (Hans Moser 1990: 27; Pollak 1992: 93–6), based on the *Bühnendeutsch* (stage German) of Vienna's Burgtheater. The notion of 'stage German' has become somewhat antiquated in Germany. It was the original motivation of the Siebs standard but has little significance in Germany today. The radio news pronunciation, though still distinctively Austrian, bears some resemblance to that of German-speaking Switzerland, where this needs to be seen in relation to diglossia (see 2.5.2). In Austria, other programmes, such as the morning programme, talkback, talks and children's programmes, are in a more everyday sociolect of Austrian German.

As there is no complete description of Austrian Standard German, its status is often confused through prejudice. Muhr (1982, 1987a) demonstrates the effects of what he calls the 'schizophrenia of the Austrian

nation' (cf. 1.4.1). He shows that there is a tendency for Austrians to use but denigrate their own national variety (*Standard-nach-innen*) and to regard as the norm a variety that is neither normally used nor acceptable within Austria (*Standard-nach-außen*). This is related to class and geographical factors (see above and cf. Hans Moser 1990) and comes to the fore in the debate over the Austrian dictionary (see 2.4.3). The result is frequent code-switching in the public domain (Muhr 1989). This creates problems in the codification process.

In a survey of language attitudes in Vienna, Moosmüller and Dressler (1988) found positive attitudes to Austrian Standard German, which was described as soft and melodious, though some of the informants reacted negatively to unrealistically normative pronunciations. A more extensive study of the attitudes of people from four states of Austria (Moosmüller 1991:16–22) revealed both positive and negative attitudes to the notion of 'Austrian German'. Evidence in favour of a 'linguistic cringe' (see 2.4.3) is to be found in the transference of certain words from German Standard as prestige forms'[3], e.g. *Mädchen* (Austrian *Mädel*), *nachhause* (Austrian *heim*), *guten Tag* (Austrian *Grüß Gott*)[4] (Eichhoff 1978: 13). German technology, tourism, imports and synchronized television for the entire German-language market as well as youth subculture have prompted the spread of GSG variants and uncertainty as to Austrian norms. On the other hand, it is with Austrian Standard that the middle and upper middle classes identify (Wodak-Leodolter and Dressler 1978: 31).

At all levels of language there are marked distinctions between local or regional Austrian dialects and Austrian Standard in both the capital city and the provinces. This was already observed by the Austrian writer Hugo von Hofmannsthal in *Wert und Ehre der deutschen Sprache* in 1927. He felt an absence of an intermediate variety for social contact between different segments of the population. Due to its belated overall industrialization, Austria still has a more pronounced class structure than Germany, and social class and educational background are indicated through the variety of Austrian German (dialect or Standard) used. As the lower sociolects of Austrian German are the ones most distant from GSG, the distinctiveness of Austrian German represents a conflict between national and social loyalty (Hans Moser 1990). Vienna is the political and cultural centre and

---

[3] According to Ebner (1969), Austrian Standard is gradually adopting the German Standard norm here.

[4] It has been pointed out to me (Leslie Bodi, personal communication) that the opposition *Guten Tag vs Grüß Gott* may be politically motivated (socialist vs conservative) and that to some in Vienna, *Grüß Gott* has a rural ring about it (Hermann Scheuringer, personal communication).

its German exerts an influence on the educated speech of the provincial cities (e.g. Graz, Linz, Salzburg, Innsbruck, see e.g. Moosmüller 1991), though there is some tension between the eastern and western varieties, and Standard German in Austria certainly varies regionally, as in Germany (see Wolf 1994). Viennese influence is weakest in Vorarlberg, which, linguistically and culturally, has much in common with neighbouring areas of Switzerland, and has been making bids for increased political autonomy.

Because of longstanding cultural links dating back to the Austro-Hungarian Empire, ASG is enjoying considerable currency in the neighbouring Central European countries, such as Hungary, Slovenia and Slovakia. This is partly due to cognate vocabulary. For instance, Nagy (1990) cites the Hungarian words *kifli* (ASG *Kipferl*, GSG *Hörnchen*, horseshoe roll), *zsemlye* (ASG *Semmel*, GSG *Brötchen*, roll), *karfiol* (ASG *Karfiol*, GSG *Blumenkohl*, cauliflower), *ribizli* (ASG *Ribisel*, GSG *Johannisbeere*, redcurrant), *kukorica* (ASG *Kukuruz*, GSG *Mais*, sweetcorn), *fotel* (ASG *Fotel/Fauteuil*, GSG *Lehnsessel*, armchair), *plafon* (ASG *Plafond*, GSG *Zimmerdecke*, ceiling), *lavór* (ASG *Lavoire*, GSG *Waschbecken*, wash-basin), *cipzár* (ASG *Zippverschluß*, GSG *Reißverschluß*, zip), and numerous others. Similar lists have been drawn up for Czech (Spáćilová 1993), Slovak (Kozmová 1993) and Croatian (Glovacki-Bernardi 1993). The motivation to use ASG words is decreased because North Germans often do not understand them or consider them non-standard. This may be why some Central Europeans like ASG but consider it inferior to GSG (Csaba Földes, personal communication). Nagy (1990) refers to menus in Central European restaurants catering for the tourist trade written in a mixture of ASG and GSG.

2.4.3   Codification

Austrian variants are mentioned in the German pronunciation handbooks, Siebs and *Duden-Aussprachewörterbuch*, in the *Duden-Grammatik*, and in the German dictionaries such as Wahrig, *Duden-Universalwörterbuch*, and Klappenbach and Steinitz. There is an *Österreichisches Beiblatt* of Siebs which Pollak (1992: 95–7) demonstrates to be inadequate in his argument for a codification of ASG pronunciation.

Now that the *Duden-Aussprachewörterbuch* has accepted a broader set of pronunciation options, some characteristically Austrian norms (especially those rules also applied in parts of Germany) have been included, something that was not the case prior to 1974. Examples of such Austrian pronunciations are the short vowels in: *Behörde, Geburt, Harz, Nische, Städte*.

However, the main opportunity for endonormative planning is the *Österreichisches Wörterbuch* (*ÖWB*). It is the official listing of the lexicon of

Standard German in Austria, with some treatment of grammar, published under the auspices of the Ministry of Education and the Arts. In contrast to earlier editions which attempted to provide an inventory of standard 'common German language', the 35th edition (1979) exercised a soli-darizing and separatist function (Dressler and Wodak 1982a), accentuating the distinctiveness of Austrian Standard German in a climate of increased national consciousness and progressive social reform. At least one third of the items in this edition had not appeared in previous editions. Some were neologisms but most were characteristically Austrian words, among them dialect expressions employed in Austrian literature written in Standard German. They were marked '*mda*' (*mundartlich*, dialectal) or '*ldsch*' (*landschaftlich*, regional). 120 items were marked as '*als bundesdeutsch emp-funden*' (felt to be West German) even if they were also employed in East Germany and/or Switzerland.[5] These included *albern* (simple, childish, ASG *blöd*), *Aprikose* (apricot, ASG *Marille*), *Müll* (rubbish, ASG *Abfall, Kehrricht, Mist*), *Sahne* (cream, ASG *Obers*), and *Sonnabend* (Saturday, ASG *Samstag*, also GSG except in the North). The dictionary also reflected the flexibility in gender usage in ASG (see below, 2.4.4.3), and took the bold step of listing the prepositions *wegen* and *statt* as taking either the dative or the genitive. (Duden 1985: Vol.9 gives only the genitive even though both prepositions appear with the dative in Germany.)

The 36th edition of the *ÖWB* (1985) retreated from some of these reforms, largely in response to criticisms of the controversial previous edition from some linguists and lay people. This may also be symptomatic of a general return to conservatism and regionalism in Austria. It was claimed variously that standards had been lowered by the acceptance of non-standard forms and a disregard for stylistic levels, that the inter-national unity of the German language was being damaged (Wiesinger 1980a), that there was a 'reactionary' overstating of the Austrian element (Reiffenstein 1983), and that the dictionary was Vienna-centric and oblivious to usage in the western part of Austria (Wiesinger 1980a, 1980b, 1988b, Dressler and Wodak 1982a). (Some of these points were also made in letters to the editor of newspapers, see Clyne 1988.) Many of the eval-uations also contained praise for some aspects of the initiatives of the dic-tionary which gave ASG its due place. Any suggestions received are taken into account by the dictionary editors (Fussy 1990). The 36th edition retained the practice of leaving ASG forms unmarked and of marking characteristically GSG forms. Thus, for instance, *Aprikose, Quark* (cottage

---

[5] The earlier term for such items would have been '*reichsdeutsch*' (Imperial German), which was no longer appropriate.

cheese, ASG *Topfen*), and *Tüte* (bag, ASG *Papiersackerl*) are still marked
while *Müll*, *Tomate* (tomato, ASG *Paradeiser*), and *Zoo* (zoo, ASG *Tiergarten*)
are not because they are also used widely in Austria. (See e.g. Wiesinger
1988b, Wolf 1994.) The 36th edition marked at least one GSG word,
Blumenkohl (cauliflower, ASG *Karfiol*) for the first time. The stylistic level
received more attention, with some Austrian items now being designated
'*Ugs*' (*umgangssprachlich*, colloquial) and others '*ldsch*' (*landschaftlich*,
regional). However, Pollak (1992: 36–8) levels criticism at the tendency in
the 36th Edition to relegate items to dialect or colloquial too quickly. The
problem is where to establish the threshold of Standard German (Pollak
1992: 42). Some multiple gender assignments (e.g. for *Monat*, *Joghurt*) are
retained, others (e.g. for *Meter*) are abandoned. (In the case of *Meter*, rein-
stated in 1990.) The addition of '*w*' (*wienerisch*), together with the adoption of Vorarlberg items (marked '*v*') was intended to appease the western
Austrians. Grammatical rules now followed the more conservative pattern
(*statt* and *wegen* with the dative, and the Austrian contraction of *auf dem* to
am being described as '*ugs*') without detracting from the essentials of ASG
grammar, such as the use of *sein* as the only auxiliary for *liegen*, *sitzen* and
stehen, which *Duden* lists as regional South German.

The 37th edition (1990) takes a position between the 35th and the 36th,
being more prescriptive than the former and less so than the latter. There is
again a declaration of national distinctiveness in its self-description:

> Ein Wörterbuch der deutschen Standardsprache in ihrer österreichis-
> chen Ausprägung (A dictionary of the German standard language in its
> Austrian expression) (1990: 37).

It is again an inciter of language reform, but in a more subtle way than the
35th edition. The distinction between national and regional differences is
clarified. Regional variants are not only indicated but marked very pre-
cisely (e.g. East Styrian, East Tyrolean). It is recognized that GSG is influencing ASG through literature, TV, tourism and trade, leading to the
coexistence of two sets of lexical items (see 2.9).

In a sample of 454 entries, Rogerson (1992) found that 78 changes had
been made in the entries between the 36th and 37th editions, largely due
to markings, such as *ugs* or *ldsch*. This represents 60% of the changes in the
sample. Only 10.96% of the corresponding entries had been changed
between the 35th and 36th editions. The 37th edition represents a more
balanced, theoretically well founded but progressive, account of the
Austrian German norms. Its direction is now probably irreversible. The
38th edition, to appear during 1995, will be greatly expanded with a total
of 60,000 items.

2.4.4 Special features of Austrian Standard German

2.4.4.1 Phonology

At the phonological level, Austrian Standard German is distinguished by the following:

> Slightly nasalized diphthong [ɛᵉ] for /aɪ/, as in [krɛᵉde] *Kreide*; diphthongs [ɔᵒ] and [ɔᵓ] as in [frɔᵒ] *Frau* and [frɔᵓde] *Freude*. In all three cases, the diphthongal character is slight and the second element lower than in GSG (Wodak–Leodolter and Dressler 1978: 35).
>
> /a/ to [o], as in [fɔst] *fast*.
> /ɛ/ to [e], as in [trefn], [gəstelt] *treffen*, *gestellt*.
> /gs/ to [ks], as in [ksɔgt] *gesagt*.

The distinction between voiced and voiceless consonants is subject to assimilation rules, e.g. [ɛksbɔt] *Export*, [ʃdundn] *Stunden*.

> Initial [st] corresponds to GSG [ʃt] in loanwords, e.g. *Stil*, *Strategie*.
> Initial [k] corresponds to GSG [ç] in loanwords, e.g. *Chemie*, *China*.
> [v] corresponds to GSG [f] in original loanwords, e.g. *Evangelium*, *November*, *Vizepräsident*.
> [s] corresponds to GSG [ts] in some loanwords, e.g. *Offizier*.
> Voiceless initial [s], as in [sausn] *sausen*.
> There is no glottal stop [ʔ], e.g. [erɪnan] *erinnern*, [tjaːta] *Theater*[6].
> Stylistic variation takes place between final [ɪk] and [ɪç] in words spelt *-ig*, e.g. [ruːɪk] *ruhig* is Austrian Standard informal register.
> [x] occurs after [r] and some front vowels (cf. [ç] in GSG), e.g. [kiəxn] *Kirche(n)*, [duəx] or [durx] *durch*.
> The sequence [ŋk] is found in words such as [aŋkst] *Angst*, [laŋksam] *langsam* (Wodak–Leodolter and Dressler 1978).
> Also /e/ is [ə] (not [e]) in numbers such as *vierzehn*, *fünfzehn*.

(See also König 1989, Moosmüller und Dressler 1988, Muhr 1987a, Lipold 1988, Pollak 1992.)

Vowels are short in words such as *Jagd*, *Städte*, *Politik*, *Kredit*, *Appetit*, *Liter*, *Titel*, *Rüster*, *Husten*, *Schuster*, *Dusche* (most of these also in SSG, but not in GSG.) The short vowel in *Kücken* is reflected in the spelling, which

---

[6] Also in *regional standard* South German.

contrasts with GSG *Küken* (with a long vowel). There is a long vowel, e.g. in [oːp] *ob* (GSG [ɔp]), [ʃeːf] *Chef*. Some words (e.g. *Kaffee* and *Motor*) are stressed on the final syllable (not the initial one as in GSG). Others (e.g. *Mathematik* and *Physik*) are stressed on an earlier syllable ([matɛˈmaːtɪk], [ˈfyːzɪk]) – cf. GSG stress on final syllable. ASG, like SSG, tends towards initial stress of adjectives, in contrast to GSG, e.g. *allerdings* (in any case), *ausführlich* (comprehensive), *unsterblich* (immortal). On the other hand, some adjectives are stressed on the final syllable in ASG whereas the stress occurs on the first syllable in GSG, e.g. *bettelarm* (poor as a church mouse), *steinreich* (filthy rich), *uralt* (ancient) (Lipold 1988: 40).

2.4.4.2 Lexicon

Many of the distinctive words in ASG reflect the separate cultural and political development of Austria. They include words in the following fields:

> **Food**   e.g. *Jause* (morning and afternoon tea, GSG *Kaffee*). *Nachtmahl* (dinner, GSG *Abendessen*), *Kukuruz* (sweetcorn, GSG *Mais*), *Palatschinken* (pancake, GSG *Pfannkuchen*), *Ribisel* (redcurrant, GSG *Johanisbeere*)[7] *Zuckerl* (sweet, GSG *Bonbon*; in Austria, *Bonbons* are always chocolate-coated); also *Schale* (cup, GSG *Tasse*).
>
> **The home**   e.g. *Kasten* (cupboard, GSG *Schrank*), *Polster* (cushion, GSG *Kissen*), *Plafond* (ceiling, GSG *Decke*), *Rauchfang* (chimney, GSG *Schornstein*), *Sessel* (chair, GSG *Stuhl*), *Stiege* (stairs, GSG *Treppe*; narrow stairs in Austria).
>
> **Institutions**   e.g. *Flugpost* (airmail, GSG *Luftpost*), *Kanzleizeit* (clergy consultation time, GSG *Sprechstunde*), *Lehrkanzel* (professorial chair, GSG *Lehrstuhl*), *Matura* (matriculation examination, GSG *Abitur*), *Ordinationszeit* (doctor's surgery times, GSG *Sprechstunden*), *Parteienverkehr* (office-hours, GSG *Bürostunden*), *Putzerei* (dry cleaner, GSG *Chemische Reinigung*), *Spital* (hospital, GSG *Krankenhaus*), *Turnsaal* (gymnasium, GSG Turnhalle), *Trafik* (tobacconist's, where newspapers and tram and lottery tickets are sold; no equivalent in Germany).
>
> **The months**   e.g. *Jänner* (January, GSG *Januar*), *Feber* (February, GSG *Februar*).

---

[7]   Transferred from neighbouring languages, e.g. Italian, Slovenian. Purism and integration of lexical transfers were never as marked in Austria as in Germany (Fenske 1973: 160).

Other ASG lexical items are: *raunzen* (moan, GSG *jammern*), *Schmäh* (trick, swindle), *sekkieren* (tease, GSG *necken, quälen*), *ehe* (anyway, GSG *ohnehin*), and *zu Fleiß* (on purpose, GSG *mit Fleiß*). Another speciality of Austrian Standard German is the preposition *auf* used with *vergessen* (cf. GSG direct object).

Lexical transfers, such as *Praliné* (chocolate, GSG *Praline*) and *Kassa* (ticket-office or cash register, GSG *Kasse*), show less phonological and graphemic integration in Austria than they do in Germany. *Kaffee* retains its stress on the final syllable in contrast to GSG, where the stress has transferred to the initial syllable. The phonological integration of *Blamage* and *Garage* in ASG is by removing the voice, i.e. [blama:ʃ], [ɡara:ʃ], not by adding a schwa [ə] as in GSG. Some words are umlauted in ASG, e.g. *(ein)färbig* ((one)colour), *Kommissär* (commissioner), *Missionär* (missionary) (Ebner 1969, Rizzo-Baur 1962: 91–2). (For a longer list, see Durrell 1992: 22–3.) *Möchte* (from *mögen* 'to like') is employed for 'would' (GSG *würde*). The letter *j* is [je:], not [jɔt] as in Germany. ASG ['ko:pjə] (copy) has been replaced by GSG [ko'pi:] by some younger people for whom the word relates only to photocopying and not to carbon copies (cf. Wiesinger 1994: 59).

Some morphemes are particularly productive in word formation in ASG, e.g.:

-*ler*   *Postler* (postal employee).

-*s-*   *Aufnahmsprüfung* (entrance exam, GSG *Aufnahmeprüfung*), *Ausnahmsfall* (exception, GSG *Ausnahmefall*), *Gesangsbuch* (songbook, GSG *Gesangbuch*), *Gepäcksträger* (porter, GSG *Gepäckträger*), *Rindsbraten* (roast beef, GSG *Rinderbraten*).

-*Ø-*   *Toilettisch* (dressing table), *Visitkarte* (no *-en*, visiting card).

-*(e)rl*   *Hintertürl* (back door), *Schnackerl* (hiccoughs), *Wimmerl* (pimple).

(Rizzo-Baur 1962: 92–8, Wiesinger 1988: 24.)

The distinctively Austrian word *Wissenschafter* (academic) is used in free variation with *Wissenschaftler*. Hans Moser (1990: 26) suggests that the former may have arisen in Austria because the *-ler* is sometimes associated there with words expressing social inferiority.

2.4.4.3 *Grammar*

Some words have different genders in ASG and GSG, e.g. Austrian *der Gehalt* (salary) (GSG *das*); or are single gender in ASG while GSG offers a choice of gender, or offer a choice where the German Standard noun can

your own regional (rather than local) dialect (e.g. Zürich, Basel, Bern German) to that of your speech partner, often by taking over lexemes and other features from Swiss Standard German. Dialect mixture in individuals results from internal mobility (Christen 1992). In contrast to Germans and Austrians, German-speaking Swiss have no intermediate variety between dialect and Standard comparable with *Umgangssprache* (see 4.1.1).

Urban dialects are far more prestigious than rural ones. Urban dialects are also expanding in influence, but there are three main focal points – Zürich, Basel and Bern – so that a uniform national dialect is not likely to develop, despite the publication of grammars and textbooks for the learning of Swiss dialects. Wolfsberger (1967) has shown that, owing to geographical mobility and the effects of the media, there is some levelling-out of dialects, especially in the direction of the standard language. This is particularly so among the younger and the more geographically mobile.

The Swiss identify basically as citizens of a particular local or regional entity (e.g. Zürich, Interlaken, St Gallen). Within this region or locality in the German-language part, the dialect is spoken as the native language and sole language of informal discourse by all classes and sections of society, i.e. it does not have a sociolectal function and enjoys high prestige (R.E. Keller 1973: 149, Ris 1979: 153, Kropf 1986). It is the primary linguistic marker of identity, for, as Watts (1991: 92) points out, the Swiss have a mistrust of central authority and central concentration of power. Competence in Swiss Standard German and not dialect identifies people socially (Ris 1979: 48, 57), while dialect indicates their regional (cantonal) origins, and this diglossia identifies them as Swiss. A uniform national dialect might, among other things, destroy the social unity guaranteed by the local and regional dialect.

2.5.2   Diglossia

Standard German is primarily the written language, as its Swiss name *Schriftdeutsch* suggests. The norms are better defined and more consciously observed in this Swiss variety of Standard German than in dialects (R.E. Keller 1973: 144). Many German-speaking Swiss resent Standard German because of difficulties encountered with it at school or because it is the symbol of anxiety, frustration and suppression within a very prescriptive approach at school (Schläpfer, Gutzweiler and Schmid 1991: 108, Sieber and Sitta 1986, 1988). There being no intermediate variety, Standard German is often rather stilted in style. It has been claimed frequently (e.g. Boesch 1968, Sieber and Sitta 1986) that Swiss-Germans regard Standard German, even in its Swiss variety (see 2.5.3), as a 'close foreign language'.

This is not simply a symbolic rejection, for Swiss-Germans have an inferiority complex about their Standard German (Albrecht and Mathis 1990a). However, young Swiss do have the opportunity of being exposed to it from an early age through German TV (Watts 1988, Sieber and Sitta 1988) and are able to mimic it well (Häcki Buhofer and Burger 1993).

Standard German is employed in the National Parliament (along with French and Italian),[9] in secondary and tertiary education, radio and television, formal church services (liturgy and sermons), the press, worldwide fiction literature (the most important contemporary Swiss exponents of which are Frisch and Dürrenmatt) and *non-fiction literature*. Whether a variety is used for the latter function is regarded by Kloss (1978: 40–6) as a litmus test as to whether the variety is now a language in its own right. Dialect is used in some cantonal parliaments, early primary education and some *fiction literature*. It is also employed increasingly on radio and TV for women's, children's and sports programmes, and, in keeping with a greater informality in the media, for the 'new' functions – 'live' interviews, talk shows and game shows, as well as on regional radio programmes, which are 65% in dialect (Burger 1984: 216). Further uses of dialect are in weddings and informal evening church services, secondary and tertiary education (explanations, colloquia, working groups, practical classes, non-academic school subjects), the military (less formal situations), advertising, and even some formal speeches (Schwarzenbach 1969, Ris 1979, Meili 1985, Löffler 1986, Sieber and Sitta 1986, 1988). In other words, dialect is making inroads into *informal* speech in *formal* domains, and even into *formal* speech, such as addresses given on the National Day, which are closely linked with national identity (Schläpfer, Gutzweiler and Schmid 1991). As a result, new words are transferred from Standard German and integrated into dialect, e.g. *Raumfahrt* (space travel) becomes *Rûmfôrt*, and *Marktforschung* (market research) becomes *Marktforschig* (e.g. in news broadcasts).

It appears that diglossia based on domains is no longer an appropriate means of depicting the relation between Standard and dialect in the German-speaking part of Switzerland. The division is more between *speaking mode*, which is unmarked and in dialect, and *reading mode*, which is marked and in Standard. The 'speaking mode' expresses spontaneity, intimacy and interaction; the 'reading mode' expresses authority, distance and formality. Sieber and Sitta (1986, 1988) designate this 'medial diglossia', i.e. diglossia according to medium (speaking or reading). By way of illustration, news broadcasts are in Standard German on national radio

---

[9] Swiss-German dialect is now sometimes also used (Norbert Dittmar, personal communication).

2.6   Liechtenstein

As far as I am aware, no study of the diglossic situation in Liechtenstein has as yet been undertaken. It is, on the whole, similar to that in the German-speaking parts of Switzerland. Standard German in Liechtenstein has not been codified. However, it is used more than Swiss Standard German. Also there is a large degree of similarity (and some convergence, Banzer 1990) between the Liechtenstein dialects, and the capital, Vaduz, houses the headquarters of many foreign businesses run by Standard German speakers, with whom a Standard German similar to that of Switzerland is spoken. (In December 1990 there were 1,021 Germans and 2,122 Austrians living in Liechtenstein on residence permits (Roland Büchel, personal communication). The language of administration is Standard German. It is the official language of the court, though dialect is sometimes employed in simple cases where both parties are Liechtensteiners. Standard is also generally used in the Landtag (Parliament). Dialect is also permitted (but is used by few parliamentarians). While the liturgical part of church services is in Standard, sermons tend to be preached in dialect (Roland Büchel, Presse- und Informationsamtsleiter, personal communication, 27 July 1992). In schools, the dialect is used as a medium of instruction officially only in the first weeks of Grade 1 (six-year-olds). Its use is permitted in class where the pupils are experiencing difficulties in comprehension or expression (*Lehrplan der Realschule*, 1991, cited in G. Wolfinger, personal communication, 15 February 1993), and there is variation in the use and tolerance of dialect by individual teachers. The reading of dialect texts is discouraged, and it is claimed that facility in dialect reading is increased by the reading of Standard German. (*Lehrplan für die Primarschulen im Fürstentum Liechtenstein*, n.d.). G. Wolfinger, head of Liechtenstein's Schulamt, referring to the use of Standard in writing and dialect in oral communication, stresses that the unequivocal emphasis in education is placed on the acquisition of Standard German although the use of dialect is increasing (personal communication, 15 February 1993).

Banzer (1990) points out that, because of the medial diglossia (see 2.5.2), there is a good deal of lexical and phonological transference from Standard German in the Liechtenstein dialects where people are speaking about academic texts or institutional matters.

2.7   Luxembourg – planning a new language, trilingualism and diglossia

The population of Luxembourg is trilingual – in French, German and Lëtzebuergesch (Luxembourgian). Lëtzebuergesch is the mother tongue, home language and language of informal spoken discourse of all the Luxembourgians, which is manifested in Middle Franconian dialects grouped into a northern, an eastern, a western and a southern division. Lëtzebuergesch dialects (described, however, as *Déitsch*) are spoken in and around Arlon and St Vith in Belgium (see 2.8.1). There is also a suprare-gional Lëtzebuergesch *koiné*, based on the dialect of the Alzette Valley in the South, or on a compromise dialect, and transmitted through the capital, where people from all over Luxembourg have gathered and worked together (F. Hoffmann 1979: 16). Although it is not given any superior status (Newton 1979: 62) it has become the mother tongue of some sections of the upper and middle classes (Fernand Hoffmann, per-sonal communication). Because of the *koiné*, Standard German is not used as a medium of inter-regional communication.

The planned development of Lëtzebuergesch towards a sort of *Ausbausprache* has been going on since (with the removal of its French-speaking territory) Luxembourg became a purely German-(Lëtzebuergesch-) speaking state in 1839, but it was precipitated by German invasions in the two world wars and a reaction against the Germanization policy of the Nazis. It is the independent status of Lëtzebuergesch, together with trilingualism and diglossia (see 2.7.1), that gives Luxembourg its identity of *national independence*. Up to 1984, post-war Luxembourg had no 'official languages' although Lëtzebuergesch was the declared 'national language' (language used by all the population) (F. Hoffmann 1984), and French, German and Lëtzebuergesch all fulfilled some of the functions of official languages. In 1984, these three languages were declared official languages. This measure was promoted by lobbying from the Enrôlés de Force (an organization of those forced to recruit in the German army in the Second World War) with the support of Aktioun Lëtzebuergesch, which had been founded to promote Lëtzebuergesch (Gerold Newton, personal communication). More codi-fication has taken place of Lëtzebuergesch than of Schwyzertütsch (see above, 2.5). There is both a dictionary and a grammar of the 'national dialect', both descriptive, but the orthography is based on that of Standard German.

2.7.1   Trilingualism and diglossia

The parameters established for diglossia in the German-language part of Switzerland (2.5) apply to a large extent to the situation in Luxembourg, which has two H languages in complementary distribution, i.e. there are few situations where there is a choice of languages between French and German. For that reason I would describe the Luxembourg situation as 'diglossia' rather than 'triglossia', with the two H languages, French and German, designated as H1 and H2 respectively, with the functions described below. (Cf. the Singapore situation, where there are three domain levels – High, Low and Medium (Platt and Weber 1980).) Lëtzebuergesch is the medium of the 'speaking mode' – of intimacy, spontaneity and interaction. German and French are the mediums of the 'reading mode' – expressing authority, distance and formality. However, there is a little more overlap between the functions of the L and the H languages than in Switzerland because of the official status of Lëtzebuergesch. For instance, the bureaucracy is required to respond in Lëtzebuergesch where possible (*dans la mesure du possible*) to any letters received in that language. Berg (1993: 163) makes the point that Luxembourgians want their mother tongue to be a written language rather than to replace the languages of wider communication. After all, they are essential to such a small country.

Any choice of languages for the written mode tends to be an expression of educational and class status. Birth, marriage, death and thank-you notices in the daily newspapers are in either Lëtzebuergesch or French. It is the intellectuals who are most likely to *write* letters in Lëtzebuergesch, and they, especially newspaper editors, help other citizens formulate discourse in the language. (Most personal advertisements can follow a preformulated schema.) Yet it is members of the lower class who insert personal advertisements in Lëtzebuergesch because they are not able to write French well either. That is, those who need Lëtzebuergesch most are least able to make use of its increasing functions.

The class structure is also expressed through the selection of the H language. Where there is a choice, e.g. for business letters, the upper and middle classes, and especially the intellectuals, use French as their H, while the lower classes prefer German, partly because it is the main language of primary education, making it more the written language of the masses, and partly because of its closeness to the vernacular. This is the reason why German is the principal language of the press.

French is used for communication with many of the Portuguese and Italian migrants, especially in the initial stages of settlement (see N. Jakob

1981). An oral test in Lëtzebuergesch is obligatory for applicants for Luxembourg citizenship. Tests are conducted by members of the police force (Fernand Hoffmann, personal communication).

It is the more educated who have the greatest opportunity to acquire, use and maintain the H languages, while the working class lack confidence in them (Davis 1994: 164).

The division between the use of French, German and Lëtzebuergesch even within domains may be illustrated by the following examples:

Education Preschools are conducted in Lëtzebuergesch. The medium of lessons in primary schools and, for most subjects, until the fourth year of secondary education, is German. After that, it is French. But in all classes, Lëtzebuergesch is used for explanations and informal interaction (Davis 1994: 62–3, F. Hoffmann 1979: 43–9, Scheidweiler 1988). German and French, but not Lëtzebuergesch, are taught as subjects at primary and secondary schools. It is the school that makes trilinguals out of a basically monolingual Lëtzebuergesch-speaking population.

Luxembourg has a Centre Universitaire offering the equivalent of first-year university courses, a teachers' college, a conservatorium and an economics college, but university students (beyond first year) have to go abroad – mainly to (the French-speaking parts of) Belgium, France, Germany, Austria or Switzerland (in that order).

Correspondence Personal letters tend to be in German (although some intellectuals correspond in Lëtzebuergesch), but French is the main language of local business and official correspondence. The balance between German and French correspondence is determined by social distance (degree of intimacy) and class (F. Hoffmann 1979: 55–65).

Law courts Evidence is given in Lëtzebuergesch, the counsels speak French (the language of the legal code), and the language of the written verdict is German (F. Hoffmann 1979).

Parliament Most debates are conducted in Lëtzebuergesch, with some code-switching to French, usually for a legal register (Krier 1990). The printed reports of debates give the speeches in the languages(s) in which they were delivered.

Literature There are three Luxembourgian fiction literatures, one in each language (F. Hoffmann 1979: 65–107). Non-fiction literature is in German or French. The number of non-fiction texts (apart from quotations from the spoken language, such as parliamentary transcripts) is small but growing (Scheidweiler 1988, Berg 1993). This would mean that, according to Kloss's litmus test (see 2.5.2), Lëtzebuergesch is still to a large extent an *Ausbaudialekt*.

Songs and musicals are now usually written in Lëtzebuergesch.

Media   The Luxembourgian newspapers are predominantly in German. However, reports from French-speaking countries are kept in the original, and some social and cultural sections of the newspapers are in French. The sports sections are entirely in German. Advertisements are in any of the languages, with companies and estate agents tending to insert them in French, and tradesmen in German. Those advertisements in Lëtzebuergesch tend to be in a more interactive style, attempting to initiate a response from the reader. Job advertisements are generally in French (Berg 1993: 43).

All the languages (and some others) may be heard on Radio Luxembourg (or RTL, Radio Télé Luxembourg), which beams beyond the national boundaries. Most of Luxembourg's TV air space has been rented out to foreign companies transmitting from surrounding countries in German or French. The one remaining channel transmits news and documentaries in Lëtzebuergesch. Those watching French-language programmes tend to be upper class, management or unskilled workers (either migrants or soap opera enthusiasts); German-language and Lëtzebuergesch programmes are favoured by civil servants, farmers or skilled workers. Younger people opt rather for English-language programmes (Davis 1994: 77). German and Lëtzebuergesch are the languages most listened to on radio, with Lëtzebuergesch the preferred language for the theatre (Davis 1994: 78–9). In 1992/93 the Municipal Theatre in the city had 29 productions in Lëtzbuergesch, 24 in French and 6 in German (Gerold Newton, personal communication). A new domain is film – there have been a number of productions since 1981, all of them very popular (Berg 1993: 73–7).

Church   Almost the entire population is Roman Catholic. The church has shifted towards Lëtzebuergesch since the Vatican Council of 1962–5 (Scheidweiler 1988). The liturgy is still largely in German but baptism, marriage and funeral services are available in Lëtzebuergesch on request. Sermons and announcements are usually in Lëtzebuergesch, as are some hymns and intercessory prayers, and passages from the New Testament and some of the Psalms have been translated into Lëtzebuergesch (Scheidweiler 1988), giving it special status as a language of the 'reading mode'. Church newsletters are usually in German but sometimes in French (depending on who edits or writes for them).

Postmarks   Official postmarks are in French, but interactive ones, especially directives, are in Lëtzebuergesch.

Signs   The street-scape in the City of Luxembourg looks entirely French, with neon signs and most billboards in that language. Street signs are in French but an increasing number have Lëtzebuergesch names as

well. Signs in shop windows and announcements are often in Lëtzebuergesch and sometimes in German.

Because of resentment against Germany, there is a taboo on the use of Standard German for anything relating to national and personal identification, e.g. street signs, letterheads, public notices, personal advertisements, tombstones (F. Hoffmann 1979: 59). German and French express authority, distance and responsibility in different ways. French is more official than German. (For instance, the printed letterhead on an account is usually in French but the handwritten part generally in German.) While Lëtzebuergesch is the language of solidarity and general interaction and French that of power and prestige, German is more a language of convenience.

Of all German-speaking countries, Luxembourg is the one where the obligatory point of code-switching into standard German is highest (Zimmer 1977: 156). Because so many communication needs are fulfilled by Lëtzebuergesch, and there are two 'High' languages, Standard German is considered even more 'foreign' in Luxembourg than in Switzerland: 'das deutsche Wort wird nicht minder als das Französische als Fremdling empfunden' (the German word is not felt less foreign than the French one) (Bruch 1953: 95). Traditionally, French has been the main basis for renewal in Lëtzebuergesch. However, more Standard German influence is now generated by the popularity of German TV and by word-for-word translations from German originals in Lëtzebuergesch TV news broadcasts. As a result, some Lëtzebuergesch words and expressions are being replaced by transfers from German in the younger generation and German transfers are substituted for French ones (even *Fernseh(er)* for *Tele* or *Televisioun*) (Scheidweiler 1988). Newton (1993) shows the contribution of French transfers in Luxembourg in the rise of the phoneme /ʒ/ and the mixing of [ç], [ʃ] and [j] in Lëtzebuergesch.

2.7.2   Problems arising from the 'official language' declaration

At present, the 'official language' declaration is having only a symbolic effect on the Luxembourg language situation. It is inevitable, however, that in time it will need to be implemented. This will require schools to teach Lëtzebuergesch as a first (and written) language and will necessitate a more extensive codification of the language (F. Hoffmann 1987). (Work on a new edition of the Luxembourgian dictionary has commenced but will proceed slowly.) F. Hoffmann (1987, 1989) has sounded some warnings on the effects of this. One is an inter-regional conflict over competition between regional alternatives. Another is the danger that Standard

German and especially French will become the province of the élites, thereby disadvantaging other Luxembourgians on the local and European job market. In particular, children from the lower and middle classes would experience interference in German orthography from written Lëtzebuergesch (e.g. Lëtzebuergesch *Saz*, German *Satz*; Lëtzebuergesch *Trap*, German *Treppe*; Lëtzebuergesch *Läffel*, German *Löffel*).

2.7.3   Special features of Luxembourgian Standard German

There is no special codification of the use of Standard German in Luxembourg, which is basically not a spoken variety. German Standard is regarded as the norm and taught in schools, though this norm is not generally adhered to. The Luxembourg intellegentsia provides the model. Language planning efforts and linguistic studies have concentrated on Lëtzebuergesch, not on Luxembourgian Standard German, as Standard German is the small language community's medium of communication with the neighbouring Federal Republic. In his booklet *Das Luxemburgische im Unterricht* (1969), F. Hoffmann, one of the best experts on Lëtzebuergesch, enumerates the *Fehler* (errors) of Luxembourgian children learning through the medium of German at school. His remarks complement Magenau's (1964) analysis of the German of the Luxembourgian press.

The three main special influences on Standard German in Luxembourg are Lëtzebuergesch, archaisms and the French language. At the phonological level, this results in a French-type intonation (what F. Hoffmann (1969: 56) calls '*Schaukelmelodie*', rocking melody); and lenization (e.g. [d] for /t/; [ʃ] for /ç/).

In vocabulary, the above-mentioned influences are responsible for the lexical or semantic transference of words not normal in some other national varieties of Standard German and for the use of words employed far more frequently in the Standard German of Luxembourg than in that of some other countries covered. This is the case especially in the fields of administration, politics, education, entertainment and commerce, e.g. *Theatercoup* (unexpected event), *Militär* (soldier), *Konferenzler* (conference delegate), *Deputierter* (MP), *Dancing* (dance-hall),[11] *Television*, *Coiffeur* (hairdresser),[11] *Spezerei* (grocery), *Camion* (truck),[11] *Camionneur* (truck driver), *Velo* (bicycle),[11] *klassieren* (to classify), *klimatisieren* (to aircondition), *Weißkäse* (cottage cheese, cf. German *Quark*, Austrian *Topfen*). *Athenäum* and *Lyzeum* (types of secondary schools), *beilernen* (to learn something extra). Prepositions cause some confusion.

---

[11] Also Swiss Standard German.

In word formation, the dominant 'special feature' is the infixed *-s* morpheme, as in *Nachtstisch* (bedside-table), *Sonntagsnacht* (Sunday night), *Sportskritik* (sports review). Also, *Bett* (bed), *Hemd* (shirt) and nouns ending in *-ment* tend to take an *-e* plural, while *Schlüssel* (key), *Teller* (plate), *Fenster* (window), *Messer* (knife) and *Zettel* (note) are often given an *-n* plural. The analytical comparative with *mehr* is often preferred. Discontinuous constituents are sometimes brought closer together (e.g. *Du **hättest sollen** am Tage vorher mit ihr fahren*, GSG, ASG *Du hättest... sollen*). Some nouns transferred from French frequently keep their French gender (e.g. *der Jury, der Programm, die Pedale*; Magenau 1964: 78–9) (F. Hoffmann 1969, Magenau 1964).

2.8   Areas where German has regional official status or special status

Although we are focusing on the national varieties of German, mention needs to be made of the status and development of the language in Alsace, East Belgium and South Tyrol. Alsace-Lorraine has passed between France and Germany many times in history, including four times in the past eighty years. East Belgium comprises territories which became part of Belgium at different times, see 2.8.1. South Tyrol, formerly Austrian, has been part of Italy since the end of the First World War. The first two tend to follow GSG norms, South Tyrol the Austrian Standard. But dialect plays an important and different role in each case.

2.8.1   East Belgium

Belgian laws are passed in French and Dutch, judicial proceedings are conducted in French, Dutch and German, which are also the languages of education (Aunger 1993: 31). Belgium is a federation of Flanders (Dutch language), Wallonia (French language) and the bilingual capital territory of Brussels. There are Dutch, French and German cultural communities. The German-language area in East Belgium comprises 'Old Belgium', which has been part of Belgium since the inception of the state in 1830, and 'New Belgium', ceded by Germany after the First World War. The former includes Arlon and St Vith, which are actually Lëtzebuergesch-speaking, as well as Malmédy and Eupen. The areas where German has official status are in New Belgium and have Eupen as their administrative centre. Other such areas are in the French-speaking region and have undergone a strong language shift. It is only in the officially German-speaking region that Standard German has any function; otherwise only

the German dialects are used by most people beside Standard French (Born and Dieckgießer 1989: 39–42). Almost all the German-language areas are part of Wallonia. In a small area transferred to Flanders in 1962, Walloon orientation has become a further confounding factor in the rate of 'German' language maintenance (Vandermeeren 1992). Regional official status was declared for German in 1971 under the general Belgian devolution plan (see Barbour and Stevenson 1990: 225–7). Born and Dieckgießer (1989: 39) estimate that there are between 100,000 and 120,000 speakers of the different varieties of German in Belgium.

There is a domain specialization (e.g. more French in public, more German in private) and a great deal of variation in diglossia/triglossia, language maintenance and language shift depending on personal, economic and political factors (Eisermann and Zeh 1979). Because French is the dominant language, a number of political and institutional terms are transferred lexically or semantically from French, e.g. *Arondissement* (suburb), *Camion* (truck), *Erster Minister* (Prime Minister), *Garagist* (garage owner or attendant), *installieren* (to induct a priest), *Orthopädist* (orthopaedic surgeon), *Protestation* (protest), *Regent(e)* (secondary school teacher), *Zivismus* (public spirit).

Some idioms are transferred from French, and grammatical deviations from GS are largely due to the influence of the diverse dialects – Ripuarian, southern Lower Franconian (similar to those employed in the province of Limburg in the Netherlands and in Flanders), Mosel-Franconian (e.g. Landwirt*en*, cf. Landwirt*e*) (Magenau 1964, Kern 1979, Cajot and Beckers 1979).

There are two German daily newspapers in East Belgium, with a combined circulation of 14,000, and a German-language Belgian radio station broadcasting for 8½ hours per day (7½ on Sundays) (Thomas 1979).

Thomas (1992) depicts the autonomy of the German-speaking group and the treatment of their language rights by Belgium as exemplary.

2.8.2   South Tyrol

South Tyrol (Aldo Adige) has now attained regional autonomy from Italy, with Austria playing a protective role. This is the culmination of a series of concessions given to the German-language majority in the area since the end of the Second World War. Following the successful efforts of the Fascist régime during the Second World War to assimilate German speakers or decrease their relative numbers in proportion to Italian speakers (see e.g. Barbour and Stevenson 1990: 238), the Autonomy Statute of 1972 gave language rights to German and Italian speakers in public use

and school language policy in a way that advantaged German speakers, who have developed a higher degree of bilingualism (Born and Dieckgießer 1989: 111). German enjoys a prestige unparalleled in either Alsace or East Belgium. Both German and Italian speakers need to be bilingual and many children from Italian backgrounds are now being sent to German schools to improve their life chances. Increasingly, there is bilingualism without diglossia. With an increasing amount of intermarriage, many children are growing up bilingually, sometimes according to the principle of one parent, one language (i.e. each parent speaking their language to the child(ren); see e.g. Saunders 1988, Taeschner 1983, Döpke 1993). The ensuing bilingualism often declines after children start school (Egger 1985). According to Born and Dieckgießer (1989: 105), there were 279,544 German speakers in South Tyrol in 1981.

There is a rich variation between dialect, which is very prevalent, and Standard in South Tyrol (Bozen Province), and variation between ASG and GSG variants in Standard (Egger 1993). *Kaminfeger* predominates over ASG *Rauchfangkehrer*, and *Mülleimer* is more common then ASG *Mistkübel*. Deviations from other standard varieties are influenced by dialect, e.g. *Häuserin* for *Haushälterin*, housekeeper, *abstehen* for *abfallen*, to lapse (in religion) or from Italian, e.g. *onorevole*, 'The Honourable' (for Member of Parliament), *Wochenabonnement* for *Wochenkarte*, weekly ticket (Italian *abonamento*), and the formulation *Pertoll Monika des Heinrich, Bauer und der Platzer Viktoria* for *Monika, Tochter des Heinrich Pertoll, Bauer, und der Viktoria, geb. Platzer* (in marriage notices) (Rizzo-Baur 1962: 108–12, Egger 1993).

2.8.3 Alsace and Lorraine

There have been periods of Francophonization and Germanization in these regions ever since the seventeenth century. France has been slow to accede to pressure for the languages of its stable ethnolinguistic minorities, and particularly to those of the Alsatians, the German-language population of the *départements* Haut-Rhin, Bas-Rhin and Moselle (i.e. Alsace and Lorraine) to be given a special status. The argument was often that Alsatians have Alsatian dialect (Elsäßerditsch), not German, as their mother tongue and Alsatian is not a language. It was not until 1 January 1993 that German could be used as a medium of instruction in early primary school. Born and Dieckgießer (1989: 87) estimate the total German-language population of Alsace and Lorraine at no more than 1.2 million, including those with a passive knowledge of the dialect. On the basis of a survey of 1979, 73% in Lorraine and 77% in Alsace can still speak the dialect.

There tends to be a diglossic situation between Alsatian dialect of German and Standard French. (Up to 1993, German was taught only as a foreign language in schools.) Standard German still retains some limited functions in church and society but is mastered only by people in the educational field or in top management. In Alsace, where the dialect is stronger than in most parts of Lorraine, identification is with Alsace in the first place and with the French nation in a more general sense (Ott and Philipp 1993). There has been a substantial language shift, started by women and the middle class, related to social status and the importance of the service industry in Alsace (Barbour and Stevenson 1990: 235, Hoff-meister 1977). The region has no German-language newspapers (following legislation of 1945) but there are predominantly German-language bilingual editions of two French-language newspapers. There is much code-switching between Alsatian dialect and French (Gardner-Chloros 1992). Dialect is most of all the language of communication of and with the oldest generation, but there has been a recent tendency towards revitalization, with the impetus coming from the left of politics, especially the conservation movement. It is used for communication and grassroots political action across the Franco-German border. As Barbour and Stevenson (1990: 236) indicate, surveys have presented a confusing picture of attitudes to the role of German language or dialect in Alsace-Lorraine identity. In a country with a highly centralized culture, the new symbolic recognition may come too late to save bilingualism in Alsace-Lorraine.

2.9   Convergence between national varieties

There is little data available on the convergence between national varieties either in one of the German-language countries or in a third country, or in correspondence. In this respect, Koller's (1992) study of the language use and attitudes of Germans in the German-speaking part of Switzerland is pioneering research. However, most of the study concerns the acquisition of a Swiss dialect by German immigrants, in the context of German pluricentricity. Koller presents the results of in-depth interviews with 100 Germans living in Zürich or Basel. Most of them were aged 30–50, had been in Switzerland for 11–20 years, were married to Swiss-German speakers, and had children. 13% had attended a Swiss-German course.

There was much individual variation on the part of Germans and Swiss. Some Germans have mastered Swiss German in a short time and use it frequently; others use Standard in all or most situations. Some receive only Swiss German from the Swiss, some mainly Standard

(making it difficult to learn the dialect), some both. This seems to be due to a reluctance to accept into the (Swiss-German) in-group, Germans evoking the negative stereotype of a German in the Swiss interlocutor – something that is identified partly by personality and cultural traits and partly by a North German accent and problems in learning Swiss German. This is compounded by an initial German misunderstanding of the different functions and status of dialect in Switzerland (2.5.1) and Germany (Chapter 4), Germans' 'ownership claims' on Standard German, and the Swiss linguistic cringe. There is a high correlation between (South German) dialect-speaking background in Germany and both mastery of Swiss German and active use of it in a range of functions. Language use with friends, contacts with Germany, age, and being perceived and perceiving yourself as a foreigner are all significantly correlated. A threshold in the use of Swiss German is attributed to proficiency, anxiety level and communicative need. Shifting to Swiss-German is often associated with integration and employment needs. Children (other people's) and shop assistants are the people most likely to be addressed in Swiss German since they do not exercise sanctions when errors are made. Family members and those with a higher socioeconomic status are the people most likely to use Standard German to the Germans.

One of the prominent examples of convergence in one's own country occurs in menus and notices directed towards German tourists in some parts of Austria. For instance, the word *Pfifferlinge* (chanterelles) will sometimes replace the Austrian equivalent *Eierschwammerl* on menus. Menus in two national varieties or a mixture of varieties are not uncommon in tourist areas (Nagy 1990).

Because of the political power position of Germany (or the Federal Republic), its national variety has frequently provided the basis for renewal across all national varieties of the German language (Hugo Moser 1985: 1680, von Polenz 1988: 212). In a discussion with members of staff of the Austrian, Swiss and GDR embassies in Bonn in late 1988 (Clyne 1992b), the participants[12] agreed that Germans living in other German-language countries will make much less effort to adapt to the national variety of that country than do speakers of the other national varieties. Austrians and Swiss will not usually adopt the auxiliary *haben* for *liegen*, *sitzen* and *stehen* even in written German if they live in North Germany. However, a need is perceived by embassies and consulates to project their 'Austrianness' or 'Swissness' publicly to the host country through their

---

[12] Otto Brandstädter, Christian Mühletaler and Erika Sauer.

language, e.g. through signs giving office hours as *Parteienverkehr* (literally 'client traffic', GSG *Amtsstunden, Öffnungszeiten*). Another example is the distinctive national character of the Standard German of Austrian, German and Swiss radio announcers.

The attractiveness of a characteristically Austrian literature beyond its borders has given Austrians the opportunity of publishing books in Germany without making adjustments to their language. In some cases, such as children's books by Christine Nöstlinger, ASG words are asterisked and explained in a glossary. However, this has not been without problems, and the author Franz Innerhofer (1993) tells of his experiences of being harassed by German publishers' editors insisting on adherence to GSG lexical and grammatical norms. He shows how Austrian literature is constantly being deprived of its autonomy.

Patterns of convergence between speakers of different German national varieties in countries of immigration is a test case which could contribute to our understanding of this phenomenon.

Austria's entry into the European Union may not affect favourably the status of its national variety as German Standard German is already very firmly entrenched as the community's German since the Federal Republic of Germany was one of the original community members. Besides, the European Community has up to now not made any concessions to O varieties (see 2.2) of French or Dutch (see 2.1). In the negotiations over EU membership, the Austrian Government secured recognition of twenty-three ASG variants as official alternatives to GSG ones, all words from the culinary domain, including *Erdäpfel* (potatoes), *Faschiertes* (minced meat), *Karfiol* (cauliflower), *Kren* (horseradish), *Powidl* (sweet plum sauce) (*Neue Zürcher Zeitung*, 1/2 August 1994).

The satellite TV station 3-SAT facilitates co-operation between the three major German-language countries. It is shared between the two German networks, ARD (Arbeitsgemeinschaft der öffentlich-rechtlichen Rundfunkanstalten der Bundesrepublik Deutschland) and ZDF (Zweites Deutsches Fernsehen), which each produce 30% of the programmes, the ORF (Österreichischer Rundfunk) 28%, and the SRG (Schweizerische Rundfunkgesellschaft) 12% (Norbert Waldmann, personal communication). There is no apparent attention paid to the pluricentric nature of German (although Swiss dialect is usually subtitled). However, the satellite does provide additional opportunities for people throughout the German-language area to get to know one another's national varieties better from an early age. English films are usually synchronized in Germany for the whole of the German-language area, and, where needed, commercials are added locally.

2.10   Some lexical differences

A number of maps in Eichhoff's (1977–8) *Wortatlas der deutschen Umgangssprachen* demonstrate the importance of the national boundary in the overall distribution of lexical selection, e.g. *Schluckauf* (old FRG), *Schlucken* (old GDR), *Schnackerl* (Austria), *Gluggsi* or *Higgsi* (Switzerland) (hiccough, Map 5). The last two are dialect words, for, in the German-language part of Switzerland, the 'colloquial language' is the local dialect. Other examples include: *das Plastik* (old FRG, Austria), *der Plast/die Plaste* (old GDR), *der Plastik* (Switzerland) (plastic, Map 77); *(die Blue) Jeans* (old FRG, Switzerland), *Niethose* (old GDR), *die (Blue) Jean* (Austria) (jeans, Map 86).

In addition, there are, of course, dialectal differences within each country. However, for some words and constructions, the older historical-dialectal model applies, i.e. North German (including old GDR) vs South German (and Austria and Switzerland), e.g. *sein/haben* as auxiliary (Map 125), though *sein* has national Standard status only in Austria and Switzerland; *Gaul, Pferd, Roß* (horse, Map 99). *Fleischhauer* and *Fleisch-hacker* (butcher) are both recorded without marking in the *Österreichisches Wörterbuch*, which, however, designates the western Austrian form *Metzger*, as *landschaftlich* (regional). *Fleischhauer* is listed as Austrian and *Fleischhacker* as 'Upper Austrian colloquial' in the Mannheim *Duden*, which previously recorded *Fleischer* and *Metzger* without comment (along with 'North German' *Schlächter*). *Fleischer* appeared without comment in the Leipzig *Duden*, which listed *Metzger* as mainly 'South and West German' and *Schlächter* as 'Low German'. The other two designations were not mentioned at all. In the post-unification Mannheim *Duden* (1991), *Fleischer* is unmarked and *Metzger* designated as 'West Central German, South German and Swiss'.

A set of words not included in Eichhoff is, for 'roast chicken', *Brathähnchen* (West German), *Broiler* (East German, see 3.1.1), *Brathendl* (Austrian) and *Poulet* (Swiss).

2.11   Brief summary

From the above it can be concluded that Austria, Switzerland and Luxembourg each have their own varieties and norms of Standard German, which differ from the German Standard German in phonology, lexicon, morphology and syntax. In terms of Ammon's (1989) model (see 2.1), only Germany (and before 1990 the Federal Republic) has full endonormativity. The second most 'endonormative' state prior to 1990

was the GDR. In the case of Austria and Switzerland, the norms have been defined but not codified as clearly as those of German Standard German. German 'cultural imperialism', semantic muddle, and a 'linguistic cringe' have resulted in attributing an inferior status to the other standard varieties and in creating a confusion between these and dialects. But a new national awareness, especially in Austria, has been reflected in a stronger identification with one's own national variety. This has, however, been limited due to the interaction between national and social-class identity. The acceptance of national variation has also increased in Germany over the past decade or so. In Switzerland and Luxembourg the domains reserved for Standard German are decreasing. In Luxembourg, most of the language planning efforts have gone into the 'national dialect', which is now a codominant official language, and the endonormative standard is set entirely by models, while all the codices are exonormative. In Austria, on the other hand, it is the Austrian Standard that has been the object of language planning in Austria (e.g. the dictionary). Liechtenstein appears close to full exonormativity, as are the German-language areas of Alsace, East Belgium and South Tyrol, supporting Ammon's (1989) contention that norm planning is related to the size of the centre.

The relation between standard, dialect and 'in-between varieties' in the Germanies and Austria will be compared in Chapter 4. Whereas the use of dialect in these countries is connected not only with regionalism but also with social stratification and/or educational background, class structure appears to be reflected in Switzerland in the levels of the national standard variety, and in Luxembourg through the relationship between French and German as High languages. Of all the German-language countries, Luxembourg is the one with the highest threshold of code-switching into the standard language. It is also the country with the fewest national bonds to Standard German and the greatest discontinuum between dialect and Standard German. Germany, of course, lies at the other end of the scale.

I would concur with Wagner (1992) that the time has come for a 'de-nationalization' (*Entnationalisierung*) of foreign language teaching. This means giving recognition to all the national varieties and, in fact, teaching about the pluricentricity of German (Nagy 1990).

2.12   Further reading

Clyne (1992a) is a collection of articles on a number of pluricentric languages with a theoretical and comparative component. The *Österreichisches Wörterbuch* gives insights into the Austrian conception of the Austrian

Standard German lexicon.[13] For different views on the debate, see Wiesinger (1990) and Scheuringer (1988, 1990) for a more conservative point of view, Muhr (1987a, 1989), Hans Moser (1990) and Pollak (1992) for a more radical viewpoint, and Reiffenstein (1983) and Dressler and Wodak (1982a, 1982b) for a more cautious one. Von Polenz (1988) offers a progressive German perspective. Bigler *et al.* (1987) and Meyer (1989) give primary data on Swiss Standard German. For more recent Swiss perspectives on Standard and dialect, see Löffler (1986), Sieber and Sitta (1986, 1988) and Watts (1988). F. Hoffmann (1979) is still the standard account of the Luxembourg situation. This will be updated by the English-language volume edited by Newton (forthcoming). Davis (1994) is an ethnographic study of the Luxembourg situation. The reader will find Eichhoff's (1977–8) word atlas useful.

---

[13] Dressler and Wodak (1982a) have cast doubt on some of the entries, e.g. the labelling of *Tomate* (tomato) as '*bundesdeutsch*' (35th edition) when this word has largely replaced Paradeiser, which has lost much of its social acceptability in Austria.

3

German in divided and unified Germany

The evolution of the national varieties of Standard German described in Chapter 2 took centuries of political and cultural development, sometimes more divergent, sometimes more convergent. The post-war division of Germany covered a period of forty-five years – four years when Germany was split into occupation zones and the forty-one years when the Federal Republic of Germany and the German Democratic Republic were separate entities. The division occurred after standardization in the German language was complete. In this chapter, I will discuss how the language differed in the GDR and the Federal Republic and particularly to what extent it has converged again.

3.1   Situation prior to 1989

The two Germanies had vastly different social and political systems, opposing political and economic alignments, and in many ways underwent separate cultural developments. This was reflected in the language, which at the same time contributed to variations in people's consciousness. During the time of division, the German language gave unique contrastive insights into the ideologies and approaches of the Eastern and Western Blocs. In the case of the two German states specifically, the Federal Republic paid a great deal of attention to coming to terms with the past (*Vergangenheitsbewältigung*) and to being seen to accept responsibility for the actions of the National Socialists. Nationalism was pushed from the 'high' culture to the 'low' culture of some groups, such as returned soldiers and refugees from the former German territories east of the Oder–Neiße Line. The GDR, on the other hand, declared itself an anti-fascist state because many of its leaders had been victims of National Socialism and this absolved all the GDR's inhabitants from their past actions. It attributed to the Federal Republic the continuation of 'Hitler-Fascism'. The GDR did select some landmarks in German high-culture history (Luther,

Goethe, Schiller – partly linked to places situated in the GDR) as its pre-history. For some time, the Federal Republic claimed the sole right to represent the German nation while the GDR claimed there were two German nations, a socialist one in the East and a capitalist one in the West. In many ways, the GDR was the more 'unchanged' Germany and the Federal Republic the more open, cosmopolitan Western European nation.

3.1.1   Linguistic variation between the German of the GDR and that of the Federal Republic

There were virtually no phonological and syntactic differences between the Standard German of the two German states. Minor exceptions were the frequent occurrence of genitives in the GDR public register (Hellmann 1978: 27) and the transitivization of a number of intransitive verbs in the Federal Republic but not in the GDR (Carstensen 1965: 80). There were, however, lexicosemantic and pragmatic differences due to the different conditions of life in the two Germanies.

(i) The need to express technological, social, economic and political change, new ideological directions and new institutions (in both Germanies but especially in the GDR) led to the creation of new vocabulary, e.g.:

GDR
Erweiterte Oberschule   extended upper school (i.e. upper secondary school)
Elternaktiv   elected representatives of parents of children in a particular class at school
Kombinat   big state-run company or agricultural concern
Federal Republic
Alternativbewegung   alternative movement
Gastarbeiter   guest worker,[1]
Mitbestimmung   co-determination in the workplace
Vergangenheitsbewältigung   coming to terms with the past (i.e. with the Nazi period)

Some of the lexical peculiarities of GDR German had their origins in the Socialist Movement from its German (i.e. pre-Russian) beginnings; many were transferred from Russian, e.g.:

---

[1] The linguistic denial of Angolan, Vietnamese, Polish and other migrant workers in the GDR may have influenced attitudes of large sections of the East German population towards them following the revolution.

with the private register, which was not nearly as different from its West German equivalent. An example of the public register is the use of *noch* (yet) + the comparative (discussed by Fix 1992a) as part of a refusal to admit weaknesses in the system, avoiding the publicly inexpressible reality that things are not completely satisfactory. For example:

> Die Leistungen der Schüler in der Rechtschreibung müssen noch verbessert werden. (The achievements of pupils in spelling need to be improved even further.)

This represents adaptation to a thought pattern imposed by the authorities. Schlosser (1990, 1991b) shows that people in the GDR were able to achieve a certain liberation through register-switching. While the Berlin wall was called the *antifaschistischer Schutzwall* (anti-Fascist rampart of protection) in the public register, it would be simply the *Mauer* in private register, to cite but a single example. Reference to discourse in the public register also necessitated switching in informal situations. The public register lent itself to ironization. Fraas and Steyer (1992) also give evidence of an intermediate, semi-public register used among intellectuals, in church and (underground) opposition. This corresponded to the public register in other parts of the German-language region. The public register had some commonalities with the H language in Switzerland and Luxembourg (see 2.5 and 2.7) in that it too fulfilled functions such as authority, distance and formality, and was regarded as unreal. It is doubtful, however, if it was the H language of a diglossic community, as Gärtner (1992: 224) suggests, because it was a register of ritual, as Fix (1993) has shown in her analysis of letters to the editor, and since there was, side by side, the 'semi-public register'. The 'unreal' functions made it a register of mistrust (cf. Fix 1992b) that they all used.

Letters and notices in the public register typically began:

> *Werte Genossen* (esteemed comrades)
> *Werter Professor Schmidt* (etc).

A specific jargon in the public domain of the GDR was that of the dreaded *Stasi* (*Staatsministerium für Staatssicherheit*, Ministry of State Security) (Küpper 1993), which contained the structural features of the public register and was strongly oriented towards earmarking enemies, e.g. the Stasi's definition of *Beeinflussung* (influence):

> Zielgerichtete Einwirkung auf den Menschen, seine Meinungen, Einstellungen und Verhaltensweisen. B. erfolgt, je nach dahinterstehenden Klasseninteressen, als Überzeugung (unter sozialistischen Gesellschaftverhältnissen) oder als Manipulation (unter den Bedingungen des imperialistischen Herrschaftssystems). (Targeted bearing on a person,

his opinions, attitudes and behaviour. B. occurs, depending on background class interests, as persuasion (in Socialist societal conditions) or as manipulation (under conditions of imperialist domination).) (Cited in Küpper 1993.)

A typical Stasi letter went:

> Sie sind gebeten, zur Klärung eines Sachverhalts beim Innenministerium vorzusprechen. (You are requested to call at the Ministry of the Interior to clarify a matter.)

Stasi employees learned to write this register at *Agitationsschule* (propaganda school).

An integral part of the vocabulary of the Stasi was *konspirative Objekte* ('buildings used by the Stasi for secret meetings', cf. the West German usage for 'buildings used for secret meetings held against the state by terrorist organizations'; Horst-Dieter Schlosser, personal communication).

It should be noted that much of the research comparing the German of the Federal Republic and that of the GDR was based on newspaper corpora and largely on the lexicon, the level of language most susceptible to rapid change and official planning. GDR newspapers transmitted different information from that transmitted by newspapers in the Federal Republic (past or present). All GDR papers displayed an ideological unity with the state and tended to report on progress in productivity by collectives throughout the country, party news, international conferences, third-world liberation movements, and visits by leaders of friendly nations. They also emphasized conflict, violence, unemployment, inflation and disease in the West. Even the more conservative newspapers in the Federal Republic carried Western news of a negative nature. Small-scale economic developments rarely gained a mention. (On the language of newspapers in the GDR and the Federal Republic, see Good 1989.)

(vii) Language planning proceeded in a different manner in the two German entities. Within the framework of *Sprachkultur* (language cultivation), the GDR officially justified prescriptivism and stricter codification by the need to equip citizens with the linguistic means to ostensibly participate in decision-making. In the Federal Republic there was little official language planning and less prescriptivism. There were, however, attempts at gender-inclusive language which did not occur in the GDR (see Chapter 7). In the Federal Republic, models for language use were provided by free market forces and the most authoritative dictionary, the Mannheim *Duden*, was in the hands of private enterprise. The Leipzig (GDR) *Duden* was an instrument of state control and its codification strictly adhered to in the public domain.

Note the respective definitions of *Imperialismus* (Imperialism) of the two *Dudens*:

> Machterweiterungsdrang der Großmächte (Urge of the great powers to expand and extend their powers) (Mannheim *Duden* 1973: 438).

> Höchstes und letztes Stadium des Kapitalismus, gekennzeichnet durch die Konzentration von Produktion und Kapital in Monopolen und den Drang zur Neuaufteilung der Welt durch Kriege (Highest and final stage of capitalism, characterized by the concentration of production and capital in monopolies and the urge to repartition the world through wars) (Leipzig *Duden* 1972: 202).

(viii) The influence of English, which played an important role in the West, was discouraged publicly in the GDR although it affected the varieties of young people and dissidents. There were a few notable exceptions, such as *Meeting* (political meeting), *Rallye* (car or motor-cycle rally), and *Broiler*, (roast chicken, actually 'young fattened chicken' – Lehnert 1986: 133–4) and *Dispatcher* (clerk on duty or in charge). The last two came via Bulgarian and Russian respectively, and those such as *High Society*, *Image*, *Trick*, *Big Business*, *Manager* and *Pop-Industrie* were supposed to express the decadence and undesirability of living conditions in the West (Kristensson 1977). Russian influence in the GDR was quite limited and was represented mainly in semantic transfers – the meaning of existing German words changed by analogy with Russian ones (see (iii) above for examples). Lehmann (1972) shows that 66% of items influenced by Russian were semantic transfers.

(ix) There was a strong collective culture in the GDR, hence the much more frequent use of the 1st person plural *wir* and *unsere Republik* than in the Federal Republic (Oschlies 1990: 44).

Contact between East and West Germans immediately before and since the dismantling of the wall has thrown some light on variations in communication patterns in the two Germanies (see Chapter 5).

As will have been gathered from 2.10, there were everyday items such as 'hiccough', 'jeans' and 'plastic' denoted by different lexemes in the two Germanies. (In the case of 'hiccough', this is based on older regional variation.) The equivalent of 'objective' was *Zielsetzung* in the Federal Republic but *Zielstellung* in the GDR.

Thierse (1993: 120) suggests that, because of their need to continually read between the lines in interpreting texts, East Germans may have developed a greater respect for the written word than West Germans and a special sensitivity to the spoken word. In a 1993 survey, 55% of East

Germans reported reading every day, as compared with 34% of West Germans, and only 8% of East Germans never read books, as compared with 24% of West Germans (*DAAD Letter* 1993: 8).

3.1.2   Language attitudes and policies prior to 1989

In accordance with their stance on the controversy – one or two German nations – there was a divergence between the GDR and the Federal Republic on whether the Standard German used in the two Germanies constituted two different national varieties. Up to the mid 1960s, West Germans emphasized the emerging differences and warned that these could damage the 'unity of German' (e.g. Hugo Moser 1961c: 21). The German of the Federal Republic was treated as the norm, and East German neologisms and style (such as the frequent stringing together of genitive phrases) were criticized, as Hellmann (1978: 17) has shown. Apart from early criticisms of American 'linguistic imperialism' in the Federal Republic in the mid 1950s, the problem of emerging language variation was largely ignored in the GDR until about 1963. After the mid 1960s, West German research on the topic placed more emphasis on documentation and tended to play down the differences and stress the common bond through language (see Hellmann 1978: 19ff.), while GDR scholars tended to highlight variation, some affording GDR German the status of a national variety (Lerchner 1974: 265). This position diminished in the early 1980s (e.g. Fleischer 1983, 1987) with increasing contact between the two Germanies and their populations. At the same time, it became clearer to West German scholars that not all change had occurred in the GDR. Schlosser (1989) subsequently argued that it was the Federal Republic that had moved away most rapidly from the common linguistic starting-point. The possible existence of a GDR national variety was acknowledged through the discussion of German as a pluricentric language (Bern 1986, von Polenz 1988, Hellmann 1989b). Hartung *et al.*'s (1974: 541) differentiation between the German language community (*Sprachgemeinschaft*) and the separate communication communities (*Kommunikationsgemeinschaften*) of the Federal Republic and the GDR gained wide acceptance.

Apart from differences in political positions, different approaches to language motivated disagreement. In the 1960s and early 1970s, a period where structuralist and generativist positions dominated linguistics, some felt justified in regarding the East and West German varieties as a single national variety because the variation was believed to be not in syntax and phonology but in lexicon. This obscured the important semantic and

pragmatic differences (see 3.1.1, 5.1.5), for it was at this level, rather than at the structural level of the German–Austrian–Swiss differences, that East–West variation occurred.

3.2   The language of the *Wende*

The peaceful revolution in the GDR in November 1989 had the effect of an instantaneous language emancipation. This applied particularly to Leipzig, where the crowds at the large November demonstration were more active and articulate than in East Berlin, creating simple, highly effective slogans. There were some aspects of GDR language that resisted change. In her address to a meeting in East Berlin on November 4 1989, the East German author Christa Wolf said: 'Jede revolutionäre Bewegung befreit auch die Sprache' (Every revolutionary movement also liberates language). But in the case of East Germany, it was the GDR variety that played an important role in the rhetoric of the revolution itself. As Oschlies (1990: 1) puts it, 'Das Wort hat die Revolution vorbereitet' (The word prepared the revolution). Schlosser (1991b) suggests that words such as *Freiheit* (freedom), *Demokratie* (democracy) and *Deutschland* had retained, in the GDR, beneath the surface of the public register, a broader 'semantic horizon' than in the Federal Republic, where the meanings were largely limited to the Federal Republic and its institutions. The central slogan of the protest movement, **Wir** *sind das Volk* (**We** are the people), was a parody on the usurping of the word by the Socialist Unity Party, which continually claimed to be speaking and acting on behalf of the people. As Schlosser (1993b) explains, the utterance, *Wir sind das Volk* would have been impossible in the West owing to the nationalist and racist overtones that *Volk* had acquired during National Socialism and before. The slogan *Deutschland einig Vaterland* (Germany united father-land), which used another word largely tabooed in the West, was derived from the old GDR national anthem, *Auferstanden aus Ruinen* (Resurrected from the ruins). These words had eventually been banned in the GDR days. In the GDR, *Vaterland* occurred in the collocation *unser sozialistisches Vaterland* (our socialist fatherland). Bodi (1993) attributes some of the naïve surprise at the unification shown by West German intellectuals to the fact that they do not have the terminology to verbalize questions of nationalism, patriotism, statehood and ethnicity due to the usurping of these issues by the right, especially the Nazis and other extremist groups in Germany.

3.2.1   The *Wende*

The word *Wende*[2] (turning-point) itself has become the term for the period of transition from the November revolution via the attempts at democratizing the GDR to its incorporation into the Federal Republic (also known as (re)unification). During this time, *Wende* and *Dialog* and synonyms of both of these words were in very common use in the GDR (Schäffner 1992, Hellmann 1993) and the metaphor of the state as a 'container' and unity as a journey gained prominence (Schäffner 1992). The revolution itself had given rise to new words, such as *(Montags)demos* (Monday demos), contrasted with *Demonstrationen*, which had been used for officially organized demonstrations in favour of the GDR state throughout its existence; *Bürgerkommittee* (citizens' committees) and *runder Tisch* (round table). Language could now be used creatively in an overt way and not just in the underground. The public register of the GDR was ironized in slogans at meetings and in graffiti. Incidentally, the term *Revolution* was often avoided for the events of November 1989 because the word had previously been occupied for Communist ideology. However, some words with negative meanings relating to the West, such as *Terror* and *Mafia*, were soon applied to the former régime so that the images of the enemy were now projected in the opposite direction (Oschlies 1989, 1990).

The events occurred very rapidly. During this period, there was a great deal of serious reflection and discussion on how a 'better' German nation incorporating the positive features of the GDR as well as of the Federal Republic could come about. In June 1990, there was still much debate on what should be the national anthem, the national day and the flag of the new united Germany. Four months later, the former GDR had become part of the Federal Republic.

The media played an important didactic role in preparing the East Germans for unification by explaining the West German institutions to them, e.g. by explaining initials: 'DGB (das heißt, Deutscher Gewerkschaftsbund)' (i.e. German Confederation of Trades Unions).

Private enterprise companies contributed to the 'semantic re-education', as Good (1993: 10) refers to it. He cites an advertisement of the Raiffeisenbank, Berlin, including the extract: '"Öffentlichkeitsarbeit" heutzutage oftmals unter PR (= Public Relations) bekannt'

---

[2] *Wende* occurs in the compounds *Tendenzwende* and *Trendwende*, also untranslatable into other languages, which stood for the conservative resurgence after the student revolution and its after-effects in the late 1960s and early 1970s.

('Öffentlichkeitsarbeit' nowadays often known as PR (= Public Relations)). Advertisements of this kind also tried to remove the old negative connotations of words such as *Profit, Management, Konkurrenz* (competition) and *Team* from the East German language user.

It was during the transition period that the designations *Ossi* and *Wessi* (for former East and West Germans) became widespread. *Besser-Wessi* came to be used to stress the paternalistic and arrogant stereotype of the West German.

A dictionary of the language of the *Wende* period is currently being produced by a team of ex-West and ex-East German linguists working within the Institut für deutsche Sprache in Mannheim. It covers 4 million items from texts concerning political change, convergence and unification from East and West Germany which appeared between the middle of 1989 and the end of 1990. In an early analysis, Hellmann (1990a) concluded that a number of words such as *orientieren auf* (to work towards) and *informieren, daß* (to inform . . . that) were persisting in the East. The transformation of SED newspapers, especially its official organ, *Neues Deutschland,* now a national newspaper, still representing the Socialist point of view but in a pluralistic context, can be observed through linguistic analysis. In a matter of days in late 1989, *Neues Deutschland* started expressing shades of modality, such as possibility and probability, and not just certainty. It began to collocate negatives with the GDR and positives with the Federal Republic and other Western countries (Hellmann 1990a). English lexical transfers, previously discouraged in the GDR, appeared instantaneously, e.g. *Crash* (for car crash), *Disk-Jockey* (replacing *Schallplattenunterhalter,* record entertainer), *jobben, Joint venture, Killer, Know-how, Marketing, Tips, Tricks.* In addition, there were some that were quite different to those employed in West Germany, e.g. *Einbruchsboom* (burglary boom), *smogisch,* found in the *Sächsische Zeitung* as recently as early 1992. Another early development was the institution of a letters to the editor column. Stores and shops, even in small places, changed their names to *Hosenshop* (or *Jeans-Shop*), *Beauty-Shop, Party-Grill, Küchenstudio, Cosmetic-Studio, Haarpflege-Salon* and *Schuh-Center. Flexibel* and *dynamisch* became the trendiest attributes – the passports to success in the new system.

Oschlies (1990) pinpoints three stages of 'linguistically overcoming the past', not only in East Germany but also in other former East Bloc countries: dropping propaganda slogans, the removal of negative weighting of words such as *Pluralismus* and *Marktwirtschaft* (market economy) referring to the West, and the dropping of typically Socialist political terms such as *Genosse.* Many place names and street names were changed during the

Wende, often back to their original names before the Communist régime (e.g. Karl-Marx-Stadt to Chemnitz, Karl-Marx-Allee (Berlin) to Frankfurter Allee, Karl-Marx-Platz (Leipzig) to Augustusplatz). Economic change prompted the replacement of *Werktätige(r)*, 'person doing work (for the good of the (Socialist) nation)', a key concept of the GDR (Good 1989: 65), by *Arbeitnehmer(in)*, 'person taking work'.

Old GDR words used by young East Germans in round-table TV discussions studied by Kreutz (1993) are frequently accompanied by hesitation phenomena such as filled and unfilled pauses, indicating linguistic uncertainty. This points to both a lack of lexical alternatives available to the speaker and the anticipation of communication breakdown with the predominantly West German audience.

The semi-public register (Fraas and Steyer 1992) was extended to take on some of the functions of the GDR public register in the new political context, including the media register. *Herr* and *Frau* replaced *Kollege/ Kollegin* in addressing work colleagues (Good 1993b, see also 5.3.1).

The main difference between East and West German academic discourse (Clyne 1987: 234) written for local consumption – a beginning and/or final section relating the topic to Socialism – immediately became superfluous with the revolution.

In turn, the language of the revolution itself became the subject of irony as people became increasingly discontented with the outcome of the revolution. For instance, soon after unification, the slogans *Wir waren das Volk!* (We were the people!) and *Wir sind ein blödes Volk!* (We are a silly people!) appeared (Reiher 1993).

The post-unification designation of the part of Germany that previously constituted the GDR was itself the subject of controversy during the *Wende*. *Die neuen Bundesländer* (The new Federal states) emerged as the clear winner among 700 entries in a competition run by the Gesellschaft für deutsche Sprache in Wiesbaden. In actual usage, this designation, *Ostdeutschland* and *die östlichen (Bundes)länder* have been most common. *Die alten Bundesländer, die Altbundesländer, die Altbundesrepublik, Westdeutschland* and *die alte Bundesrepublik* seem the most frequent designations for the parts that previously formed the Federal Republic.

Fewer opportunities are available to express these adjectivally, and *ostdeutsch* and *westdeutsch* are the most usual designations. The inhabitants are predominantly referred to as *Ostdeutsche* and *Westdeutsche*, although in the East, one comes across *Ostbürger* and *Westbürger*, and *Ostler* and *Westler*, which are reminiscent of the GDR variety. The East German states are still generally referred to as one unit, e.g. 'Das größte Möbelhaus *der neuen Bundesländer*' (The biggest furniture store in the new federal states).

3.3   Convergence of East and West?

3.3.1   Attitudes and processes

It has frequently been observed that political unification has not yet turned the German people into a single united nation. This comment does not refer to regional variation, which will be discussed in Chapter 4, but to the East–West division. In October 1992 (two years after unification), a public opinion found (Infos, reported on the *Tagesschau*, 5 October, 1992) that only 35% of West Germans and 13% of East Germans felt that East and West Germans had come closer since unification (see Table 3).

The cost of unity has been greater than had been expected or promised. Increased taxes to pay for economic recovery in the East at a time of unprecedented economic austerity (for post-war West Germans), resulting increases in inflation and spending cuts have displeased West Germans. East Germany is taking much longer to catch up with West Germany than people had believed it would. The East European markets on which the GDR had relied are no longer available. East German technology and methods have been found to be inefficient and uncompetitive by Western standards, leading to the demolition of some industries in the new states. East Germans, whose planned economy had ensured full employment, have thus experienced high levels of unemployment. Although East Germany is better off than the other successor states to the East Bloc countries, its population is constantly making comparisons not with them but with the West German states, being part of the same political entity. West Germans, in turn, are blaming the East Germans for the fall in their standard of living. In this confrontation situation, the East Germans are maintaining a pride of identity. All this is reflected in language. There are those East Germans who have adapted their language to that of the West Germans. This applies most of all to East Berliners, for the City of Berlin, which was split between 'two worlds' in the days of the wall, is officially a single metropolis despite stark contrasts between the two parts. There are other East Germans who are striving to maintain their distinctive identity. It is only the East Germans who are expected to make an adjustment. There is virtually no convergence in the opposite direction, just as they have become part of the Federal Republic. The onus is on the East Germans to avoid miscommunication. This is so especially for the 350,000 East Germans who commute to work daily in one of the West German states (*Wochenpost*, 10 February 1994, pp. 36–7).

A continuing process since unification has gone on under the name of

Table 3 *Relation between East and West Germans in comparison with before unification (%)*

	West Germans	East Germans
East and West Germans as distant	26	39
More distant than before	25	33
Closer than before	35	13
Satisfied with unification	45	58

Source: based on Infos Poll (1992).

Abwicklung (winding up). It involved dismantling the remains of the East German system and the institutions which existed under it. It includes the privatization of nationalized industry. Another important example is the East German universities. In order to bring the very favourable staff–student ratio in East German universities in line with West German norms, about half of the academic positions have been cut. (This proportion, of course, includes the Departments of Marxism-Leninism, which gave the students compulsory instruction in the party line in the days of the GDR.) Those academics remaining have had to reapply for their jobs and have had to undergo an investigation into their past political activities, including checking files for possible collaboration with the Stasi. Committees sitting in judgement over the future of the *Ossis* have comprised mainly *Wessis*, something that has caused additional bitterness. The opportunity to peruse Stasi files has itself influenced the language, giving rise to semantic extensions, such as *aktenkundig* (formerly 'on record' or 'notorious', now also meaning 'knowing your (Stasi) file') and *Aktenneid* envy of someone else for having a file (Bodi 1993 in his discussion of Schädlich 1992), and *Aktenschluß* (termination of opportunity to check files – *Wochenpost*, 16 December 1993, p.3).

3.3.2   Tenacity of old words, importation of new ones

Various commentators have made predictions about the convergence or continuing divergence of the German language in East and West. Schlosser (1992) does not expect a common variety in the short term. He argues that the semantic systems will be based on the old *Weltsicht* (way of looking at the world) even if there are new words to express the concepts, and that there will be a continuing East German identity. He believes that East Germans will come to terms with the past by lexical taboo (as was the case with Nazi words in West Germany) and that the demand for new vocabu-

lary will be satisfied from the West. However, switching between East and West German modes of speaking will be maintained, although the switching between public and private register had long become unnecessary and obsolete (Schlosser 1990, 1991b).The outspoken East German member of parliament Wolfgang Thierse (1993), on the other hand, believes that the special features of German in the East will disappear without trace.

Even before unification, linguists had made predictions about which words would survive. Hellmann (1990a), for instance, speculated that *andenken* (to plan), *abnicken* (to give something the nod) and *Kollektiv*, and possibly *Datsche*, might belong to such a category. In a subsequent paper (Hellmann 1990b), he argued that *Broiler*, *Plaste* and *Zielstellung* were too well established to yield to West German equivalents. Oschlies (1990: 64) made stylistic effectiveness the basis of his list, which includes *Feierabendheim* (old people's home, literally 'knocking-off-time home'), *Grobmüll* (hard rubbish, literally 'rough rubbish'), *Oberweltkriminalität* (white-collar crime, literally 'upper-world-criminality').

In fact, many GDR words are being retained consciously and semi-consciously in written and (spontaneous) spoken German. Fraas (1993: 261), an East German linguist now working in the West, comments:

> Wenn Deutsche Ost und Deutsche West miteinander reden, suggeriert die gemeinsame Sprache eine breite Verstehensbasis, die offensichtlich real sehr viel schmaler ist (When Germans from East and West talk to each other, the common language suggests a broader basis for understanding which in practice is very much narrower).

This she attributes to their different *Erfahrungswelten* (worlds of experience). There has clearly been resistance to language change as well as a positive reaction to the change. For instance, East German newspapers have received letters opposing the change. The following extract is taken from a letter which appeared under the heading 'Umgangssprache bitte mehr berücksichtigen' (Please use more colloquial language, literally 'Please take colloquial language more into account') in the *Sächsische Zeitung* of 19/20 December 1992:

> In zunehmendem Maße werden in den Medien Amerikanismen, Worte und 'Wortschöpfungen' verwendet, die uns fremd sind. Hinzu kommen Worte, die in unserem Sprachgebrauch nicht üblich sind (Bayern-Import). (To an increasing extent, our media use Americanisms, words and 'word creations' which are foreign to us. In addition, there are words not usual in our language usage (Bavarian import).)

The writer then goes on to give as examples the 'Americanisms' *kids*, *food zu shoppen*, the South and West Germanisms *samstags* (on Saturdays, East

German / North German *sonnabends*), *Metzger* (butcher, *Fleischer*), *Brotzeit* (tea/supper, *Abendbrot*), the West Germanism *Aktionspreis* (bargain, *preisgünstig*) and *Kita* (= *Kindertagesstätte*, child-minding centre). He concludes by expressing the wish that the *Sächsische Zeitung* be written in a way corresponding to the local *Umgangssprache* (colloquial language, see 4.1.1). Another correspondent complained to the same newspaper (21 April 1992, p.4) about the difficulty of English transfers such as *Boss, Team, City* and *joggen*, which had replaced *Chef, Kollektiv, Innenstadt* and *eine Wald- oder Dauerlauf machen*, and about an unpronounceable word for *Federball* (*Badminton*)! *Kita*, along with *Tram* (for *Straßenbahn*), are given by Schönfeld (1993: 201) as West Berlin words that some former East Berliners take over and others reject. (*Tram* was an instance of language planning by the Berlin Senate – West Berlin did not have trams!) Some Bavarian words and expressions, including the greeting *Grüß Gott!*, have crossed the border, especially through the assistance of Bavarian TV. Even East Berliners have adopted via West Berlin some southern expressions such as the modal particles *halt* (Northern: *eben*) and *eh* (*ohnehin*) (Schönfeld 1993: 205).

In an article in Lerchner's collection, Gärtner (1992: 229–30), having discussed the political discourse of the GDR, expresses the view that the new 'free market' discourse is even worse with its subtle manipulation. In recent years, East Germans have become increasingly aware of variations in language use, e.g. Porsch's (1992: 191–2) comment that West Germans simply fetch (*holen*) things that cost money, and have themselves 'declared sick' (*Sie lassen sich krank schreiben*), i.e. get themselves a sick day, the actions of the doctor being of no explicit significance. There are some differences in the newspaper advertising in East and West. This is commented on in correspondence to the *Sächsische Zeitung* (15/16 August 1992, p.17). West German advertisements emphasize the image of the product and East German advertising emphasizes its function and use and additional information is often given. (Certain companies in the West have specialized in advertising in East Germany.) However, Gläser's (1992) analysis of East German advertisements indicates that entry into the world of private enterprise has been accompanied by a full range of advertising techniques already available, similar to those in Western countries.

Semantic variation between old GDR and West German words is sometimes grasped and sometimes not. East Germans have, on the whole, substituted *Supermarkt* for the old *Kaufhalle* because of store signs and because of the realization that the *Kaufhalle* is a chain of stores which are socially stigmatized by their low prices. However, several East Germans living in West Germany have expressed the belief to me that *Dispatcher*

has the same meaning in the West that it did in the East. In the West it means 'mail order business' or a person working in such a company. In the East it is (and was) used to denote a person in charge or on duty in a particular department, e.g. 'Suchen Sie unseren *Dispatcher* beim Empfang auf (Look for our representative on duty at the reception) (circular concerning a 1993 conference held in Leipzig).

The German of young people in the East is influenced by English more than was previously the case. This is creating a more marked communication gap between the generations, since the compulsory foreign language in the GDR was Russian. But words such as *Highlights, Knowhow, Marketing, Safe-sex* and *Star*, and *starten* with a meaning beyond cars and sport may be found in daily newspapers. Schönfeld (1993: 198) states that anglicisms (including idioms, such as *Sinn machen* 'to make sense') are spreading from the western part of Berlin and employed frequently also by East Berliners of all ages working together with West Berliners.

Some well-known GDR words have experienced less tenacity than some people had expected. This includes the well-known East German marked item *Plaste* (from Russian *plastmassa*), replaced in the media by *Plastik*, also in compounds such as *Plastiktüte* (plastic bag) and *Plastikgeld* (plastic money), although it is no doubt used colloquially in many situations between family and friends. *Broiler* and the West German equivalent *Grillhähnchen* are both to be found on signs on stands. Trucks of producers of roast chickens from West German states prominently displaying the word *Grillhähnchen* may be seen on East German streets. Schönfeld (1993: 202) indicates that, in East Berlin, *Broiler, Grilletta* and *Ketwurst* are used more by the older generation and that younger people prefer to use the West German equivalents, *Grillhähnchen, Hamburger* and *Hot Dog*. Several East Germans have indicated to me a reversion to the use of *Broiler* as from 1992 as a (nostalgic) 'identification marker'. Words such as this symbolize membership of a *Schicksalsgemeinschaft*, a community of fate, whose collectivist cohesion has been destroyed by their new (sought-after) life style. Schönfeld (1993: 202) refers to an East Berlin roast chicken stand with a sign: 'Hier dürfen Sie noch Broiler sagen' (Here you can still say *Broiler*).

It is ironically words more closely associated with the old order that recur frequently, both in the media and in casual everyday conversations. East German newspapers such as the *Sächsische Zeitung* (Dresden) and *Wochenpost*, a former SED newspaper which is now a nationwide weekly giving an East German perspective on German and foreign events, often use *(unsere) Republik*, the old media designation for the GDR, to cover the new unified political entity or just the Federal Republic:

Nach den Morden von Solingen muß sich die *Republik* beweisen. (After the murders [of people of Turkish descent] in Solingen the Republic has to prove itself.) (*Sächsische Zeitung*, 3 June 1993, p.1.)

Die gelähmte *Republik* (The crippled Republic) (*Wochenpost*, 13 May 1993, p.1).

Am anderen Ende der *Republik* (At the other end of the Republic) (*Wochenpost*, 28 October 1993, p.4).

Doch kontrastiert die progressive Fusion . . . wie es in der Geschichte der *Republik* noch nicht gab (Yet the progressive fusion contrasts . . . in a way it never has yet in the history of the (Federal) Republic) (*Wochenpost*, 4 October 1993, p.7).

Wir sitzen im Zentrum der politischen Wissensbildung *unserer Republik.* (We are sitting in the centre of the political knowledge-formation of our Republic.) (*Wochenpost*, 24 February 1994, p.4.)

Among other such words are *Fakt* (fact, *Tatsache*), *Objekt* (building) and *Brigade* (small collective, see 3.1.1), e.g.:

Fakt ist, daß sich die Lage nicht verbessert hat. (It is a fact that the situation hasn't improved.) (Conversation in Leipzig.)[3]

Die beiden *Objekte* sehen identisch aus. (The two buildings look identical.) (Academic colleague from Leipzig.)

Sehen Sie dieses *Objekt*? (Do you see this building over there?) (Directions given in the former East Berlin.)

. . . das derzeit auf einem militärischen *Objekt* in der Nähe von Berlin eine Gefährdungsabschätzung vornimmt (which is currently undertaking an assessment of the potential danger of a military installation? near Berlin) (*Sächsische Zeitung*, 30 October 1992, p.17).

Es arbeiten zusammen Leute aus verschiedenen Nationalitäten in einer *Brigade*. (There are people from different national groups working together in one 'brigade' – in West Germany.) (Academic colleague, originally from East Berlin, now working in West Germany.)

Eingabe (submission, East German nearest equivalent of 'complaint', *Beschwerde*) and *einen Antrag durchstellen* (West German *stellen*) occurred in conversations in Eisenach in October 1992. *Meeting*, frequently used for

---

[3] According to Horst-Dieter Schlosser (personal communication), *Fakt* was used occasionally but infrequently in spoken discourse in the Federal Republic before 1989.

3.3.3   Discourse and pragmatic aspects

(See also 5.1.5, 6.3.8.) As Schlosser (1989, 1993b) has shown, the big problem of communication is at the pragmatic and discourse levels (see also Stevenson 1993). In conversations with East Germans in Eisenach (1992) and Leipzig (1993), it became clear that, owing to the differences between the practices in the two Germanies, East Germans were not well equipped to communicate with the bureaucracy of the new Western-based system. Among the problems were writing letters of application for pensions and allowances (which did not need to be done in the GDR), making complaints (which was not permissible in the GDR – the nearest discourse form being the *Eingabe*, submission), and doing taxation returns. Many of the forms are not comprehensible to East Germans and they do not have the pragmatic formulae to construct some of the letters to the bureaucracy. It has been observed frequently that East Germans speak more softly than West Germans, even when the door is closed, and that they hedge more in round-table discussions (Kreutz 1993). This may be due to the experience of recent life in a totalitarian régime. My own impression on a visit to Leipzig was that dialect speakers there speak quite loudly and Standard speakers stand out by speaking very softly. It has been brought to my attention (by Ulla Fix) that this may be attributable to sub-cultural differences, unassuming behaviour being regarded as both morally respectable and cultivated in the GDR education system (see Chapter 5). Together with the continuing features of the GDR variety, this may be a yearning for the past when there was a feeling of security in that at least everyone knew what was required and what was certain (Schlosser 1993c, Beneke 1993: 223).

According to Beneke (1993: 235), communication is more teacher-centred in West Berlin schools, where the pupils are involved in more confrontative discussions than in East Berlin, where communication is more consensus oriented. In her study of letters to the editor, Fix (1993) indicates a movement from more collective approaches before the *Wende*, when letters basically demonstrated support of the party line, to a more individualistic one.

In letters being written in the East, people are still being addressed as *Herr Kollege*, and correspondence is still being concluded with the routine *Mit kollegialem Gruß* (With collegial greetings), which was the less ideological equivalent of '*Mit sozialistischem Gruß*' (With Socialist greetings) at the time of the GDR. But changes are gradually occurring. An announcement of the *Deutsche Reichsbahn* on East German railway platforms in October 1992 headed *Werte Passagiere* had been replaced by one

headed *Verehrte Reisende* by August 1993. Clearly, the previous formulation was too close to *Werte Genossen*!

3.4   Brief summary

Over forty-five years, the western and eastern parts of Germany were separated and aligned to different political and economic systems. There were different viewpoints in the two Germanies on whether there had developed two distinct German national varieties of German. The discussion was determined partly by political motives and partly on linguistic positions. Most of the linguistic variation between German in the Federal Republic of Germany and in the GDR was lexical, semantic and pragmatic. The grammatical and phonological levels were hardly affected. The strong contextual nature of the variation speaks for two emerging national varieties of a completely different nature to German–Austrian–Swiss variation. Collectively, the language communicated different meanings, different functions to the people of the GDR and the Federal Republic, and they identified at least to some extent with their varieties. If they did not, it was with their own national variety that they chose not to identify for reasons of political disillusionment – usually in particular with the public register which was an instrument of oppression and which provided the vehicle for the peaceful revolution of 1989.

If there had not been a GDR national variety, the convergence discussed in this chapter would not be necessary. It is, in fact, a somewhat slower process than sometimes anticipated. The process of divergence has stopped. The reversal is in progress, involving innovation, disintegration of the past structures, and integration to the West (H. Fleischer 1993). Some East German speakers are adapting to the West German variety faster than others. Among factors to be considered are: nostalgia and resistance to the loss of identity, partly due to the unification process and its effects; complete rejection of the GDR past; the superfluousness of much of the former GDR variety under the new conditions. Much of the language changes reflect a change from a collectivist to an individualist society which is partly being resisted. It should not be forgotten that convergence, like unification, has been a one-way process. The present situation can tell us a little about the salience of national varieties developed over a brief period, which are, as mentioned, quite different from the German–Austrian–Swiss national variation. In the future, the GDR variety could become regionalized or simply a generational phenomenon.

3.5   Further reading

A number of good monographs and collections of readings on this topic have appeared recently. I would recommend Schlosser (1990) on the German of the GDR, Oschlies (1990) on the peaceful revolution – it has comparisons with other East Bloc countries – and Welke, Sauer and Glück (1991) and Lerchner (1992) for before–after comparisons. Contributors to the latter are all East Germans. There is also a special issue of *Muttersprache*, edited by Hellmann (No. 103, 1993), devoted to communication difficulties between East and West Germans. Older but still valuable surveys are Hellmann (1978) and W. Fleischer (1987). A retrospective survey of the linguistic division may be found in D. Bauer (1993). The papers in Reiher and Läzer (1993) are predominantly in this area. The reader is also referred to von Polenz's (1993) summary article.

4

Language and regionalism in Germany and Austria

Languages are not only means of communication, mediums of cognitive development and instruments of action. Through the variety of languages used, speakers also identify their geographical origins, local loyalty, migration history, and their social background and group membership. Dialects are geographical varieties, while sociolects are social varieties. Examples of how geographical varieties can at the same time have the function of sociolects are given below. This chapter also discusses the tenacity of dialects in general and in comparison with one another and the social factors governing this, as well as the changing functions of some dialects.

4.1   Standard German and dialects as regional and social markers

For the historical reasons outlined in Chapter 2, regionalism, and regional identification through language, were and continue to be strong in German-language countries. A speaker's regional identification can occur along a continuum from local dialect via regional dialect, even to regionally coloured Standard German. The latter is characterized by secondary (i.e. not the most typical) phonological features and intonation patterns (i.e. 'regional accent') being transferred from dialect (a locally or regionally identified variety) to Standard German, and through the choice of lexical items associated with a particular region. There are certain meanings for which there is no single supraregional German Standard German lexeme, e.g. 'Saturday' (southern and western, *Samstag*; northern and eastern, *Sonnabend*), 'butcher' (east central, and some west central, *Fleischer*; southern and central, *Metzger*; northern, *Schlächter*), so that regional identification in speech is unavoidable. Other instances include diminutives, where northern *-chen* suffixes and southern *-lein* suffixes are equally standard. 'Regional accent' in Standard German contrasts with the normative

Deutsche Hochlautung (originally *Bühnenaussprache*; see especially Barbour and Stevenson 1990: 148–59).

Dialects themselves, though generally not codified, are autonomous systems with regard to phonology, grammar and lexicon. For instance, some dialects have phonemes that do not exist in others, or in the standard language. Bavarian dialects have the bilabial /β/, some Low German dialects velar /γ/. The distribution of phonemes varies between dialects. In Swiss dialects alone, /x/ comes in initial position. Many dialects (especially Upper German ones) lack a preterite (*er kam*) and generalize the perfect (*er ist gekommen*), while some Central German dialects tend to use the pluperfect (*er war gekommen*) instead. Low German dialects have a uniform case in place of both accusative and dative, while there is systematic confusion between the dative and accusative in Berlin (dialect), and the accusative is generalized in Upper Saxon and Ripuarian (Rhenish). The verb meaning 'to speak' is *reden* in most Austrian and Bavarian dialects, *schwätze* in Swabian, *kalle* in Ripuarian (Rhenish), and *schnacken* in some Low German dialects. (For detailed examples, see Durrell 1992: 13–17, 20–2, R.E. Keller 1961, 1978, and for a more comprehensive treatment, Barbour and Stevenson 1990.) Of course, owing to contact between dialects and between dialects and Standard, dialects can no longer be regarded as homogeneous (see Mattheier 1980: 199). Regional and social variation in pragmatic rules and discourse patterns will be discussed in Chapter 5.

In 2.3, I briefly outlined the dialectal divisions within the German-language area. To an increasing extent, Standard (High) German (based on Central German) has replaced Low German (Low Saxon). For several centuries, many people in northern Germany (what is now the states of Bremen, Hamburg, Lower Saxony, Mecklenburg-Vorpommern, Schleswig-Holstein, and parts of Sachsen-Anhalt, as well as the north of the former German provinces east of the rivers Oder and Neiße) were bilingual in a Low German dialect and Standard (High) German. In some (mainly rural) areas there are still a large number of bilinguals. Many of them code-switch whole passages from one variety to the other (Stellmacher 1977: 151–63). Through switches, speakers quote what has been said in Low German, express their emotions and reactions or give examples. Low German speakers will also often transfer lexemes or grammatical forms and constructions into their High German (Stellmacher 1977: 164–7) and Standard German lexemes into their Low German (Herrmann-Winter 1974). Because the Low German dialects are so distant from Standard (High) German, they do not form a continuum but are completely discrete systems. However, in the North German *regional*

dialects of (High) German, there is the substratum from the Low German dialects influencing the High German of even those who no longer speak a Low German dialect.

In southern Germany and Austria, the Bavarian, Upper Franconian, and Swabian and other Alemannic dialects have continued in general use. In the South, and to a lesser extent in Hessen and parts of the Rhineland, dialects are widely employed alongside regionally coloured colloquial Standard German (for terms, see Barbour and Stevenson 1990: Chapter 5). The fact that North German colloquial speech is closer to Standard German than is its equivalent in the South has given the River Main (the boundary between North and South) a new significance as a linguistic boundary (Durrell 1989).

A public opinion poll conducted in 1966 by the Institut für Demoskopie in Allensbach (Noelle and Neumann 1967) showed that while 71% of people surveyed in Bavaria and 64% in Baden-Württemberg said they mastered a dialect, this was the case for only 46% of respondents in northern Germany and West Berlin (including, however, 51% of informants in Hamburg and 67% in Schleswig-Holstein). This question was not asked in a subsequent Allensbach survey on dialect use in 1980. It should be noted that these statistics are based on self-reporting, and are probably not completely comparable due to the greater prestige of dialect in the South and respondents not being given a frame of reference for dialect (Stephen Barbour, personal communication). A representative sample of people in the Low German-speaking areas of the Federal Republic (1984) showed the proportion speaking Low German ranging from 80% in the north of Lower Saxony and Bremen, 77% of Schleswig-Holstein and 73% in Hamburg to 51% in the north of North-Rhine-Westphalia. 53% of those in northern Lower Saxony and Bremen believed they spoke Low German well, as did 47% of Schleswig-Holsteiners but only 29% of those in Hamburg and 27% of the people in the northern part of North-Rhine-Westphalia (Stellmacher 1987). Schluppenhauer and Werlen (1983: 1417) found only 16% of North Germans to be 'monodialectal', 8% speaking only Standard and 8% only Low German.

Bavarians (Alemannic-speaking), Badensians and Swabians (Württembergers) are culturally very different from North Germans, and they have all had their separate histories. Bavarians have a lot in common with Austrians (including the main features of their dialects).

Any comparison between the German-language countries must take into account that most of the dialects in Austria are Bavarian in origin, and Bavarian dialects are the most retentive. On the other hand, many of

the dialects still in use in the East German states are Low German,[1] and Low German dialects are among the less retentive in the western states. It was a written form of East Central German, based on the ancestors of the GDR's Upper Saxon varieties, which formed the basis of Standard German, together with a substantial contribution from *Das gemeyne Deutsch*, the sixteenth-century southern standard. It will be interesting to see if the growing importance of Berlin, following its resumption of the status of capital of the unified Germany, will have any linguistic implications. Despite Vienna's importance as the political and cultural capital of Austria, many people in the provinces feel that it is remote for geographical reasons. Nevertheless, Eastern Austrian has had a dominating effect on ASG, as has Northern German on GSG.

4.1.1   Variation

Within a given area speakers will select their code(s) from a series of varieties along a continuum from the narrowest local form to something approaching Standard German. To many linguists, only the narrow local forms at the bottom of the continuum are dialect (*Dialekt, Mundart*). They postulate a three-tier categorization which incorporates into a middle category, *Umgangssprache* (colloquial language), any point on the continuum between local dialect and Standard (*Standardsprache, Hochsprache, Einheitssprache, Gemeinsprache, Literatursprache*). Hain (1951) shows, in her analysis of the situation in Hessen, that there are numerous transitional varieties between the two poles. This is confirmed by the research of Schönfeld (1974, 1977), Herrmann-Winter (1974, 1977, 1979) and E.S. Dahl (1974) in the northern areas of what was then the GDR, as well as by the writings of Engel (1961, 1962) on Swabian, Kufner (1961) on Munich dialect, Rein (1983) on Bavarian dialects in general, and Macha (1991, 1992, 1993a) on Rhenish. The continuum has led to disagreement amongst researchers as to the number and nature of the varieties. Schönfeld and some other East German scholars add the categories *hochsprachenahe Umgangssprache* (colloquial language approaching Standard), *mundartnahe Umgangssprache* (colloquial language approaching dialect), and *umgangssprachlich beeinflußte Mundart* (dialect influenced by colloquial language) to the two extremes. This contrasts with the three non-standard varieties described by Engel (see below).

---

[1]   Apart from the Central German dialects of Saxony and Thuringia and a few Upper German dialects.

Rein (1983: 1447, based on research by Gfirtner 1972) shows a reduction in the number of syllables in accordance with lower level on the Standard–dialect continuum, e.g.:

> Des hams uns ja no net xagt. (dialect)
> Das haben sie uns ja noch nicht gesagt. (Standard)

In her study of Standard and dialects in Austria, Moosmüller (1991: 144) presents acoustic evidence of greater vowel length and a higher rise in the last syllable in dialects.

As Bausinger (1967: 295) has commented, the multidimensionality of the German language has been obscured by the term *Umgangssprache*. It is ill-defined, with definitions ranging from 'Sprache des Alltags' (everyday language: Wahrig 1968) to 'Hochsprache auf großlandschaftlicher Ebene' (standard language at the level of a large region: von Polenz 1954). It can refer to a type of usage or to a (geographical or social) variety. Its norms are not defined (Bichel 1973, 1980). *Umgangssprache* is seen more as what it is not than as what it is. It contrasts with dialect in that it covers geographical varieties beyond the local one. It also contrasts with standard language in that it covers varieties that do not adhere (completely) to the (artificial) norms. It includes both 'colloquial standard' and 'colloquial non-standard' in Barbour and Stevenson's (1990: 141) terminology. Summarizing a number of studies, Mattheier (1980: 164) generalizes that the dialect–Standard constellation is determined by four factors: – urbanization, local loyalty, the importance or otherwise of 'official' situations, and the value system associated with the particular variety. While Rhinelanders distinguish dialect and Standard, they regard anything in-between as a mixed form. Inhabitants of the Ruhr consider the intermediate varieties to be 'careless German' and Bavarians, with their strong local identification, differentiate between Standard, regional *koiné* and (local) dialect.

Engel (1961, 1962), in his pioneering study of the phonology, syntax and lexicon of Neuler, a village near Aalen (Württemberg), distinguishes the following three non-standard varieties, based on speaker–hearer relations.

> *Bauernsprache*[2] (peasant language): *i hoo* ən Mordsd*uu*rscht, aber
>   koe' B*ii*r m*aa*g'e net.
> *Bürgersprache*[3] (townspeople language): *i han* en Mordsd*u*rscht,
>   aber B*ii*r m*aa*g'e net.

[2]   Also termed *Mundart.*
[3]   Also termed *provinzielle Umgangssprache.*

Honoratiorensprache[4] (notables language): *i hab* en Mordsd*u*rscht,
aber B*ii*r m*a*g e n*e*t.
Standard German: Ich habe einen großen Durst, aber Bier mag
ich nicht. (I am very thirsty but I don't like beer.)

Bauernsprache:[2] 's g*å*t ə bä*a*sr L*uu*ft hae't, aber *e*m Bus isch waarə.
Bürgersprache:[3] 's g*å*t ə be*e*ser W*e*nd heit, aber *e*m Bus isch s
war*m*.
Honoratiorendeutsch:[4] 's ge*e*t ə be*e*ser W*i*nd heit, aber *i*m Bus isch
s warm.
Standard German: Es geht ein böser Wind heute, aber im Bus
ist es warm. (There is a bad wind today but in the bus it is
warm.) (*å* corresponds approximately to [oː].)

Historically, *Bauernsprache* is the dialect of the village, *Bürgersprache* that
of the nearby town of Aalen, and *Honoratiorensprache* the dialect of the
state capital, Stuttgart, which has influenced the speech of the whole
region. According to Engel, the use of *Bauernsprache* is restricted to the
intimate circle (e.g. family sphere, pub). Standard German is associated
with foreigners and people from the other German-speaking regions.
The other two varieties are used in the everyday sphere, and here variety
and register selection may overlap. *Bürgersprache* is employed in general
interaction in the area around Aalen, while *Honoratiorensprache* is used by
and to local dignitaries (doctor, mayor, clergyman, teacher) and to
Swabians from other areas. In this respect, dialects are at the same time
sociolects. Most speakers have the competence to code-switch between
varieties in much the same way as bi- and multilinguals switch between
their languages. A similar hierarchy has been described for Lower
Austrian dialects by Wiesinger (1980b), a dialect in Hessen by
Friebertshäuser (1987) and by Zehetner (1985) for the Freising dialect
in Bavaria. Incorporating the insights of more recent studies and using
Wiesinger's (1980b) terminology, Friebertshäuser has defined the functions of the varieties as follows:

> *Basisdialekt* (base dialect): local, rural, conservative, non-mobile
> population, in private conversations.
> *Verkehrssprache* (language of communication): regionally
> distributed, influenced by town, either more modern or
> more extensive in communication radius, private or semi-
> official.

---

[4]   Also termed *württembergische Umgangssprache*.

Umgangssprache (colloquial language): retains a distinct regional
link, avoiding primary dialect features; everyday language of
mobile, middle to higher socioeconomic group (business
people and officials).
Standard: oral realization of written language.

The variability of the 'intermediate' varieties and the stability of the
Standard and local dialect also applies in cities, as Veith (1983) found in a
study in Frankfurt-on-Main.

In Austria, Tatzreiter (1978) shows that the lexical and phonological
differences between neighbouring local Styrian dialects are levelling out
in that 'new dialects', which are closer to Austrian Standard German, are
being formed. There are also transitional varieties between the old and the
new dialects, determined by the speaker's communication networks. The
formation of 'new dialects' is common to small communities that are
mainly agricultural and ones that are not. A similar tendency is attested by
Hutterer (1978: 326), based on the radiation of the Graz town dialect.
Surrounding rural dialects replacing, for example, *Dirndl, Ertag, Pfinztag*
and *i hān* by *Mädel, Dienstag, Donnerstag* and *i hob* (girl, Tuesday, Thursday, I
have) respectively. The latter are the equivalents in the town dialect, which
is also becoming the regional dialect (cf. Engel on Württemberg
(Swabian), above).

The factors influencing choice of variety are the ones operating in language contact situations (Fishman 1965, Cooper 1969): domain (contex-
tualized sphere of communication, e.g. family, work, school,
neighbourhood, church); interlocutor (speech partners will accommodate
to each other's speech, as Giles (1977) has shown for bilinguals); role-rela-
tionship; type of interaction (public or private, e.g. business transaction,
lecture, sermon, carnival, private conversation – this factor being identified by Mattheier (1980) as a key one in the dialect–Standard dichotomy);
topic (more personal or emotional topics in dialect; more neutral, abstract
or objective, e.g. politics or occupation, in Standard, cf. Rein 1983: 1452);
locale of interaction (e.g. village, town or city; home, street or pub). In the
Austrian context, Muhr (1987a) has identified the following as factors in
Standard–dialect variation: degree of formality, the function of the
speaker, occupation, interlocutor and degree of emotionality. People will
use Standard particularly in their function as an expert, in presenting the
views of others, talking to foreigners or speaking in an official or institutional context. (Here, as with the GDR public register (see 3.1.1), some of
the dichotomies for diglossic situations (see 2.5.2, 2.7.1) apply in a more
limited way.) There is general consensus on the significance of social

Table 4 *Respondents using dialect in three domains (%).*

Family	70
Friendship	67
Work	35

Source: based on 1980 survey, Allensbach (1981).

group and situation in the choice of variety (Löffler 1985, Macha 1993a, Rein 1983). Speakers code-switch between varieties to express their social identity, contrasting *us* and *them*, and to differentiate between the official and informal domains (Kallmeyer 1994, especially Gumperz 1994). Code-switching between varieties is undoubtedly not a new phenomenon, but one that had been ignored by dialectologists propagating the myth of a 'uniform local dialect', as Hard (1966: 29) has pointed out. Barbour and Stevenson (1990: esp. 61–71) discuss the working methods of traditional German dialectology, which made no provision for variation within the speech of one locality or even of one speaker. This helps explain the sparsity of studies on German urban dialects (Dittmar and Schlieben-Lange 1981, Debus 1962) with their complex sociogeographical stratification and dynamic variation. (On urban communication patterns, see Chapter 5.)

Research in many areas of the German-language countries confirms the occurrence of variation, as do the results of a public opinion poll on dialects (Allensbach 1981 – there is no more recent nationwide survey). According to this, the domains for which dialects are employed are as shown in Table 4. Domain specialization (dialect for family/ friends, Standard for work) is general among German dialect speakers, most markedly among white-collar workers (Ammon 1979: 30). Hain (1951) observed, in her research in Ulfa (Hessen), that the farmer will speak differently to his wife and his farmhand and that the young people will use different forms when talking to the elderly and to their own peer-group.

Domain specialization in Bavaria is exemplified in Rein and Scheffelmann-Meyer's (1975) study of Walperskirchen, 30km north-east of Munich.[5] Local dialect is the medium of all everyday communication, including interaction with local officials and shopkeepers, and that of the

---

[5] There are parallel situations in the villages of the Saarland, except that there are many people who do not speak Standard though they understand it (Wolfgang Klein, personal communication).

work domain. It is also the medium of clubs and societies, including youth groups. Standard German is the language of school (except for grade 1) and also of the church (though parish council meetings tend to be conducted in regional dialect). In municipal politics, local dialect is spoken by people functioning as individuals; only in their capacity as office-bearers do they employ Standard or, more usually, regional dialect (*Umgangssprache*), which is considered more proper for formal domains and prepared speech. Standard and regional dialect are the appropriate mediums for general politics in this triglossic community.

Research in the GDR indicated a high degree of situational variation among speakers, such as code-switching to a higher register at central work meetings (rationalized as part of Socialist work ideology or motivated by the behaviour of others) (Schönfeld 1977 in Berlin) and to speak to superiors (Herrmann-Winter 1979 in Greifswald) and the use of non-standard varieties to express 'mateship' (Schönfeld 1977). Both Schönfeld and Herrmann-Winter noted a strong reluctance of speakers to use non-standard varieties to children for fear of disadvantaging them at school.

Senft's (1982) study, based on participant observation and interviews among local workers in a metal factory in Kaiserslautern (Rhineland-Palatinate), indicates a high degree of uniformity in both phonology and syntax within the variety spoken by his (35- to 47-year-old) subjects. Listeners responding to tapes of other workers in the factory were able to detect differences in syntactic complexity between the speech of the sectional head and foreman on the one hand and workers on the other. Senft asserts that the listeners had been influenced by the content and discourse development. He finds, on the whole, that the informants rated male voices mainly on linguistic and personal characteristics and female ones on sociopsychological (emotional) factors.

4.1.2   Who speaks dialect?

The Allensbach public opinion poll on dialects (Allensbach 1981) gives us the breakdown of dialect-using respondents throughout the old Federal Republic shown in Table 5. The results of this poll and the previous one in 1966 also give us a general profile of dialect, non-Standard speakers in the western part of Germany (Noelle and Neumann 1967, Heuwagen 1974, Allensbach 1981): they have low incomes and low social aspirations, they are working class, live in small rural municipalities, and are South German.

South Germans (especially Bavarians and Swabians) have a high degree of local identity (*Ortsloyalität*, Mattheier 1980). Dialect is more likely to

Table 5 *Respondents using dialect in three domains by education and place of residence (%)*

	Family	Friends	Work
With primary education	74	70	38
With secondary education	60	58	25
Places with less than 5000 inhabitants	78	78	47
Places with 100,000 inhabitants and more	57	53	28
North Germany and (West) Berlin	54	55	36
North Rhine-Westphalia	65	60	22
Rhine-Main/ South-West	78	75	37
Bavaria	77	74	43

Source: based on 1980 survey, Allensbach (1981).

function as a marker of identity in South Germany than in most of North Germany.

Ammon (1973a) has defined the following as the principal factors determining whether a person is a dialect speaker:

(i) the communication radius of the speaker
(ii) the speaker's self-image

Macha and Wegera (1983) make the valid point that the sharp dichotomy between town and country should not be stated too strongly because 'urbanization' often affects the varieties of country areas first, with cities containing 'linguistic relics' (1983: 273), but this varies between regions. Social group and occupation are perhaps the more significant factors. Ammon (1973a) names social contacts and social mobility as important variables. These are all connected with occupation, in particular with the division between physical and intellectual work in industrial societies and also with the power structure (Ammon 1973a). On the basis of his research on Swabian and Franconian speakers, Ammon (1973b) draws the conclusions listed below.

(i) Socioeconomic status correlates strongly with the selection of language variety (Noelle-Neumann 1976). Unskilled industrial workers are more likely to speak Standard than are agricultural workers. Skilled workers and self-employed tradesmen are more likely to speak it than are unskilled workers. People in non-manual occupations tend to speak Standard more than those in manual occupations. Ammon (1979: 29) constructs the follow-

ing sociolinguistic hierarchy (with those at the bottom using most dialect and least Standard):

Entrepreneurs

Leading employees

Self-employed business people

Self-employed tradesmen

Self-employed farmers

Lower-level employees

Factory workers

(This is confirmed by Macha's (1986) research on the German side of the Dutch–German border.) Working-class people gravitate between dialect and a 'mixture' of dialect and Standard German; the middle class often vacillate between this 'mixture' and Standard German (Ammon 1979: 32–3). However, Hasselberg (1981) found 26% middle-class monodialectal speakers among his 7,004 children in Hessian *Gesamtschulen* (comprehensive schools).

(ii) Males are more likely to speak Standard than are females, especially women who are not in employment away from home. This appears to contradict conclusions from English-speaking countries, e.g. Mitchell and Delbridge (1965 in Australia); Labov (1966 in the US); Trudgill (1974 in Britain), who all report women using standard varieties more than men because it is the prestige norm. These results are confirmed in a Viennese study (Wodak-Leodolter and Dressler 1978, see below) and one in Berlin (Schlobinski 1985) and they overlap to a large extent with the findings of research in the former GDR (see below). But among the *rural* women in Ammon's study, dialect is more prevalent in the Franconian and Swabian areas because it appears to be the local norm in the small townships in these regions.

(iii) Young people are more likely to speak Standard German than are old people. (This point will be taken up in relation to the 'decline of the local dialect', see below, 4.2.1. For recent developments, see 4.3.) Macha (1993a), in a comparison of surveys in the Rhineland, demonstrates a rapid decline of dialect competence there over three generations among villagers, from 88% of grandparents and 76% of parents to 19.2% of children. While parents address grandparents in dialect, they speak Standard to their children, who generally do not gain competence in dialect, which has ceased to be a first language. 77.7% of 53–65-year-olds but only 21.3% of 17–28-year-olds consider themselves to

have such a competence. Dialect is employed between masters, journeymen and apprentices in some trades leading to its perpetuation in this context, though even here age plays a role, as does contact with customers, sales representatives and deliverers. There is a high degree of reflection on language variation and movement up and down the sociolectal continuum when assessing what the preferred variety of the interlocutor is. Thus there is now an unstable co-existence between varieties and an interpenetration of domains (Macha 1991, 1992).

Mattheier (1980: 27–9) uses public opinion polls to show that, with few exceptions, more women know and employ dialect than do men, but women are also more likely than men to devalue and reject the dialect in areas where it is being abandoned. While women speak more dialect in the family, men use it more in the work and friendship domains. Women have a greater tendency to react to social conventions in their replies to questions on language use (Mattheier 1980: 35–7).

Our understanding of the relation between gender and dialect use is enhanced by a study of the language use and attitudes of siblings aged 14 to 40 in the village of Fritzdorf, 20 km south of Bonn (Sieburg 1992). The female siblings consistently and consciously use less dialect in the parental home, with colleagues or schoolmates and with friends than do the male siblings. The female siblings take over norms and attitudes concerning language use from outside the family and set new patterns which are partly adopted by the males. One important factor is the tendency for the women to adopt non-manual jobs. 67.2% of those who have left school are in white-collar occupations while 49.1% of the males are in manual jobs. Dialect use is important in some 'male' manual jobs (see 4.2.1). Men are more likely to employ dialect in public domains than women, who tend to limit its use to the private domain (if at all). This is associated with social pressure on women and the stereotype of the 'refined woman'. The Fritzdorf pattern may be attributed partly to the general language shift occurring in the Rhineland and the proximity of the village to Bonn.

Löffler (1985: 21) summarizes two tendencies:

(i) Women (notably older women and housewives) are more likely to maintain the dialect while men are more open to a change to Standard.

(ii) Women (notably younger, urban, working women) opt for the more prestigious and fashionable Standard variety while men are prepared to stick to stigmatized forms (see the above discussion). Mothers are more likely than fathers to use Standard with their

school-age children for the sake of their education. While both boys and girls accept the supremacy of Standard in official situations, girls are far more inclined to accept its supremacy in informal contexts. All this gives an indication of gender roles in Germany.

Using a matched-guise technique (Lambert 1967), Johnson (1989) tests the attitudes of Year 10 pupils, aged 15 to 19, to recordings of one male and one female Berliner, each speaking Standard and Berlin urban variety (the informants believe each realization to be from a different person). There was no significant difference in the girls' and boys' ratings of the Standard and Berlin urban variety speech for speaker's honesty, friendliness, intelligence, manners and school marks. The Standard speaker was rated more highly on all counts. However, boys did rate the 'Standard speaker' considerably higher on friendliness than did the girls. Regional origin (Berlin or elsewhere) caused a greater difference in responses than did gender, with non-Berliners rating Standard speech relatively more highly. Using Schlobinski (1985) as an example, Johnson (1992) offers a feminist critique of the models and methods of analysis in some variation studies involving gender. She criticizes the construct of social class based on income, education and profession, which can misplace women, the disaggregation of gender and class so that the position of working-class vs middle-class women is not readily discernible, and the problematization of females only as the marked gender (e.g. reference to their insecurity) in explanations.

In most of the areas of South-Western Germany, Vorarlberg (Austria) and Liechtenstein where Graf (1977) studied the use of the subjunctive in dialect, the ratio of Subjunctive I (e.g. *sei*) to Subjunctive II (e.g. *wäre*) was much higher in the speech of older women than in that of older men.[6] In the middle and younger age groups, however, the pattern was reversed. Thus it was the women who conformed to the change, even within their dialect speech. In Senft's (1982) study of the speech of Kaiserslautern metal-factory workers, in which the age group (35–47) was kept uniform, no major sex-specific differences were registered in phonology or syntax.

On the basis of conversations and interviews with 75 speakers in the industrial and business growth centre of Osterholz-Scharmbeck, 20 km

---

[6] There are two subjunctive moods in German. Traditionally Subjunctive I, based in form on the present tense, is used in indirect speech and Subjunctive II, based on the form of the past, is employed to denote the hypothetical. However, the latter is also used increasingly for indirect speech. Graf showed that Subjunctive I is still alive in Alemannic speech and that it is a marker of dialectality.

north of Bremen, Stellmacher (1977) established age, along with low socioeconomic status and an informal communication situation, as factors correlating with dialect usage. Sex and degree of mobility do not stand out as significant factors in dialect usage. However, any differences between Ammon's and Stellmacher's findings could be due to regional factors. In a study of the Regensburg town dialect, Keller (1976) found that the younger generation initiated changes but that there were phonological and lexical instances where the variety of the older and younger generations overlapped but differed from that of the middle generations.

The results of Wodak-Leodolter and Dressler's (1978) research based on interviews in Vienna are of significance for two reasons. Firstly, many other studies on dialects in Germany and Austria were conducted in rural areas and provincial towns, but Vienna is one of the largest cities in the German-language area (the third largest after Berlin and Hamburg). Secondly, the data could test whether the social function of dialects in Austria is similar to that in Germany. It should be noted that Wodak-Leodolter and Dressler focus on phonological aspects. They reach the following conclusions:

(i) Working-class people (those with only primary education) tend to use local dialect, occasionally switching to higher varieties. Such switching is commonplace among the lower middle class (those with secondary or technical education), a parallel to the uncertainty and hypercorrection among the lower middle class in New York (Labov 1970). The middle and upper classes in Vienna (those with higher education) generally employ Austrian Standard German or regional dialect.

(ii) Women employ less dialect and more Standard than men. They are more conscious of language and adhere to prestige norms more strongly due to their insecurity. The discrepancy with Ammon's findings is probably due to urban–rural differences as well as to the distinction between housewives and women employed outside the home.

(iii) Young members of the middle class are more likely to speak dialect than are older ones (see below).

(iv) Intra-individual code-switching occurs significantly in the lower middle class, with its social insecurity, and in 'upwardly mobile' speakers, who have been able to move up the social ladder but have a confused identity. It occurs less in the working class. Wodak-Leodolter and Dressler (1978: 50) claim that this type of language behaviour is 'non-existent' in the middle and

upper middle classes. (However, this is perhaps due mainly to the interview situation.) The older generation of the lower middle class, especially women, produce the most hypercorrect forms.

Sound changes in Vienna are currently occurring both 'from above', with the lower middle and working classes and the upwardly mobile adapting to the middle class, and 'from below', with the middle class breaking the taboo on local dialect. However, Moosmüller (1991), in a more recent study, indicates that the middle class has now moved away from this tendency.

On the whole, it can be seen that the point on the continuum from which one's speech is selected in a particular situation is intricately interwoven with class structure. Barbour and Stevenson (1990: 106) make the important point that most German research on linguistic variation has avoided testing class as a variable and that the term 'class' is less established than in English-speaking countries – except in Marxist frameworks.

The relation between language and social status can be informed by reference to GDR studies. Schönfeld (1974) conducted a comprehensive survey of a village near Stendal in the Ostaltmark (Saxony-Anhalt). The older the speakers there, the more likely they were to use the local Low German. Another factor correlating with use of local dialect was a low level of education. The regional dialect (*mundartnahe Umgangssprache*) was employed by those with no more than eight years of formal education, the sons and daughters of tradesmen, and rural labourers. It was not usually employed by those whose fathers were members of the intelligentsia or white-collar employees. A person who learned to speak in a village was 1.1 times as likely to master a dialect than those who migrated from a town or city. While older women used and mastered dialect more than their male peers, younger and middle-aged women tended more towards the use of, and attitudinal support for, Standard German than younger and middle-aged men. There was a strong attitudinal preference for Standard except among the 16–25 age group, the majority of whom are completely tolerant towards all language varieties. Otherwise, attitudes were occupation-determined.

Herrmann-Winter (1977) investigated the acceptance of regional grammatical and lexical forms in and around Greifswald (Mecklenburg-Vorpommern). She tested attitudes towards: plural -*s* (as in *Jungens*); dative of possession (e.g. *Peter sein Fahrrad*, Peter his bike, for *Peters Fahrrad*, Peter's bike); discontinuous preposition-pronouns (e.g. **Da** *kann er nichts für*, for **Dafür** *kann er nichts*, He can't help it); *tun* + infinitive (e.g.

tut er glauben, he does think, for *glaubt er*, he thinks); and diminutives ending in *-ing* (e.g. *Größing*). Those with the highest qualifications (intellegentsia, 'leaders' in industry) seemed to be most tolerant of deviations, though this does not necessarily mean that they would employ them themselves. Those with a trades certificate were least likely to accept the deviations – something that can be compared to the hypercorrection and linguistic insecurity of the lower middle class in the US and Austria (see above). The 'leaders' in agriculture would use local dialect in everyday situations and observe Standard norms more in situations where Standard is employed. It is suggested (Herrmann-Winter 1977: 230) that they prefer Standard to regional intermediate varieties in order to 'prove their qualifications'.

In a subsequent study, Herrmann-Winter (1979) investigates both the speech and the language attitudes of speakers in Greifswald and the surrounding industrial and agricultural areas. Among other things, she elicited colloquial words and expressions, neologisms, technical jargon and grammatical constructions that make up the speakers' everyday repertoire. The highest number of phonological deviations from Standard (i.e. non-obligatory regional features) were recorded among workers in industry and trades, mastercraftsmen and in the over-65 age group, and the fewest among the intelligentsia, those with twelve years of schooling, schoolchildren, and others under the age of 25. The importance of the elicitation situation needs to be stressed, for many of the words and expressions would have been acquired in a formal work situation.

Schönfeld (1991) shows in a comparison of several sets of data, that there is a great deal of variability between regions, between places and between individuals in the tenacity and use of dialects. In some areas of East Germany, dialect took more than a hundred years to die out; in others there was a shift over a few decades. Individual variation may be determined by an early development of a relationship with another person through a particular variety and/or it may correlate with value systems, a subject he recommends for further study. On the whole, however, the GDR studies cited above suggest that social position and function in the workforce are by far the most important factors in code selection, followed by age. The youngest and the most educated, while tolerant of variation, are unlikely to actually use dialect. People's social background at home and their own training and occupational status co-determine their speech. The results may be a linguistic manifestation of the establishment of the intellegentsia as the dominant class of East Bloc countries, including the GDR (Konrád and Szélenyi 1978). There are no post-unification studies to date, to indicate if this situation has altered in

the East German states and whether dialect is gaining in importance as an identity marker in the face of East–West tensions (see 3.3). While it is difficult to make direct comparisons between studies conducted in different ways, the relation between Standard German use and social and educational status, between (old) age and dialect speaking, and the importance of the speech situation appear common to Germany (East and West) and Austria.

An important breakthrough within the political limitations of interviewing on either side of the wall at the time was achieved by a team under the direction of Norbert Dittmar (Schlobinski 1985). They were able to study German in three Berlin districts, Wedding (West), Prenzlauer Berg (East) and Zehlendorf (West). The first two are traditional working-class districts, separated by the wall at the time of the study. The researchers found that the Berlin 'dialect' – which is really a dialectally flavoured colloquial non-standard – had remained more intact in Prenzlauer Berg than in any district of West Berlin and that attitudes were more positive towards dialect in the East. This is due in part to the planned housing policy in the GDR keeping Prenzlauer Berg more homogeneous than its western counterpart. Dialect was most stigmatized in middle-class Zehlendorf. Dialect has variously the function of main variety, social symbol and relic (see Mattheier 1980: 166–71). Other factors identified were complex social networks and the role of Berlin dialect in promoting cultural identity against the threat of the Saxon of the then GDR hierarchy. In the West, *Berliner Schnauze*, the local urban style, is still employed as a register for a humorous informal atmosphere and to express a close social relationship within the urban milieu. The way in which discourse patterns such as this function to provide social cohesion is discussed in relation to Berlin and Mannheim studies in Chapter 5.

4.2   Decline or resurgence?

4.2.1   The decline of the 'local dialect' and development of 'regional dialects'

Many linguists have claimed that German dialects are declining or have died. (Spangenberg 1963, Hard 1966, Leopold 1968 and Schönfeld 1974 have all argued in this direction). As the theory runs, dialects have been, or are being, replaced by a more uniform *Umgangssprache*. The terminology muddle surrounding *Umgangssprache* has already been mentioned (4.1.1). Taking into account the various conclusions on the relation between German varieties, I would agree with Hasselberg (1981: 33–4) that there

is a continuum between Standard and dialect, the only two 'systems', and that dialect begins well before the extreme of the continuum. What the proponents of the 'death of dialect' are probably really saying is that the narrowest dialect cum lowest sociolect, Engel's *Bauernsprache*, is rapidly declining to be replaced largely by the other geographical varieties, Engel's *Bürgersprache* and *Honoratiorensprache*. Lerchner (1983) puts it another way – the continuum of dialectal codes has provided the basis for new regional 'sub-standards'.

In her examination of the speech of collective farmers in the north of the GDR, Herrmann-Winter (1974) observes the rise of a regional North German compromise variety strongly influenced by Standard norms as well as by the dialects. (This is spoken north of the line Anklam–Demmin–Rostock.) The finding is based on speech samples and conversations. Phonological features of the regional dialect include the diphthongization of /eː/ and /oː/ to /eɪ/ and /ou/ and a change from /yː/ to /øɪ/; variation between /g/ and /j/; a dark [ɫ]; /s/→/z/ and /b/→/v/; and /sv/→/sw/, as well as the de-affricatization of /ts/ to /s/. Tatzreiter's study of 'new dialects' in the Steiermark (Styria) has already been mentioned above (4.1.1). So it appears that where local dialects were still spoken, they were yielding to regional dialects. This is borne out by the tendency for younger speakers to shed the local features of their dialect leading to a levelling in the broader regional varieties (see Herrgen and Schmidt 1985).

The above-mentioned development is not surprising. The local dialect is the variety of closed rural communities, which no longer exist in most parts of Germany or Austria. Many villages have been urbanized and incorporated into towns and cities, which has brought about not only a breaking of isolation but also a mixing of populations. Mattheier (1980) sees this as part of a modernization process which has been continuing since the sixteenth century, in which cosmopolitan features have gradually spread from town to country. In the most recent period, even large, previously rural areas have become industrialized. Moreover, many villagers commute to work in a nearby industrial town or city every day while maintaining their small farms and their place in the village community. Some people work in towns and cities during the week and return to their villages for the weekend.

One of the studies of this situation, by Hofmann (1963), predates the international sociolinguistic boom. It was based in the village of Nauborn (population 2,400), about 3 km south of Wetzlar (Hessen). 70% of the inhabitants at the time commuted daily to Wetzlar, and therefore belonged to two communities (Wetzlar and Nauborn). The total popula-

tion of Nauborn was divided up according to age, sex, occupation, education and employer (Leitz, optical industry, or Buderus, steel works). Hofmann also took into account voting patterns and affiliation with local and other organizations. The study is restricted to phonological aspects of language, the speech of the commuters being compared with that of elderly non-commuters in Nauborn and that of Wetzlar workers. The least deviation from the local dialect is observed in Buderus workers aged 45–59, who constitute a very conservative group. Workers in the optical industry, who are much less conservative, have more contact with the town population and have therefore been influenced more by its speech. They often use compromise forms or vary between alternatives. The children are influenced more by Standard German through schooling than by the town dialect.

A more extensive study of this problem was the one investigating the speech of all the men aged between 21 and 65 in the village of Erp, south-west of Cologne. 70% of the population commute to work in the nearby industrial area, only about 15% are involved in agriculture, and many people from Cologne have moved into the area. (The somewhat problematic limitation of the research to men is motivated by the fact that hardly any of the women were commuters.) The corpus includes natural conversations, interviews in natural, careful and very careful style, and responses on language attitudes (Besch 1975, Besch and Mattheier 1977). 64% of the informants were primary dialect speakers, 23% used regional dialect (*Umgangssprache*), and 13% spoke Standard only. There were four prevailing attitudes:

    (i) Dialect was the main medium of communication.
    (ii) There was a positive attitude towards the dialect.
    (iii) Standard was growing in importance and dialect declining.
    (iv) Dialect speakers were discriminated against. (Hufschmidt 1983)

Standard was generally regarded as necessary and desirable. Within the new middle class, those with higher incomes and aspirations devalue language maintenance; those with lower income and aspirations tend to be bidialectal, especially if they have strong local ties, as do the old middle class (farmers, craftsmen and tradesmen). Those marrying into old established local families are under pressure to learn the dialect. When informants were asked to mark in on a chart which variety they would use to thirteen interlocutors (Klein 1983), they – especially the new middle class and commuters – had some difficulty in distinguishing intermediate varieties between the extreme forms of dialect and Standard, suggesting that the detailed distinctions are not of great importance (see Mattheier 1983).

Commuting is a factor in the decline of the local dialect also in Austria. Resch (1974) found that 47% of young people, aged 18–30, who commute to Vienna daily or weekly from the village of Gols in the easternmost state of Austria, Burgenland, use the Viennese diphthongs /aɪ/, /au/ or /ɔy/. Only 30% in this age group retain the phonological system of the local dialect. However, 70% of commuters over the age of 30 have kept the original dialect; 48% of skilled workers show the adaptation (cf. 32% who retain the phonology of local dialect); but only 9% of unskilled workers have changed to Viennese diphthongs. The adaptation to Viennese urban dialect is strongest among those whose first employment was in Vienna and those from ethnic minorities (Croatian or Hungarian) and occurs more among daily than weekly commuters. Compromise forms are very prevalent among weekly commuters of all ages.

An additional reason for the decline of the local dialect could be the changes in family structure from the stable three-generation extended family to the more mobile nuclear family, which is less self-sufficient.

Generally, the post-war decades have been a period of unprecedented mobility in Europe – often across regional or even national boundaries. Mobility was particularly strong in the early years of the Federal Republic because of the arrival of refugees from the GDR, 12 million expelled from the former German provinces east of the Oder-Neiße Line and *Volksdeutsche* (ethnic Germans) from Eastern and South-Eastern Europe. Many of them were resettled in rural areas of the Federal Republic, where vastly different dialects were spoken. In 1950, 34.7% of the population of Schleswig-Holstein, 26.6% of Lower Saxony, 20.8% of Bavaria and 18.2% of Württemberg-Baden were people who had been expelled (Hugo Moser 1979b: 323). While Pomeranians and East Prussians predominated in Schleswig-Holstein, Silesians in Lower Saxony and Sudeten Germans in Bavaria and Württemberg-Baden, there were smaller groups from each 'home-region' throughout the Federal Republic (Hugo Moser 1979b: 330). It was only those expellees who remained at home all day whose language was unaffected by the move – old people and housewives. Those at work tended to adapt towards the regional variety of the area of resettlement. Children became bidialectal, employing their parents' dialect at home and the regional dialect of the area elsewhere (Moser 1979b). Today the effects of this great migration have largely worn off, although it may have contributed to a levelling-out of some regionalisms in Standard German. (Moser (1979b: 335) gives some examples for Württemberg.) The second generation of those who had been expelled, like the second generation of Eastern European refugees all over the world, has come to terms with the permanence of its new environment. This new attitude has

increased with the passage of time and with the growing certainty that the eastern provinces will not return to German control. A similar situation developed in Austria, where some *Volksdeutsche* from Central and Eastern Europe, speaking non-Austrian dialects of German, were resettled.

Erdmann (1992) investigates 'what happens when a language which used to be the majority language (Low German) is suddenly confronted on its home turf by an invading language (the near-standard German of postwar East German refugees) with an equal number of speakers' (1992: 5). This is carried out through a sociolinguistic survey of 218 families, personal interviews with 26 three-generation families, and a language attitude test conducted with 13 second-generation informants in Dahlenburg-Bleckede, near Lüneburg, North Germany. Generally speaking, it is the first generation that initiates the language shift in response to the forced population changes, the second generation implements the shift, and the third is characterized by a loss of competence in Low German. The second generation's active competence in the dialect decreases sharply but passive competence is still strong. Active competence has virtually disappeared by the third generation, whose passive competence tends to be limited. There are, however, differences between the occupational groups. Farmers, the homogeneous and traditional local prestige group, have shifted because of the educational aspirations they have vested in their children, and their children's opportunities are being challenged by competition from the refugees using the educational prestige variety. The white-collar occupations shifted due to a need to use Standard at work. However, Low German has been actively maintained among male construction workers because of the covert male prestige and solidarity between the construction trades identified with the non-standard variety in this group. A strong pro-Low German attitude among teachers offers 'top-down' support for dialect maintenance. Among issues opened up by this study are the effects of the entry of women into the construction industry on Low German as a male in-group variety and the impact of possible future East–West mobility on shift from dialects.

In a longitudinal study in progress, Auer *et al.* (1993) are conducting three-monthly narrative interviews among East Germans in West Germany. They are finding that maintenance of the original dialect depends on the extent to which dialect was, in fact, spoken originally by the person and on their present network (mainly West Germans or East Germans). The effects on the rest of the network do not seem to be included in the scope of the project.

Further reasons for the decline in the use of local dialect or in its gravitation towards regional standard have been the communications

explosion, best exemplified by the universal pastime of television-watching, and the sharp rise in the number of people receiving secondary (and post-secondary) education. Both the media and school are Standard German domains and Standard German has become the language of children's primary socialization in many areas. The regional mix in the armed forces during the Second World War also led to some levelling (Schönfeld 1991: 186).

Initially there was a negative policy towards dialect in the GDR, linking it with the feudal era (see Besch 1983: 1409, also Schluppenhauer and Werlen 1983: 1415, Schönfeld 1991: 175). Schönfeld's (1974, 1977) studies suggest that a strong standardization process was brought about by schools in the GDR. As is the case in several of the regions discussed in above-mentioned studies, parents spoke Standard to their children for the sake of their education while school attendance appears to have minimized the use of dialect in the younger generation, as has a higher level of education in general. A factor specific to the GDR was the collectivization of farming, which brought together in rural settings people from different regional backgrounds.

Another reason for the avoidance of local dialect is, of course, the difficulties that it causes in inter-regional communication. The most substantial study so far on this question is Schmitt (1992), which investigated the mutual intelligibility of local dialects in the Rhenish-Franconian and Moselle-Franconian groups (see Map 2) from Rheinland-Palatinate and the Saarland. He played 45–65-year-old people with a strong local identity and manual occupations tapes of sentences and a continuous passage from each of six other local dialects spoken by people over 60 in the two adjacent regions. There were also questions asking for ratings of expected intelligibility of the various dialects. The expectations were only partly fulfilled because they were based almost entirely on a mental geographical map. However, the dialects of the same region did turn out to be most intelligible to the informants. Rhenish-Franconian dialects were more comprehensible to Moselle-Franconian speakers than vice versa. This Schmitt attributes to the greater homogeneity of the Rhenish-Franconian dialects and their closer proximity to the Standard language. Dialects that shared fewer features with their own dialect sounded faster to the informants.

4.2.2   The resurgence of regionalism

The decline of the local dialect and the variation in the use of dialect and standard language as outlined under 4.1 and 4.2.1 are general phenomena

in highly industrialized societies. A counter-phenomenon of similar dimensions is the resurgence of ethnic and regional awareness. It has generally led to a more positive attitude to regional and minority languages rather than to a reversal of language shift (see Fishman *et al.* 1985, Fishman 1991). Even in nations such as Britain and France, where centralized control has been well established over many centuries, ethnic and regional minorities are beginning to assert their rights. The nineteenth-century nation-state is declining in importance. There is a 'higher' level at which there is a tendency towards internationalization – the European Union with its directly elected parliament is an example. But at the 'lower' level people want to identify, not so much with a nation-state, but with their own region, or ethnic minority. In Fishman's (1972: 285) terms, there is diversification and massification at the same time. All this is largely a reaction to centralized bureaucracy and over-development. The 'opting out' mentality longs for close human contact, good air and scope for creativity, according to Dahrendorf (1979: esp. 49, 156). A way in which people can express their own existence and individuality, demonstrate solidarity and regain confidence is through an exclusive variety of communication, i.e. through the dialect – though often the regional rather than the local one. This has led to changes in the functions and status of dialects in Germany and Austria over the past two decades.

A comparison between the 1966 and 1980 public opinion polls on dialect use (Allensbach 1981) shows a decline in the percentage of dialect speakers but a rise in the proportion of dialect users among them. While the proportion of people who master a dialect has decreased from 59% to 53%, the number of those who can speak a dialect but never use it has dropped from 29% to 16%. (Among 30–44-year-olds from 15% to 8%.) According to the 1980 survey, dialect is used mainly in informal domains and in personalized local activities. At the same time, 83% of respondents preferred to remain living in their home region. Schönfeld and Pape (1981: 187–8), in a survey of research on GDR varieties of German, recorded a dialect resurgence there, with the dialect increasingly acquired not from the parents but from the peer-group. Stellmacher (1987), in his work in north-western Germany, finds positive attitudes to dialect there, with many regretting their lack of competence in it. 90% of his informants allow their children to learn it on the street or from grandparents (who, however, are sometimes reluctant to pass it on). On the whole, it is the oldest and youngest groups who hold the most positive attitudes to dialect.

Dialect serves as a marker of solidarity and group identification. This has no doubt played a role in the positive attitude towards local dialect

among Stellmacher's (1977) younger informants and towards *mundartnahe Umgangssprache* among the younger generation in Schönfeld's (1974) GDR study. It has led to the younger members of the Viennese middle class employing more dialect than their older counterparts (Wodak-Leodolter and Dressler 1978). The 1980 Allensbach survey found that 46% of young people speak dialect at work – for them, the domain boundaries between dialect and Standard are breaking down. In contrast, people over 30 normally employ Standard German at work. Family and friendship, however, continue to be their primary domains of dialect use. This trend is confirmed by Zehetner's (1985: 171) research in Bavaria. It is the middle generation, the 25–45-year-olds whose language is furthest from the dialect while younger people tend to produce the sounds and words of their grandparents. This quite conscious development can be attributed to nostalgia and/or regional identity. Another reason for the *Mundartwelle* (dialect wave) is, according to Schluppenhauer and Werlen (1983: 142), a tendency towards informality, also reflected in the increased use of *du* (see 5.3).

4.3   New functions of dialects

Dialects are being employed for functions that did not exist in the past or for which they were previously not deemed appropriate. These include radio talkback programmes and, on some stations (e.g. WDR 3), weather reports; radio, TV and street advertisements; slogans and pamphlets of residents' action groups; pop music and cabaret; as well as 'serious literature'. The fact that radio in Germany is organized on a regional basis and is intended to cater for a region facilitates some use of dialect (Straßner 1983). This is hardly possible on television in Germany.

Dialects, being 'discriminated varieties', have become languages of protest, part of an emancipatory strategy. Forced monolingualism in the standard language is seen as an ideological instrument of domination. Pop groups using dialect, such as Die Prinzen in Leipzig, played a role in the GDR revolution. Young people are identifying with pop groups singing in dialect (see 6.2). Teaching, social work and psychotherapy in dialect have yielded fruitful results. It is in this context that F. Hoffmann (1981) pleads for an interdisciplinary approach to dialectology.

For many decades, dialect speaking was identified either with conservatives, who resisted change, or with Fascists, for whom German rural varieties were a 'healthy' part of the *Blut und Boden* (blood and soil) ideology. But in the late 1960s and early 1970s, dialect speaking was propagated by young educated socialists who were trying to establish solidarity with the

working class. It became, in a way, an index of 'social conscience' or of ideology. The resurgence of dialect in Germany and Austria is closely connected with the conservation movement, which has a young, 'green' and radical profile and is associated with action against nuclear power.[7] The 1980 public opinion poll (Allensbach 1981) shows an increase in dialect use among those with tertiary education. Some of the (regional) dialects are used across national boundaries, e.g. Alemannic (South-West Germany, Switzerland, Alsace), Bavarian (Bavaria, Austria, South Tyrol), and serve as a link between groups in different countries challenging the nation-state and the pollution of the environment.

With the dialect resurgence has come a 'rediscovery' of dialect as a potential medium of literature – whether poetry (e.g. the Viennese – Artmann and Jandl, and the Bernese – Eggimann and Marti) or drama and film (the Bavarians – Fassbinder, Kroetz and Sperr, and the Austrians – Qualtinger and Turrini). F. Hoffmann (1981) contrasts three types of contemporary dialect poets:

(i)   those 'democratizing' literature by writing poems, intended as social criticism, in the 'language of the masses' (e.g. Andrae, Haid, Kusz)

(ii) those 'liberating' poetry from the standard language and treating dialect like any other language as material for literature (e.g. Bellmann, Bünker, Kruse)

(iii) those who use dialect to extend their potential for language play, thereby developing a new relationship to reality (e.g. the Austrian 'concrete poets' – Achleitner, Artmann, Jandl, Rühm)

4.3.1   Austria as a special case

The experiments currently made by Austrian creative writers, producers of pop music (see also 6.2) and intellectuals in the interpenetration of stylistic registers and sociolinguistic domains through dialect are probably a cause of the confusion of linguists as to whether dialect use in Austria has actually been increasing (Wodak–Leodolter and Dressler 1978, but cf. Moosmüller 1991), or whether it is giving way to Standard German under North German influence (Eichhoff 1977–8: 13). Reiffenstein (1977) sees Standard increasing at the expense of dialects in a general way, but dialect making inroads into literature and politics – which is probably an appropriate assessment of the situation. According to Reiffenstein,

---

[7]   See below, 6.3.

there is no diglossia in Austria as Austrian Standard German and dialects are not employed in complementary distribution. However, there are domains (e.g. law, school, church) which are distinctly the province of Standard German. In the cities, there is no domain which is equally clearly the province of dialect, whether in a local or regional form. There is, at the lexical level, a tendency towards Standard, though non-standard phonological rules are being preserved and even extended.

It must be taken into account that, in most parts of Austria, regional identification through language is at the same time national identification, for a regional dialect is distinctively 'Austrian' as opposed to 'German'. This is part of the dilemma discussed by Muhr (1987a) and Pollak (1992) and explained by Muhr in terms of the '*Standard-nach-innen*' and the '*Standard-nach-außen*' (see above, 2.4.2). The main exceptions to the national-regional-syncretism are the Alemannic dialects in the western state of Vorarlberg, which is increasingly desirous of expressing its regional peculiarity and is hoping to attain greater autonomy, a tertiary educational institution, and other benefits commensurate with its cultural and geographical distance from 'Austria proper'.

4.4   Educational aspects of the dialect–Standard question

There are indications that Standard German is mastered better by the upper classes than by the working class in empirical research in at least Württemberg (Ammon 1972: 95), Bavaria (Rein and Scheffelmann-Meyer 1975) and Hessen (Hasselberg 1976b: 77). The problems at school of monodialectal speakers (using only a non-standard dialect) have been the object of a number of studies and the findings are set out below.

(i) Dialect speakers, even in Bavaria, take four years of schooling before they reach the level of Standard German attained by bi-dialectals (speaking Standard and dialect) by the time they enter school. Errors were made by dialect speakers in the fourth grade (9-year-olds) of a Bavarian primary school in 11.75% of oral utterances and 16.3% of written ones. 71% of the errors in oral utterances and 40% of those in the written language were due to interference from dialect (Reitmajer 1975).

(ii) Dialect speakers encounter greater difficulties in acquiring literacy skills than do Standard speakers, as has been empirically shown for the Swabian area by Ammon (1975).

(iii) There is interference from the phonology of the dialect in the orthography of Standard German. This has been examined in

speakers of Rhenish-Franconian, Bavarian, Swabian, Alemannic and Pfälzisch (Ammon 1979: 33). In Zehetner's (1985: 206) Bavarian study, dialect speakers make an average of 10.63 errors per 100 words and Standard speakers 7.62. However, Zehetner does stress that the dialect is not the cause of all errors, and Naumann (1989) points out that there are fewer spelling errors than a contrastive analysis would predict.

(iv) Dialect speakers obtain results in German inferior to those of pupils who speak Standard at home. They feel uncertain in class and are reluctant to take part in group discussions (Ammon 1975: 101; Hasselberg 1972, 1976: 103–4). This is because Standard German is *the* language of schooling in the Federal Republic. There are sanctions against speaking dialect in class, or at least teachers initiate the use of Standard 'by their example'. Dialect speakers are also less likely to be admitted into *Gymnasien*, the schools which lead to tertiary education (Hugo Moser 1972: 196), although here other factors (class, schooling, etc.) have to be taken into account. Nevertheless, Hasselberg (1981) found that only 20% of *middle class* monodialectal speakers in 26 Hessian comprehensive schools were expected to pass Matriculation (cf. 57% Standard or bilingual middle-class speakers).

It is clearly not easy to determine causes and effects in the relation between language, class and social and educational inequality. But this is by no means a problem specific to the German language. Barbour (1987) argues that middle-class speech also deviates from Standard norms, albeit not as much as does that of the lower class.

There have been three different responses to these problems:

(i) The argument for Standard German   This was argued very strongly by Ammon in his earlier work (1972, 1973a, 1973b, 1975, 1979). He saw only advantages in adopting the standard language, due to its extensive communication radius, its use in formal domains, and its monopoly on the written form of communication (Ammon 1979: 36). The advantages of the dialect, such as its role in collective and personal identification, he claimed (1979: 37), could be transferred to the standard language.

(ii) The argument for extending the permitted domains of the dialect   This argument was widely debated in the long educational and political controversy surrounding the guidelines for German in schools proposed in the early 1970s by the SPD government of Hessen. The

guidelines contained an emphasis on the teaching of communicative competence in whatever variety or varieties of the language the pupil has available to him/her. They attempted to separate the ability to communicate effectively from the exclusive use of Standard German in the school domain. In fact, it was argued (Christ *et al.* 1974) that, through the imposition of Standard German, working-class children are either muted or cut off from their home background. Standard German was seen as the sociolect of the middle class and the school as an assimilationist agent which conceals class struggle. These arguments were countered partly by the denial of such conflicts, partly by an appeal against the 'politicization' of language and education, partly by evoking the cultural heritage of Standard German which might be destroyed, and perhaps most effectively by referring to the need to communicate on a wide radius (cf. Christ *et al.* 1974), to say nothing of the needs of children moving to another region. In a far more limited way, Mecklenburg-Vorpommern has introduced Low German as an optional subject in its schools. Pre-school projects have also been introduced, with songs and role-plays (*Rheinischer Merkur*, 27 December 1991, p.15).

(iii) The difference hypothesis Labov's (1970) 'difference hypothesis' that no varieties are inferior, though they may be different, was strongly supported in the Federal Republic by Dittmar (1973) and other sociolinguists. They emphasize the functional differences of Standard German and dialect.

A series of contrastive analyses (phonological, lexical, grammatical) has been produced by linguists specializing in dialects and edited by Besch, Löffler and Reich. They contrast Standard German and dialect and have treated Alemannic, Bavarian, Hessian, Rhenic, Swabian and Westphalian dialects. Their intention is to equip German primary school teachers with data to enable them to understand transfers in the Standard German of dialect speakers and to use dialects as a basis for teaching Standard German. There is also a volume on Berlin dialect by Schlobinski and Blank (1985) outside the series. It is intended for upper secondary school use. Barbour (1987) makes the valid point that the series contrasts a formal and normative Standard German with traditional dialects, ignoring the more commonly used (colloquial) varieties along the continuum.

There is probably another powerful argument for making all people in strong dialect areas bidialectal, namely that monodialectal speakers of Standard German can be social outcasts in many such areas. Some of the assumptions of the contrastive series (the value of contrasting dialect and a standard language, and the homogeneity of each system) are challenged by Mattheier (1980: 132–6). He also argues the need for *content-*

based materials for disadvantaged dialect-speaking children (not just for teachers' use).

On the whole, it may be concluded that nowadays, with the decline of the narrow local variety, dialects are not communication barriers but they tend to reflect and exacerbate social barriers.

4.5   Attitudes to dialects and their speakers

Some dialects are generally evaluated more or less favourably than others. König (1978) and Jakob (1992) both indicate that dialects have a fairly consistent sliding scale of popularity, prestige and stigmatization among German speakers. Jakob refers to a study carried out in the 1960s which found Viennese to be the most popular dialect of German (19% popularity), followed by Hamburg, Cologne and Munich, with Frankfurt (8%) and Leipzig (2%) trailing the list. It is clear from Jakob's study that there is no way of separating the 'internal' (language) and 'external' (speaker) aspects of the prestige scale. Incidentally, the Austrians in Moosmüller's (1991) study consistently give Viennese a negative rating compared with most provincial dialects, surpassed only by Burgenländisch. This she attributes (1991: 153) to the 'dusty', industrialized image of Vienna and the 'backward' image of the Burgenland.

Using a range of different methods, Hundt (1992) elicits attitudes to speakers of Bavarian, Hamburg, Palatinate and Swabian dialects (including matched-guise tests) from speakers from all these areas. There is considerable consistency in the stereotypes, e.g. Hamburg speakers are rated intelligent, arrogant and lacking in emotions; Swabian speakers miserly, small-minded and sociable; Bavarian speakers primitive, attached to their area, and sociable; and Palatinate speakers slow, boring, and sociable. While the subjects cannot always reconstruct the features, they probably identify bundles of them. It appears that there are a combination of reasons for the assessments, including extralinguistic ones and distance from Standard German.

The question could be put: 'Is there anything inherent in a dialect which gives it a negative stigma or is it that the status of the majority of the speakers is transferred to the dialect?' – something that occurs in many regions in different countries. A long-standing prejudice against Saxon dialects – or Standard German spoken with a Saxon accent – was reinforced by the Saxon dominance among functionaries in the last years of the GDR. However, the prejudice has waned due to the role of Saxons in leading the East German revolution and the association of Saxon accents and dialects with the *Wende* (Peter von Polenz, personal communication).

Since dialects also have a sociolectal function (see 4.1), attitudes to dialects are also an indicator of social prejudice (see Moosmüller 1991, above). In Vienna, Wodak, Menz and Laluschek (1989: 106) found that dialect speakers are interrupted more than Standard speakers, are given less information and ask fewer questions in communication with doctors. Moosmüller's (1991) study shows that, across class, gender and age, Austrians uniformly assign Standard speakers to higher-status occupations than dialect speakers.

On the other hand, Fónagy (1963) has found that certain sounds have particular images for listener-informants from diverse language and other backgrounds, e.g. back, more open vowels and diphthongs are unpleasant in contrast to front, more closed vowels. This would suggest that the sounds themselves could be responsible for the stigmatization of a dialect, just as stereotyped attitudes are held for specific languages. This subject would warrant closer investigation.

4.6   Brief summary

In Germany and Austria, there is an overlap between dialects and socio-lects, so that dialects are both socially stigmatized and instruments of regional pride and collective identification. They are used far more in the South than in the North of the Federal Republic, where they are more stigmatized. There is variation along a continuum between local dialects with a narrow currency via regional dialects to the standard language. Improved communication and educational opportunities, urbanization, internal migration and commuter mobility have led to a great decline in local dialects in favour of regional ones.

The decline of the local dialect indicates at least some greater social mobility in both Germany and Austria. However, in both countries, even in the areas formerly part of the GDR, social status and/or function in the workforce as well as age are still the main personal factors determining one's language variety. There is widespread situational variation. Domain, topic, role relationship and emotional state co-determine choice of variety. This is particularly so in southern Germany, where dialect and Standard German tend towards a diglossic relationship.

There is also a tendency towards the heterogenization of Standard German with a broad variation in regional features in German Standard.

A regional resurgence is characterized by a more positive attitude towards (regional) dialects and their use in new functions. Despite contin-uing language shift away from dialect use in many parts of Germany, partly motivated by the dominance of Standard in education, some young

people are learning it outside the nuclear family. This dialect revival is indicative of increasing regionalism and the lessening of class differences and it reflects anti-establishment political ideologies, which have played a role in the use of dialect in politics and contemporary literature.

The disadvantages for dialect speakers in West German schools have led to constructive action to alleviate the problems of the pupils, including the development of materials for teachers which will enable them to use dialects as a basis for teaching Standard German.

4.7 Further reading

The reader is referred to Barbour and Stevenson (1990), which deals more comprehensively with the issues discussed in this chapter. R.E. Keller 1961 and Russ 1990, written from the traditional and structural viewpoints, also intended for the English reader, deal specifically with German dialects. In German, two books focusing on sociolinguistic and pragmatic aspects are Mattheier (1980) and Löffler (1985). The massive two-volume *Dialektologie. Ein Handbuch zur deutschen und allgemeinen Dialektforschung*, edited by Werner Besch *et al.*, is a very useful reference book. Some of the numerous studies in this field are discussed in this chapter. Ammon (1979) is also a good general survey, while Ammon's books (especially 1973) concentrate on the educational implications of variation in German.

5

Communication patterns

So far we have concentrated our discussion on the more traditional areas of linguistic description – phonology, morphology, and syntax, lexicon and semantics. With recent advances in pragmatics beyond the theoretical level and in discourse analysis, more studies will provide information in an area of language that is very intricately bound to cultural values systems. We have referred, in Chapter 3, to research indicating how the sociopolitical differences between the GDR and the Federal Republic affected the pragmatic and discourse levels and to the difficulties this is causing East Germans in the post-unification era. This is the tip of the iceberg; this chapter will focus on national and regional variation at these levels.

5.1 Some national and regional specifics in communication rules

Coulmas (1979) has argued that the pragmatic conditions for the appropriate usage and communicative function of routine formulae relate to cognitive systems of beliefs, preferences, norms and values. He demonstrates that a proper analysis needs to be reached by a contrastive approach. This applies to both national and regional differences.

If, as has been suggested in Chapter 2, there are national cultural differences between the German-language countries, they will be reflected in the communication patterns of the language. The variations in cultural values systems displayed by the regions of each of the countries can be expressed in pragmatic and discourse rules. The same applies to differences resulting from social structures. Communication patterns, often relating to issues of politeness (see Brown and Levinson 1987), will affect the success of communication as well as attitudes to other German-language groups.

5.1.1 Germany and Britain

House and Kasper (1981) conclude that Germans communicate with a greater degree of directness than do British English speakers. They had twenty-four informal everyday situations – complaints and requests – acted out by two pairs of native speakers, one English and one German pair. House and Kasper establish eight levels of directness for each of the speech acts. For *complaints* there is a heavy concentration on level 6 (the third most direct level) among the Germans (e.g. *Du hättest meine Bluse nicht ohne meine Erlaubnis nehmen sollen!* You shouldn't have taken my blouse without asking my permission. Or: *Du hast meine ganze Bluse ruiniert!* You have ruined my blouse). The British English speakers show a spread from level 3 (e.g. Terrible, this stain won't come off!) to 6, while the least direct level (Odd, my blouse was perfectly clean last night), was far more frequent among the English than the German informants. For the *requests*, level 6 was by far the most frequent among the Germans (e.g. *Du solltest das Fenster zumachen!* You should close the window). The English, on the other hand, concentrate around level 3 (e.g. You can close the window). The most indirect level, 1 (It's very cold in here) is considered far more by the English than the Germans.

House and Kasper also categorize modality markers which downgrade or upgrade the impact of the utterances in both languages, e.g.:

> downgraders: *please, kind of, just, I guess,* [ɛ:], and their German
> equivalents *ja, mal, eben, wohl, denn*
> upgraders: *absolutely, well, I'm sure, you must understand,* and their
> German equivalents

Downgraders are used by the English informants 1.5 times as often as by the German subjects in the same situations (2.7 times as much for the complaints). There is an overall tendency for the German speakers to use upgraders 4.6 times as often as the English informants, who hardly employ them at all with requests. The role of intonation needs to be considered in this area. It is difficult to isolate cultural from individual characteristics in the discourse situations tested; but since national stereotypes and inter-cultural communication breakdown are based on differences in communication rules, any progress in quantifying them is of great importance. It is unfortunate that House and Kasper do not reveal the regional origins of their subjects. The above conclusions concerning German are confirmed in Blum-Kulka, House and Kasper's (1989) study of complaints and requests of Argentinians, Australians, French-Canadians, Germans and Israelis, where Argentinians and Israelis exhibit more and

Australians and French-Canadians less direct ways of realizing speech acts than Germans.

Schlieben-Lange and Weydt (1978) contend that, in West Germany, questions are asked and decisions are made in a small group first, whereas in the US, discussions and questions are more likely to take place immediately in the entire group.

5.1.2   Austria and Germany

In many respects, Austrians communicate in a way more similar to Czechs, Slovenians, Hungarians and Northern Italians than to Germans (especially North Germans). Many communication routines date back to the Monarchy, the period when all these cultures were part of a poly-ethnic empire, some are of far more recent vintage. An Austrian novelist remarked that present-day Vienna has many clocks, all showing different times. This is certainly reflected in pragmatic aspects of language, especially those related to politeness.

Titles are employed more widely than in Germany (especially the western part) and still transferred to the wife of the person concerned (e.g. *Frau Professor, Frau Hofrat*).[1] This reflects the hierarchical class system and the acceptance of authority. Honorific formulae considered archaic or expressing distance in the Germanies (e.g. *Mit vorzüglicher Hochachtung* with excellent respect, rather than *Hochachtungsvoll*, respectfully) are still used in letters. The expression *Aber bitte* (Mind you!) is used outside hon-orifics to draw the hearer's attention to a particular point. On the other hand, the farewell routine *baaba*, originally from young children's register and baby talk, is specific to Austrian German.

Austria is one of the areas of Europe where, to achieve your goals in communication, you need to 'overstate' your case. Understatement in rhetorical or ironical usage, as is practised in Britain and Scandinavia, and to a much lesser extent in the Netherlands and parts of North Germany, is ineffective or misunderstood in Austria. This is particularly the case in requests, advice, warnings and promises. House and Kasper's downgraders (1981; see above, 5.1.1) often accompany overstatement due to Austrian politeness rules.

Some differences between Austrian and West German communication routines may be exemplified in telephone booth notices warning would-be vandals:

---

[1] *Hofrat*: a high rank in the Civil Service.

Table 6 *Subjunctives in requests – Austrians and Germans*

	n	Austrians (%)	Germans (%)
kannst	62	45	55
könntest / würdest	148	60	40
hättest	137	60	40

Source: Muhr (1993b: 35)

Table 7 *Neutral and negative evaluations – Austrians and Germans*

	n	Austrians (%)	Germans (%)
Neutral formulations	115	48	52
Negative evaluations	42	78	22

Source: Muhr (1993b: 36).

> Dieses Telefon kann Leben retten. *Zerstört es nicht!* (This telephone can save lives. *Do not destroy it!*) (Austrian)

> *Schützt dieses Telefon!* Es kann Leben retten. *(Protect this telephone. It can save lives.)* (West German)

The Austrian version overstates, in a pessimistic way.

Muhr (1993b) has made contrastive studies of the responses of 163 Austrians and 163 (West) Germans from a diversity of regions, using a version of Blum-Kulka, House and Kasper's (1989) discourse completion test, where a situation was depicted in writing and the respondent was required to supply the appropriate speech act, such as request or complaint. Austrians fairly consistently produced longer utterances than Germans, both in the number of words and in the number of illocutionary elements. Austrians also used more subjunctives in the same situation, e.g. in a request to clean a dirty kitchen. In the same completion test, Austrians used far more negative evaluations (e.g. *Ich möchte nicht in diesem Saustall zu kochen anfangen.* I wouldn't want to start cooking in this pigsty) and marginally fewer neutral formulations.

Muhr (1993b) is part of a larger study (Muhr, forthcoming) which comes up with similar results in other situations – Austrians produce longer utterances, many subjunctives and modal verbs, and explicit requests. In the questions on job search, 87% of the subjunctive modal

verbs came from Austrian respondents, who also used 14% more words (Muhr, forthcoming: 139). The length of the realizations is related to a Central European discourse style, requiring explanations of justifications, and apologies as part of complex directive/request sequences in the interests of politeness (see Clyne 1994), e.g.:

> Entschuldigen Sie, ich möchte nicht lästig sein, doch ich kenne Sie vom Sehen, da wir in der gleichen Straße wohnen, und sah Sie auch mit dem Auto hierherkommen. Wären Sie bitte so nett und würden mich mit nach Haus nehmen – der nächste Bus fährt nämlich erst in einer Stunde. ('Excuse me, I don't want to be a bother, but I know you by sight since we live in the same street, and saw you came here by car too. Would you be kind enough to give me a lift home – the next bus only leaves in an hour (doesn't leave for an hour)?) (Austrian)

> Ich möchte, wenn es Ihnen recht ist, mit Ihnen nach Hause fahren. (If it's alright with you, I'd like to have a lift home.) (German) (Muhr, forthcoming: 97.)

Germans produce more statements but they are shorter; Austrians employ long introductions and take longer to get to the actual point.

In another study, involving 23 middle-class and 23 working-class Austrians, Muhr (1988) investigates the Austrian attitudinal response to German modal particles and their anticipated Austrian equivalents in situational contexts. *Etwa*, as in:

> Hast du *etwa* Salz in den Kaffee getan? (Have you put salt in the coffee or something?)

is unusual in Austria and restricted to the written register. The nearest equivalent, *vielleicht*, is rated as 'more impatient'. *Denn* is considered far more acceptable. The position of *denn* in a polite utterance is limited to a position after the noun in ASG:

> Wo kommst du *denn* her?

whereas the following is also acceptable in GSG, with a difference in emphasis:

> Wo kommst *denn* du her?

Mal, as in:

> Kannst du mir eben *mal* einen Gefallen tun und den Dienst tauschen? (in library) (Could you just do me a favour and swap duties?)

is considered by the Austrians to be German German, brash, and impetuous. The same applies to *eben*. To Muhr's Austrian respondents, *halt* is not the Austrian equivalent. It is warm and friendly while *eben* sounds cold and aggressive. Moreover, *halt* tends to be used towards the end of an intonational sequence, *eben* in a continuing one.

Generally speaking, Austrians have a more creative and lighthearted and less prescriptive approach to language than Germans. This is reflected not only in Wittgenstein and other philosophers, but also in contemporary Austrian literature (e.g. Jandl, Handke), which tends to play with language more freely than German literature. It may be related to life in the multicultural Austro-Hungarian Empire. An area in need of study is *Schimpfen* in Austria, especially in Vienna. This speech act combines elements of swearing, grumbling, whingeing, abusing and nagging, and is an everyday public response to the powerlessness of the individual.

5.1.3   Switzerland

While English people tend to 'share a text' in verbal interaction by negotiating the choice and development of the topic, German-Swiss simply present their position (Watts 1989). Those Swiss 'who fail to do so', Watts concludes in his cross-cultural comparison (1989: 160), tend to be regarded as 'very passive communicative partners'; those who do so 'often (appear) argumentative, certainly competitive, perhaps even dogmatic to outsiders'.

5.1.4   Luxembourg

Luxembourgian communication routines are based on egalitarianism, a preference for order, discipline and tradition, but a lack of respect for authority, leading to directness. Closeness to the land is reflected in symbolism in everyday speech and proverbs (F. Hoffmann 1969). This is in spite of the industrialization of large parts of Luxembourg and the fact that 78,000 of its people live in the capital. Understatement and black humour occur frequently in written and spoken discourse.

5.1.5   East–West differences

First the peaceful revolution in East Germany and then German unification have provided an opportunity to study the effects of political division on discourse patterns and pragmatic rules.

For example, in the GDR, a request for an article in a shop was performed by *Haben Sie..?* (Do you have..?) as opposed to *Ich hätte gern...* (I

would like...) or *Geben Sie mir bitte...* (Please give me...) in the Federal Republic. Other pragmatic variation has been found in the communication routines for renting a flat, opening bank accounts and resolving work patterns (Hellmann 1989b). It has been claimed that East Germans communicate in a more indirect way, that they employ a more collaborative type of discourse, that in communication with West Germans they suffer a conversational imbalance, that they behave in an uncertain manner (Ylönen 1992). East Germans communicate in a slower, quieter, more monotonous way, while West Germans speak faster, with more marked pauses and more clearly accentuated intonation (Reséndiz 1992). Oschlies (1989: 20) claims that they are more gentle with one another than are West Germans (Oschlies 1989: 20).

In contact between East and West Germans, the westerners tend to use speech acts of instructions and set conditions while East Germans simply express agreement (Ylönen 1992). It is likely that this is the result of socialization in the GDR and recent life-style rather than of longstanding regional variation. It may well be that the differences will become part of East German cultural communication styles. In Chapter 3, I indicated the effects that East Germans' lack of competence in specific discourse patterns for certain kinds of bureaucratic communication (e.g. applications, tax returns, formal complaints) are already having on their ability to cope with communication in particular domains in unified Germany. Research on attitudes of East and West Germans to the varying styles, e.g. in job interviews, would enhance our understanding of the dimensions of intercultural communication breakdown.

5.1.6   Regional differences

Schlieben-Lange and Weydt (1978) have made some observations on regional differences in communication rules within the Federal Republic. For instance, they contrast Swabian and Rhenic reactions to compliments – the Rheinlander accepts a compliment, the Swabian plays down the cause of the praise. Another routine that they describe is the Rhenic greeting which consists of the addressee's name articulated with greeting intonation. The utterance *Da können wir mal sehen* (We'll just see) in response to a request has a dilatory function in the Rhineland and Bavaria, but is a promise in Württemberg. Schlieben-Lange and Weydt refer to questions that, in South-Western Germany, represent both a quasi-monologue and the acceptance of a formal obligation to take turns. Such questions are misinterpreted by Northerners as rude, since they give the impression of a reproach in a situation where thanks or some other speech act of acknowl-

edgement would be usual in their own repertoire. Similarly, the utterance *I mag hald net* (I just don't want to) or *Halt so* (That's how it is) in Bavaria fulfils the formal obligation to take turns. In most other regions, a detailed reason would be necessary for the sake of politeness.

Apart from such potential for communication breakdown, there are differences in the degree of verbality between regions of West Germany. Swabians, Westphalians and Schleswig-Holsteiners are generally known for their non-verbality in comparison with Rhinelanders, Berliners and Bavarians. I have also observed different types of proxemic behaviour between different regions, especially for sitting in public places, such as trains and restaurants. Swabians (particularly Stuttgarters) and Schleswig-Holsteiners employ more distant proxemic rules than Rhinelanders and Bavarians, something they all tend to be conscious of. The Swabian satirical writer 'Thaddäus Troll' (1970: 114) tells of a country innkeeper's daughter saying to her father: 'Was machet mer bloß, Vadder, do kommet femf Schduagerder, ond mir hent bloß vier Disch!' (Whatever shall we do, father, there are five Stuttgarters coming, and we've only got four tables.) On the other hand, Bavarians are noted for their *Gemütlichkeit* (an atmosphere of jovial togetherness). In suburban trains around Stuttgart (*Nahverkehrszüge*), people will at first 'monopolize' a double seat, with no-one sitting opposite. When the train becomes crowded, new passengers will occupy seats diagonally opposite the others. The same applies generally in the area north of Hamburg, but in Bavaria and the Rhineland, passengers tend to sit next to and/or opposite each other. More distant proxemic patterns are associated with less conversation. Such differences as the above could be explained by recourse to the social and religious history of Germany.

5.1.7   Social variation

Dialects are both markers of distinctiveness and, in rural communities, instruments of social cohesion. The same can be said for urban dialects, which are often also sociolects, indicating membership of certain sections on the social hierarchy.

The ways in which an urban dialect is employed in the resolution of inter-personal conflicts are demonstrated in the Berlin study by Dittmar, Schlobinski and Wachs (1986). Whereas in a small rural settlement, conflicts are resolved through the social control of those who are at the top of the social hierarchy, in an anonymous urban centre, this is done by interactional eloquence. The Berliners' feeling of one's own superiority plays an important role. This reflects its historic position as Prussian and German capital city and is expressed through quick-wittedness, humour,

effective verbal routines and/or self-assertive aggressiveness. The rhetorical formula *sag ick* (I say) reflects asymmetrical verbal fighting. The many nicknames of buildings, activities and occupations in Berlin, e.g. *Schwangere Auster* (*Kongreßhalle*, congress hall, literally 'pregnant oyster'), *Dreckbuddl* (*Putzfrau*, cleaning lady, literally 'filth bottle'), *ausbuchteln* (*unter großer Anstrengung einen Aufsatz schreiben*, to write an essay under a great deal of strain), *trommeln* (*angeben*, 'to drum' for 'to boast'), display verbal creativity, as do graphic comparisons.

As part of a large study of the use of linguistic variation as an instrument of social cohesion by different groups in a number of Mannheim suburbs, Keim and Schwitalla (1993) contrast the style of two groups of women. One is a literature circle, the other a craft group. The literature circle members avoid any topics that are taboo, keeping the level of conversation at the general when they talk about other people. They engage in ironical and joking behaviour. The members of the craft group, on the other hand, more overtly comment on serious violations of norms in their gossip. Members of both groups display collaborative discourse, in which they help each other in formulating a position (Schwitalla 1992).

Among other groups studied in the project (Kallmeyer 1994) are a political circle, sports clubs, a youth group, and pupils of a *Gymnasium*. Code-switching between varieties at different points on the continuum between local dialect and Standard is used to characterize and cite people of other groups. There is a strong 'us–them' dichotomy (Gumperz 1994), which is expressed through phonology, prosody and the lexicon as well as through tempo and volume, especially in gossip and the telling of jokes. Asocial types ('Asos') are portrayed as using aggressive, brutal, violent language and sexual terms in everyday conversation. The young working class are characterized, by *Gymnasiasten*, as having rough voices and elongating vowels and final syllables. The *Gymnasiasten* believe that they themselves speak softly and quietly. While the literature circle members engage in collaborative discourse, the narrator tends to dominate when anecdotes are shared in most of the other groups.

Schenker (1978) concludes, on the basis of interviews on linguistic etiquette with 500 people in the city of Trier and the nearby village of Maxweiler, that less privileged people are more conservative in their communication rules (e.g. titles, who greets whom first, pronouns of address). Villagers, women, older people and members of the lower class use and value transmitted norms more than townspeople, men, the younger generation and the middle class respectively. The exception is in the use of *du*, which the villagers of Maxweiler prefer because their dialect does not have a *Sie* form.

5.2   Attitudes to language, and some consequences

Germans, but not Austrians (see above, 5.1.2), tend to take a more prescriptive attitude to language than do English speakers. To Germans,
language is a serious matter, related to ideology. This limits the use of
verbal humour and verbal irony in everyday discourse. The kind of
'ping-pong pun game' that is played by many English speakers is
not known to, or understood by, most German speakers. Verbal humour
and verbal irony are, at best, the province of creative writers (including journalists who write for such periodicals as *Der Spiegel* and
Die Zeit) and cabarettists. House and Kasper's (1981) research indicates
that Germans overstate while English people understate (see above,
5.1.1).

German children do not have as rich a tradition of children's riddles
and rhymes based on linguistic creativity and polysemy as do English-
speaking children. This can be seen by comparing German collections
of children's humour (e.g. Helmers 1971) with English-language ones
(e.g. Opie and Opie 1959/1967, Turner 1969). The German children's
joke centres far more around situations than on linguistic aspects such
as polysemy.[2] Most of the children's verbal humour referred to by
Helmers appears to be based on a reaction to linguistic errors made by
the informant or by someone else, i.e. a prescriptive attitude to language. The stereotypical linguistic riddles on which many English
speakers have been brought up – such as 'When is an X not an X?' or
'Knock, knock, who's there?'[3] – have no equivalent in German. (One
exception is the pattern: 'What is the difference between an X and a
Y?', which is common to both cultures.) Perhaps the best source of
verbal humour in German is bilingual puns, which are the province of
an older, more élitist group. It may be that the *general* tendency
towards, or away from, verbal humour is one that is developed early in
life.

---

[2]   This is borne out in Baulch's (1979) comparison of jokes told by German and Australian
schoolchildren. However, there are local differences, e.g. some *ad hoc* rhyming in Bavaria and
ritual insults in Saarland mining areas (Wolfgang Klein, personal communication).

[3]   For example: Q: When is a tree not a tree?
                     A: When it is a lava*tory*.

Q: Knock knock, who's there?
A: Mike ...
Q: Mike who?
A: *My* keys are locked in your car and I can't get into mine.

5.3   The German address system

Although the German system of pronouns of address is generally perceived as a *du* (singular) + *ihr* (plural) [informal] / *Sie* [formal] dichotomy
(e.g. by Brown and Gilman 1960), there are actually seven modes of
address in use:

(i)   *Du* as the informal pronoun of address in the singular.
(ii) *Ihr* as the informal pronoun of address in the plural.
(iii) *Ihr* as the plural pronoun of address for a group of two or more
      people, of whom at least one is addressed as *du* and at least one is
      addressed as *Sie*.
(iv) *Ihr* as a marked plural pronoun of address for a group of two or
      more people addressed as *Sie*, e.g. *Wieviel Bücher habt ihr in der
      Bibliothek?* (How many books are there in your library?) (stress-
      ing that the speaker is referring to the speech partner's institu-
      tion and not to his or her personal library).
(v)   *Sie* as the plural pronoun of address for a group of two or more
      people, of whom at least one is addressed as *du* and at least one
      as *Sie*. This is intended to be polite, and the utterance is oriented
      to the speech partner(s) with whom one is ordinarily on *Sie*
      terms.
(vi) *Sie* as the formal pronoun of address in the singular.
(vii) *Sie* as the formal pronoun of address in the plural.

The rarest pattern is 5, and 2 and 3 are much more common than 4 and 5.

In the past, the use of *du* has been a manifestation of a fairly closed
system of relationships. English *friend* corresponds to both *Freund(in)*
(friend) and *Bekannte(r)* (acquaintance) in German, but there are fairly
strict boundaries between these. *Freundschaft* (friendship) is a rather exclusive mutually binding relationship, particularly when it involves people of
opposite sexes. *Du* relations have been more common among people of
the same sex than between the sexes.[4] The 'traditional' pattern of pronoun
selection is as follows:

(i)   *Sie* is the unmarked pronoun of address; *du* is marked as the
      pronoun of solidarity (Brown and Gilman 1960).
(ii) Members of a family address each other as *du*.
(iii) *Du* is used to children under the age of fifteen.

---

[4] *Du* is also used generically, i.e. instead of *man*, where no specific person is addressed, e.g.
*Wenn **du** einsam bist* (If you are lonely). It is also employed in advertising to establish 'direct'
interaction, e.g *Leidest **du** an Kopfschmerzen?* (Do you suffer from headaches?)

(iv) Young children tend to call everyone *du*. (Bates 1976: 283 points out that Italian children acquire the polite form between the ages of three and four. The situation among German monolinguals may be the same.)

(v) *Du* is employed in prayer.

(vi) People may, as a sign of friendship, *decide* (i.e. make a verbal agreement) to use *du*. Sometimes this is associated with a ritual drink (*Brüderschaft trinken*). The use of *du* is then reciprocal.

(vii) Older people (especially those of higher status) may asymmetrically address younger people (especially those of lower status), i.e. the older person uses *du*, the younger one *Sie* (this is what Brown and Gilman term the 'power semantic'). As Ervin-Tripp (1971: 20) explains, a senior person can dispense the younger one from this by suggesting a symmetrical informal mode of address. For instance, parents-in-law would do this to comply with rule (ii) (above).

Du has also become traditional in parts of the labour movement and in some political parties as well as on the shop floor and in clubs.

The *Sie* partner in a gathering of people on *du* terms will show up as an outsider. *Siezen* is a way of excluding someone from a group (*jemanden schneiden*). Selective *du* relationships may cause 'diplomatic' problems in the work domain. They may give the impression of favouritism. The influence of alcohol will frequently mean the suspension of normal *Sie* relationships. In a drinking situation, and sometimes on walking tours at high altitudes, *du* relations may be initiated which have effect only for the particular occasion.

5.3.1   Recent changes

The past two decades or so have seen a marked change in the rules for *du* and *Sie*, particularly among the younger generation, who are using *du* more widely than did previous generations. According to a longitudinal study on representative samples conducted by the Institut für Demoskopie at Allensbach (Allensbach 1993), 34% of (West) Germans prefer to use *du* to people whom they have not known for long, as opposed to 25% in 1974. This tendency is strongest (59%) among the 16–29 age group and hardly affects the 60-and-over group (14% rapid *du*). Table 8 shows that in 1993, each age group was prepared to adopt *du* faster than the previous generation by a considerable margin. Also, a return to more conservative practices is much less apparent than might be expected as people age.

Table 8 *West Germans adopting* du *quickly (%)*

	1974	1980	1984	1993
16–29	44	56	54	59
30–44	24	29	26	40
45–59	19	20	19	24
60+	13	16	9	14

Source: Allensbach (1993).

Table 9 *Adopting* du *quickly by age group 1993 (%)*

	16–29	30–44	45–59	60+
I use *du* soon	56	38	24	15
It takes me longer	6	26	42	60
Depends	38	36	34	25

Note:
This includes East Germans, see below, 5.3.2.
Source: Allensbach (1993).

There are actually few in the under-45 age groups who indicate reluctance to employ *du* to new friends (see Table 9). Unfortunately the question neither indicates specific situations nor defines 'fast' or 'slow'. This makes it difficult for respondents to commit themselves to a blanket response.

Nowhere is the change in rules more conspicuous than in universities and other tertiary institutions – a result of the anti-authoritarian upheavals which commenced in 1967. As Bayer (1979) has shown, there are two competing interpretations of address systems – one based on an unmarked pronoun for formality vs a marked one for intimacy, the other based on an unmarked pronoun for solidarity vs a marked one for social distance. Before the late 1960s, German students addressed each other and their lecturers as *Sie*, which was the unmarked pronoun of respect and formality as citizens and 'bearers of social roles'. *Du* was used only among 'special friends'. As from the late 1960s, students, protesting against traditional social values, adopted a general *du* as the unmarked pronoun for communication among themselves (regardless of sex). *Sie* became a marked form of social distance. Some university staff (especially younger and sub-professorial staff) adopted the reciprocal *du* for communication

Table 10 *Preference for early* du *by political voting pattern (%)*

	CDU/CSU	SPD	FDP	Greens	Others
Approve	53.6	62.2	40.1	89.7	50.0
Disapprove	45.1	35.7	59.9	10.3	48.0
Don't know	1.3	2.1	0.0	0.0	2.0

Source: ZDF–Politikbarometer (1985).

among themselves and with students. Those that did not were seen as upholding social distance rather than maintaining an atmosphere of mutual respect, due to confusion between the two competing interpretations. Since the 'student revolt', status-marked situations (e.g. seminars, congresses, committee meetings) no longer need to bring about a temporary withdrawal of the *du* relationship, leading to a public exhibition of social relations (especially among the younger generation). Teachers who had been members of the student movement introduced *du* communication between teachers and their secondary school pupils in the 1970s. It will be seen from Table 9 that the group of student age in the early 1970s were in the vanguard of the change and have, on the whole, maintained rapid *duzen*. Titles such as *Herr* (*Frau*) *Professor* and *Herr* (*Frau*) *Doktor* were dropped in West Germany in most face-to-face communication (e.g. between students and secretaries and staff) in the late 1960s. They have been replaced by *Herr* or *Frau*. *Professor* and *Doktor* (without *Herr* or *Frau*) are still used considerably in East Germany.

Another small representative survey conducted by the ZDF-Politik-barometer in 1985 on whether respondents approved of people using *du* sooner gives us a wider range of factors for cross-tabulation. For instance, supporters of the Greens and the SPD prefer early *du* usage more than do supporters of the CDU/CSU or of the FDP (see Table 10). The strong correlation between Greens voters and early *du* usage may not be surprising considering the Greens' commitment to grassroots networking and its links with alternative life-styles. The apparent 'middle position' of CDU/CSU supporters between that of the FDP and the left-wing parties warrants some explanation. Although CDU/CSU voters are more conservative, they are also less bourgeois and these parties have their heartland in Bavaria and Baden-Württemberg, where *du* usage is strongest within Germany (see 5.3.2).

Common ideology is a feature promoting *duzen*. Not only – as previously – membership of the same party (especially the Social Democratic and

Table 11 *Gender and preference for early* du *(%)*

	Men	Women
Approve	64.9	52.4
Disapprove	34.1	45.4
Don't know	1.0	2.2

Source: ZDF-Politikbarometer (1985).

Communist Parties), club or student group, but also similarly radical or progressive political and social views will automatically start a *du* relationship (the 'solidarity semantic' as discussed by Brown and Gilman 1960). The decision to employ *du* may be governed by environment and/or dress. *Du* is more likely to occur as a spontaneous form of address in the *Mensa* (student cafeteria) of a university than on a tram, and between two young people with long hair, scruffy clothes or between two people wearing the uniform of railway conductors than between people with no such common 'externals'.

In the 1985 survey, men approved of the more rapid change more than did women, once again supporting the link between women and the prestige *status quo* (cf. 4.1.2).

Unlike the Allensbach survey, the ZDF one enables us to distinguish between Germans who have had tertiary education or at least completed thirteen years of schooling and those with lower levels of secondary education. It provides evidence that the most educated are leading the attitudinal change. Those with completed apprenticeships also show strong support for the change. (This is borne out by the Allensbach survey, see below.)

Besch (1994) characterizes the community of most common *du* users as young, male, educated non-church-going Green voters. He also refers to instances where harsh fines have been imposed on people *duzing* police (1994: 253).

The traditional 'co-occurrence' rules for forms of address are:

$$du \quad + \quad \text{first name}$$
$$Sie \quad + \quad \left\{ \begin{array}{l} Herr \\ Frau \end{array} \right\} \quad + \quad \left\{ \begin{array}{l} \text{surname} \\ \text{title} \\ \text{title + surname} \end{array} \right.$$

In addition, there is the less usual:

$$Sie + \text{first name}$$

Table 12 *Educational attainment and preference for early* du *(%)*

	Primary	Primary and apprenticeship	Secondary	Matriculation and university
Approve	46.0	62.5	56.5	68.1
Disapprove	51.0	35.2	42.8	31.9
Don't know	2.2	2.2	0.7	0.0

Source: ZDF-Politikbarometer (1985).

where the 'first name' part is non-reciprocal. This occurs sometimes when the younger partner turns fifteen (and therefore has to be addressed as *Sie* but has been addressed by the first name by the much older interlocutor over a long period of time). Another use of *Sie* + first name is in TV or radio interviews with popular sportspeople or entertainers (the first name probaly reflecting an Anglo-American practice). There are at least two other co-occurrence possibilities:

> *du* + no name
> *du* + name of occupation[5]

The first of these co-occurrences stems from the fact that group member-ship, common job or institution and common ideology are *du*-promoting factors, and some latter-day *'Duzbrüder'* (people on *du* terms, e.g. students) do not know each other's names. The second co-occurrence (e.g. *'Du, **Schlosser**, komm mal her!'* 'Hey, locksmith, come here, will you?'), pro-moted by a common work situation and the guild tradition (and a some-what 'playful' disposition) has been overheard frequently among groups of tradesmen. Both these combinations are associated with an only partial fulfilment of the criteria for either *du* or *Sie* address. Besch (1994: 254) records the use of *du* + title + surname to female colleagues in depart-ment stores. The 1993 Allensbach survey indicates that 67% of skilled tradespeople and 59% of unskilled tradespeople but only 49% of lower-level professionals / white-collar workers and 35% of more senior ones reported using *du* with most or all of their work colleagues of similar rank.

Since the mid 1970s, there has been a slight relaxation in some of the new developments. Students in most universities still address each other as *du*, but the use of *du* among young people is more situationally deter-mined than completely unmarked. It is far less usual than say in 1972–3,

---

[5] Concerning *du* + title in Austria, see below, 5.3.2.

for university staff and students to *duz* each other.[6] *Du* relations between teachers and their secondary school classes are now again quite rare. Some relaxation of the new rules, the reduced general pressure for orthographical reform (7.1.1) and the subsiding of the 'language barriers in education' debate (7.3) were reflections of a change of course (*Tendenzwende*) towards social and political conservatism in the Federal Republic but need to be balanced against the more universal informality in communication in recent years. Such linguistic manifestations require careful diachronic study. The situation has made it difficult to describe a clear-cut pattern. It is not unusual for people who do not meet very frequently to forget how they last addressed each other and to renegotiate this.

The question can be posed: 'Will *Sie* become defunct as a pronoun of address in the foreseeable future as has occurred with the corresponding pronouns in Scandinavia and appears to be happening in the Netherlands at present?' As the tempo of the change in the German-speaking countries is quite slow, no such prediction can be made. Among other things, the present development is not yet secure enough not to be undermined by a major sociopolitical pendulum swing in the future. It is likely, however, that communication across national and linguistic boundaries within and beyond Europe would strengthen the trend that has already evolved. If, for instance, people have interacted in an inter-cultural setting where an unmarked pronoun and first names are used, it is difficult for them to revert to *Sie* and title + surname when they communicate in a German-language setting.

5.3.2   National and regional differences

It should be noted that the use of rules of address varies nationally and regionally, with *du* traditionally being used more in South Germany and Austria than in North Germany, and more in rural areas than in urban ones.

The ZDF (West German) survey shows strongest support for early *du* usage among Bavarians and people in North-Rhine-Westphalia, followed by those in Rheinland-Pfalz and Baden-Württemberg. The regional factor is distorted by the larger number of people with left-wing political views in North-Rhine-Westphalia.

In Austria, the frequent *duzen* together with the importance of accepting your place in society has led to a mixing of titles and *du*. Muhr

---

[6] This comment is based on participant observation and discussions with German colleagues.

Table 13 *Region and preference for early* du *(%)*

	North	Centre	South
Approve	53.0	57.2	59.3
Disapprove	45.3	41.1	40.2
Don't know	1.7	1.7	0.4

Source: ZDF-Politikbarometer (1985).

Table 14 *Reported* du *use, East and West Germany, by education (%)*

	West Germany			East Germany		
	Primary	Secondary	Total	Primary	Secondary	Total
I use *du* soon	33	34	34	31	21	29
It takes me longer	34	36	35	29	37	31
Depends	33	40	31	40	42	40

Note:
Secondary includes higher.
Source: Allensbach (1993).

(1993b: 31) cites, for instance: '*Du, lieber Herr Hofrat!*' or '*Lieber Hans, sehr geehrter Herr Präsident!*' In some German universities (e.g. Free University of (West) Berlin, Bremen, Frankfurt, Marburg), a radical tradition dating back to the student revolution of the late 1960s has led to a wider application of *du*.

The 1993 Allensbach survey covered East Germans as well as West Germans. It showed a greater reluctance to enter into rapid *du* relations (see Table 14). Of note in the East German results is the high degree of non-commitment among both the more and less educated, reflecting lack of certainty, and the tendency for *du* to be used less among the more educated. This can be attributed firstly to the absence in the GDR of the massive social changes in the Federal Republic in the 1960s and 1970s and secondly to a negative reaction to the routine use of *du* between party members (except between the sexes where there is a large age difference). As I have mentioned in 3.3, in relation to *Werte Passagiere*, forms of address prevalent in the GDR public register are now becoming taboo. Moreover, the greater use of *Sie* in the East than in the West may also reflect a need to 'size up' a person to ensure that they can be trusted before using *du* to them.

5.4   Discourse patterns

The specific way in which discourse is organized by people from a particular culture is at least partly influenced by cultural attitudes concerning
time and space. We have already referred to research suggesting that
Austrian discourse is longer than its German equivalent. There are also
indications that German discourse is less symmetrical and linear than its
English equivalent (see below).

A study of later-year secondary school assignments in various subjects
from the Federal Republic of Germany and Australia, with teachers' or
examiners' comments on them, and of German- and English-language
essay-writing manuals (Clyne 1980) suggests that essay-writing plays a far
less central role in the German education systems than in those of
English-language countries, where essays are a major medium of assessment *across the curriculum*. In German-language countries they are largely
language exercises and the formal rules are of lesser significance than in
English-language countries. In German-language countries, *content* is
paramount in expository discourse. This is true also of academic treatises.
The German stress on 'content' may entail 'excursions' from the main line
of the argument in order to provide a complete treatment of the issue,
including a historical, theoretical or ideological perspective. From an
English point of view, which is more oriented towards linearity, this may
seem digressive and is not always tolerated, e.g. in reviews or other evaluations across cultures. On the other hand, German scholars sometimes
find English learned papers limited in dimensions by the more rigid linear
structure. (For a contrastive study of academic discourse in linguistics and
sociology by English and German speakers, see Clyne 1987, Clyne, Hoeks
and Kreutz 1988.) Meetings of German-speaking organizations (clubs,
societies, committees) traditionally tend to run in a somewhat more
informal way than their English-speaking counterparts (Clyne and
Manton 1979) although there is considerable variation due to innovations
in recent decades in some German institutions. Again, linearity is less
important. (The Westminster rule that only one motion be before the
chair at a time is followed less in German organizations.) English discourse, especially in meetings, allows for a more flexible *tempo*, e.g. hurry-
ing up business by moving 'that the motion now be put', or delaying it by
deferring it to a subcommittee. German (especially North German)
society attaches great importance to *oral expression* as a mark of education,
while in Britain and Australia (except in certain middle- and upper-class
groups), but not necessarily in North America, the emphasis is far more
on written expression. On the other hand, in West German university

seminars in the humanities and social sciences, students have tended to demonstrate their general knowledge and expertise in public exhibitions of eloquence using academic register. However, there are indications that this has changed in the generation following the post–1968 student movement (e.g. Greiner 1982). While in the English-language cultures, it is the author's responsibility to present material in a readable form, the tendency in German-language cultures is for the reader to take responsibility for understanding the content which the author is making available (Clyne 1987). This distinction is supported by Luchtenberg (1994a), who shows that American computer software manuals are generally presented in a more user-friendly way than German ones.

5.5   Brief summary

Communication patterns, which are driven by cultural values, vary between German-language countries, between East and West Germany, between regions and social classes. Germans appear to perform requests and complaints with a greater degree of directness, and upgraders are more frequently employed in German than in English. Many communication rules have regional currency, leading to communication breakdown within the Federal Republic. Some communication patterns are regarded in Austria as German German and rejected. There is some evidence that Austrian discourse tends to be more verbose than German discourse, in the interests of politeness. It has been suggested that East German discourse is generally slower, quieter, more indirect and more collaborative, reflecting the demands for conformity. There are some forms of discourse for communicating with bureaucracies for which East Germans are not well prepared because of the recent past.

Germans, but not Austrians, tend to take a more prescriptive (and less creative) attitude to language than do English speakers. Hence, verbal humour and verbal irony are rare in everyday speech and usually restricted to creative writing and cabaret in Germany. German children play less with language than do their English-speaking counterparts.

The 'traditional' system of address in Germany has been modified considerably. This is particularly so in universities in West Germany, where, since the student movement, students have replaced a system based on formality (unmarked) vs intimacy (marked) by one based on solidarity (unmarked) vs social distance (marked). *Du* is now used in a generalized way between students, and, where lecturers did not adopt this pattern, this was often (mis)interpreted as an indication of social distance. Common work and common ideology, especially if inclined towards the left,

promote *duzen*. *Du* use is also stronger in southern Germany and Austria than in northern Germany, among men than among women, and especially in the younger generation. *Du* use is increasing. Educated East Germans are more cautious about the use of *du* than are educated West Germans. *Siezen* is sometimes an instrument of exclusion. The use of *du* may be stimulated by the outward appearance of the speech partner. *Sie* + first name is employed non-reciprocally, for instance by older people addressing younger interlocutors whom they knew as children. *Du* + no name and *du* + name of occupation are promoted by solidarity semantics. A prediction of *Sie* becoming defunct as a pronoun of address would be premature.

German expository discourse tends to be less linear and less formally organized than its English equivalent, something that could be attributed to the differing role and rules of essay-writing within the education systems. There are some parallels in the structure of expository discourse and meetings.

5.6   Further reading

The area of this chapter that has been studied most is the address system. Apart from Brown and Gilman's (1960) seminal paper, I recommend Bayer (1979), which covers a subsequent period but a narrower field of investigation.

6

Gender, generation and politics – variation and change in language and discourse

This chapter deals with variation in lexicon, semantics and/or discourse patterns according to gender, generation or political ideology. It will include a consideration of language changes that have arisen from a recognition of women's rights.

6.1   Language and gender

It has been argued that there are two ways that language usage discriminates against women: firstly in the way in which they have been conditioned to use language, and secondly in the way they are treated in language usage.

6.1.1   Women's use of language

Trömel-Plötz (1978a) has suggested that women have a lesser tendency than men to employ swear-words, vulgar expressions and intensifiers, but a greater tendency to use hedges, tag-questions, diminutives and euphemisms such as:

> Es scheint, daß... (It seems that...)
> Ist das nicht so? (Isn't that the case?)
> ...nicht wahr? (isn't it?, hasn't she?, doesn't he?)
> Ich bin eben nur eine Hausfrau. (Well, I'm only a housewife.)
> Das ist nur eine Idee von mir. (That's just an idea of mine.)

This is supported by Kuhn's (1982) analysis of university seminars conducted by nine different lecturers. It shows that the female lecturers employ almost twice as many downgraders (including particles and subjunctives in situations where they are not needed), far more tag-questions, and ten times as many personal addresses than the male lecturers. The distinction between a predominantly confrontational male style and a more

co-operative female one is also borne out in role-plays conducted by Kotthof (1984), where a male and a female student were required to obtain the signature of a reluctant male lecturer. A conversational analysis of a half-hour university seminar (Klann 1978b) shows that male students speak far more than the female students and initiate more new topics while both groups contribute more or less equally to the discussion of the topics. The male students are more controversial, the female students' style is more co-operative and conflict-avoiding.

6.1.2   Towards gender-inclusive language – the role played by women

Since the late 1970s, there has been an increased awareness of the place of language in gender roles in German-language countries. It has been prompted by a greater consciousness among women in Western countries of their own identity and by early critical work on language and gender in the United States (e.g. Key 1975, Lakoff 1975). This has led to changes in language usage among some German-speaking women as a symbol of resistance to the male-dominant *status quo*. In turn, some of the changes have been followed in the wider community. It has necessarily triggered a reappraisal of the relation between natural and grammatical gender in German (see below) and reintroduced the question of the role of language in thought and culture. Feminist linguists in the Federal Republic (such as Guentherodt 1979, Hellinger 1980, Pusch *et al.* 1980–1, Pusch 1980, 1984) have agitated for language policy changes to inclusive modes of address and occupational terminology and references to the sexes. The problem, as in English, is that women are often referred to as if they were men. Where one of a group is, or may be, male, reference to the entire group and all its members requires the masculine. Pusch (1984: 7), in her book *Das Deutsch als Männersprache* (German as a men's language), quotes from her passport; '*Der Inhaber dieses Passes ist Deutscher*' (The owner (masc.) of this passport is German (masc.)). But there are differences between English and German in relation to gender questions, as Hellinger (1990) explains. She differentiates between grammatical, natural and social gender. The fact that German (unlike English) has retained gender markings in grammatical categories means that the problem of gender assignment is more pervasive, but that there are also more pairs of forms (*Student/Studentin*) available. As Hellinger puts it, both languages have the capacity to give their users the opportunity to treat men and women equally. On the other hand, it has been argued (e.g. Guentherodt 1979) that German lends itself less to gender-inclusive language than does English. For instance, because German has grammatical genders with

marked articles, names of occupations have to be either masculine or feminine. In English, the main problem is pronominalization, which entails distinguishing the sex, and also the word *man* (German, *Mensch*). The German pronouns *man* (one), *jeder* (everyone), *jedermann* (everybody, literally 'everyman'), *niemand* (nobody), and *wer* (who(ever)) are masculine and so are their possessives, although they can relate to either sex.

Inapt instances of masculine pronouns referring to women cited by Trömel-Plötz (1978a) include the following:

> *Man* erlebt *seine* Schwangerschaft und Geburt jedesmal anders. (*One* [based on 'man'] experiences *one's* [literally 'his'] pregnancy and birth differently every time.)

> Jemand spricht über *seine* Entbindung bei Leboyer. (Someone is talking about *his* delivery by the Leboyer method.)

> Wer hat *seinen* Lippenstift im Bad gelassen? (Who left *his* lipstick in the bathroom?)

Kalverkämpfer (1979) criticizes Trömel-Plötz for ignoring the importance of economical principles in language, i.e. the need for an unmarked form. This is answered by Pusch (1980, 1984), who stresses that it is nearly always the masculine form that is unmarked.

This raises the question of pronoun reference in a more general way. Strictly speaking, **das** *Kind* (child) takes the neuter pronouns *es* and *sein*, regardless of the sex of the referent. Moreover, *Mädchen* (girl) is neuter. There is an increasing tendency, however, in spoken discourse, to refer back to a particular girl as *sie*, at least in spoken discourse, e.g. *Das Mädchen war krank. Sie konnte nicht kommen.* Or even: *Das Mädchen, die ihm das Geschenk reichte, war schüchtern.* According to Duden (1989), both are ungrammatical:

> Da Mädchen ein sächliches Hauptwort ist, werden bei den Fürwörtern (Pronomen) und Eigenschaftswörtern, die sich auf Mädchen beziehen, entsprechend auch die sächliche Form verwendet . . . Nur bei größerem Abstand zwischen Mädchen und dazugehörendem Fürwort wird entsprechend dem natürlichen Geschlecht die weibliche Form . . . (sie, ihr) gewählt.

> (As *Mädchen* is a neuter noun, adjectives and pronouns referring to *Mädchen* also use the neuter accordingly. Only where there is a considerable distance between *Mädchen* and the pronoun referring to it is the feminine form used in accordance with natural gender.) (Duden 1989: 245.)

Although both of the above examples are ungrammatical, the first but not the second is used in writing. Incidentally, similar problems occur with the unmarked animal nouns, *der Hund* (dog – masculine) and *die Katze* (cat – feminine).

Similarly, feminists and feminist journals are using feminine relative pronouns to refer back to *jemand* and *wer*, e.g.:

> Jemand, *die* mir helfen kann (Someone who can help me).

> Wer von euch hat denn *ihr* Kind gestillt? (Which of you breast-fed her baby?) [German would require a masculine relating to *wer.*] (Cited by Pusch 1984: 89.)

The rules for transforming (so-called unmarked or 'generic') masculine occupational terms into feminine equivalents can be conceived as a hierarchy according to the level of gender equality (or lack thereof) achieved, e.g.

(i) N-*mann* → N-*frau*

e.g. *Kauffrau* (businesswoman), *Fachfrau* (expert), *Kamerafrau*, *Ombudsfrau*. These were propagated by women's groups to replace category (iv) below. (i) is still a relatively small category.

(ii) N → N+-*in*

(-*in* added to a traditional agent noun)

e.g. *Archivarin* (archivist), *Ministerin* (minister (in politics)), *Notarin* (notary), *Pastorin*, *Professorin*, *Programmierin* (computer programmer), *Redakteurin* (editor), *Tankwärtin* (petrol-pump attendant). These are employed in variants of the types:

> *Lehrer und/oder Lehrerin*
> *Lehrer/in*
> *LehrerIn*

(iii) N → *weiblich(er)* + N

e.g. *weiblicher Soldat* (female soldier), *weibliche Lehrkräfte* (female teachers).

(iv) N-*mann* → N-*männin*

(-*mann* changed to -*männin*, literally 'female man')

e.g. *Amtmännin* (senior clerk), *Fachmännin* (expert).

The last two categories are now probably totally unacceptable to a large section of the population of the German-language countries but still employed by older and more conservative speakers. The potential of -*mensch* or -*person* as suffixes (cf. English -*person*) has never been realized in German, so that there is no gender-unmarked singular *Schutzmensch* or *Schutzperson* (policeperson), *Fachmensch* or *Fachperson* (expert) to go with plural *Schutzleute* and *Fachleute*, for instance. Linguistic principles such as economy are invoked in the debate on the 'split' masculine/feminine forms (*Lehrerinnen und Lehrer*), including the potentially ambiguous and difficult to read *Innen* suffix (e.g. *ArbeiterInnengruppe* – 'group of male and female workers' – which could be misread as 'inner group of (male)

workers'. But in language policies the interests of social equity do need to be addressed (Schräpel 1985).

The gender-marked article in German makes the solution of adopting a 'less sexist' term such as *camera operator* or *office assistant* instead of *camera-man* or *office boy* less effective. The change from *Pumpenmann* (pump man) to *Pumpenwärter* (pump attendant) and from *Steuerfachmann* (taxation expert) to *Steuerverständiger* has facilitated feminization to *Pumpenwärterin* and *Steuerverständige,* but still based on an 'unmarked masculine'.

But the fact remains that the female form is based on the male one and not vice versa. (Generic female forms are few, e.g. *Person* (person), *Schreibkraft* (clerk/typist), *Arbeitskraft* (worker), *Lehrkraft* (teacher).)

Male derivatives of traditionally female terms are not possible. There is no *männliche Reinmachefrau* (male cleaning lady), *männliche Bardame* (male barmaid, literally 'male bar-lady'), *männliche Krankenschwester* (male nurse, literally 'male sick-sister'); no *Reinmachemann* (cleaning man), *Barherr* (bar-gentleman) or *Krankenbruder* (sick-brother). Traditionally female occupations have been renamed with an unmarked masculine to make a feminine derivative possible, e.g. *Krankenschwester* has been replaced by *Kranken-pfleger/in* and *Kindergärtnerin* by *Erzieher/in.* However, in practice, many hospitals in Germany advertise in newspapers for '*Krankenschwester/Pfleger*'.

As Schräpel (1985) points out, inclusive language can emerge only from a reciprocal relationship between language policy and language change. Although the women advocating and initiating changes were originally a small minority, their 'resistance' to the *status quo* represented 'ein Schritt zu einem neuen Selbstbewußsein' (a step towards a new confidence) (Schräpel 1985: 216).

In some feminist circles, *man* (*one,* indefinite pronoun, derived from and homophonous to *Mann,* man) was replaced by *frau* (woman), *man/frau* or, occasionally, *mensch* (person); *jedermann* by *jedefrau.* A marked male indefinite pronoun *mann* was also created. *Freundlich* became *freundinlich* and *Freundschaft* was replaced by *Freundinschaft* (Pusch 1985). The following usage stands out in feminist newspapers such as *Emma* and *Frau und Film* and in feminist leaflets:

(i) recurring slogans, similar to those of other protest groups, e.g. *Diskriminierung, Emanzipation, Unterdrückung* (suppression), *Abbau der Herrschaft* (abolition of domination), *Abbau des Sexismus* (abolition of sexism)

(ii) the generalized use of *du* and *ihr,* even in formal situations, and irrespective of whether the interactants were previously known to each other, obviously as a symbol of solidarity (see above, 5.3);

(iii) strong or 'vulgar' use of language, for instance in appeals and letters to the editor, departing from the submissive image of women, e.g. *Scheiße* (crap, shit), *beschissen* (rotten)

(iv) the polarization of *Frauen* and *Männer*, e.g. *Frauenprogramm* (women's programme), *Männerwelt* (men's world).

There are two points of view in the quest for non-discriminatory language: 'splitting', with a masculine form and a feminine form side by side (*Lehrer/Lehrerin* or *LehrerIn*), and a form that is said to be neutral (*Lehrer*). It can be argued either that a person's sex should not be an issue or that it should be mentioned within a context of equity. The proponents of what is sometimes called provocatively the 'depatriarchalization of language' overwhelmingly prefer the former solution. This has been implemented gradually throughout the German-language countries, in a restrained way. However, Pusch (1980, 1984) therefore proposes that male *and* female genders be assigned to the unmarked occupational term, with a neuter gender employed where the identity of the referent is not clear, and the plural taking -*s*, e.g. *der Lehrer, die Lehrer* → *das Lehrer, die Lehrers*. This would involve a more dramatic change in German grammar than the speech community is likely to tolerate. As Pusch herself admits, the *das* form could be interpreted as a 'dehumanization'.

6.1.3   The legal position

Since 1970 in Austria and 1972 in the Federal Republic of Germany, the legal form of address for adult women (married or otherwise) has been *Frau*. This has avoided the need for an unmarked female form of address like English *Ms*, which in some circles is regarded as socially or politically marked (Pauwels 1987).

Legal language in Germany uses the 'unmarked (generic) masculine' (*Der Spiegel* 1989, Hellinger 1993). Not only pronouns but also nouns such as *Richter* (judge), *Empfänger* (receiver), *Täter* (culprit), *Mörder* (murderer), *Schuldner* (debtor) have appeared only in their masculine forms (Stickel 1988). In the mid to late 1980s, a number of states of the Federal Republic introduced changes in the wording of laws so that women do not feel excluded before the law. Stickel (1988) argues that occupational terms should be gender-specific in reference to individual women for identity purposes but 'generic' (i.e. with masculine ending) in general as they do not add to the meaning.

The German (Federal) Government's committee on legal language (BRD-Report 1991) recommended the *status quo* – 'generic masculine'

for legal language on the grounds that its interpretation was to cover both men and women and therefore does not contravene equality in the Constitution, and support for the tendency for visible feminine alternatives in official language (*Amtssprache*). This is done through splitting or the avoidance of human nouns, e.g. *Ministerium* for *Minister*. Among arguments advanced against changes in legal language were costs and rather ugly formulations (Hellinger 1993). In accordance with Council of Europe guidelines of 1990 urging member states to use inclusive language in legal texts and in teaching, the Swiss Report (1991) recommends inclusive language (including visible feminine forms) in law and administration. The report draws heavily on the recommendations of German feminist linguists (e.g. Guentherodt *et al.* 1980). Both *Antragssteller/innen* and *AntragsstellerInnen* (applicant) are deemed acceptable in the changes which are being implemented during 1994 (Hellinger 1993). The Austrian situation is similar to that in Germany (Anne Pauwels, personal communication).

As with other sociolinguistic developments (see e.g. 5.3), inclusive language was not promoted in the GDR, where *Ich bin Lehrer* was used by women and regarded as egalitarian, so that the East German states are somewhat slower in the implementation of gender-inclusive language.

6.1.4   Implementation – advertisements as an example

An examination of computer job advertisements in nine consecutive weekend issues of the *Süddeutsche Zeitung* (from 20/21 June 1992 to 14/15 August 1992) showed the following breakdown of designations:

> masculine title with appended feminine suffix in the singular or
>   plural, 36 instances, e.g. *Programmierer/in, Software-*
>   *Entwickler(in), Organisationsberater(innen), Organisations-*
>   *Programmierer(innen)*
> masculine form as unmarked ('generic'?), 26 instances, e.g.
>   *Programmierer, Software-Entwickler*
> full form for both masculine and feminine equivalents, 2
>   instances, e.g. *Mitarbeiterinnen und Mitarbeiter, PC-Trainer/ PC-*
>   *Trainerin*

In addition, there are advertisements in which the designation is given through an English transfer, e.g. *Technical support representative, systems analyst, technical support engineer*. This avoids gender marking, among other things.

A perusal of other advertisements suggests that the above situation is

not atypical of executive positions. However, in the corpus there is an absence of computer advertisements designating the job or field, not the person to be appointed, e.g. *Professur* (professorship), *Sanitärkollektion* (sanitary collection), *Vertrieb* (sales/marketing).

The graphic presentation *-In(nen)* is most common in academic advertisements, e.g. *ProfessorIn*, *LehrerInnen*, occasionally *VolkswirtIn* (economist). (In addition, it is particularly prevalent in the columns of the alternative newspaper *Tageszeitung*, e.g. *BesucherInnen* (visitors), *BürgerInnen* (citizens), *BosnierInnen* (Bosnians), *EuropäerInnen* (Europeans), *LeserInnen* (readers).)

6.2   Generational variation

The gulf between the parents' and young people's generations has been marked in Germany throughout the post-war period. Rejection of the 'older generation' is part of a teenager's identity in the transition from child and adult. Teenagers use their in-group register to distance themselves from dominant cultural patterns, identify with a common shared set of norms and values (Schlobinski 1989: 2), exclude others, give expression to their disaffection and disorientation, and make sense creatively of what to many of them seems a rather nonsensical world. This is why it makes use of words and expressions that are tabooed as vulgar or an impoverishment of the language in established society.

There has been controversy over the extent to which there is a homogeneous variety spoken by young people in Germany. Part of the discussion has been provoked by the use of the unfortunate term *Jugendsprache* (youth language), which makes it sound as though youth have a homogeneous variety. However, this is also the term that many young people use themselves. The main features that have been described are:

  (i) Greetings: e.g. *Dear friends, Hallo friends, Na du Bär!* (Oh you bear (for a young male)), *Hi, Hey Freaks!*
 (ii) Deliberate clustering of interjections: *Naja, Hm* or *Äh!* Or the repeated use of *Ey!*
(iii) Idioms: e.g. *auf den Keks gehen* (to get on the biscuit, instead of *auf die Nerven gehen*, 'to get on your nerves'), *Bock haben auf* (to feel like, literally 'to have a buck (he-goat) on'), *eine Schnecke angraben* (to flirt with a girl in a roundabout way, literally 'to dig on a snail'), *sich aufspulen* (to film, literally 'to wind yourself up'), *er tickt nicht richtig* (he's off his rocker, literally 'he isn't ticking right'), *in die Kiste hüpfen* (to kick the bucket (die), literally 'to hop in the box').

(iv) Integrated anglicisms, especially from Anglo-American youth register: e.g. *antörnen* (to turn someone on, (for drugs, music, a person)), *reinmoven* (to move in), *rumfreaken* (to muck about, literally 'to freak around'), *eine coole Sache* (a cool thing), *groovy*, *super, cool, crazy* (adjectives expressing positive attributes).

(v) Onomatopoeia, as in comics: e.g. *Plöp!* (for opening a beer bottle), *Glok! Zosch!* (for drinking beer), *Grint!* (for machines). (See also 8.3.1.)

(vi) Neologisms and semantic extensions, partly from the field of sexual taboos: e.g. *geil* (originally 'lustful') now an adjective expressing positive attributes (also: *supergeil, affengeil, superaffengeil*), *nerven* (*auf die Nerven gehen*, to get on your nerves), *Grufti* (< *Gruft*, poetic word for 'grave') and *Komposti* (< *Kompost*, for 'oldie' (old person)).[1]

(Some of these points are taken over from studies by Henne 1980, 1986, Heinemann 1990, Müller-Thurau 1983.)

Important agencies in the dissemination and use of the youth register are advertisers, employing a stylized form to attract young people, and youth magazines such as *Bravo*. The state school acts as an 'informal distributor' of this type of German, some of which had its origins in drug and pop culture, especially in the United States, or in anarchist (*Sponti*) or alternative groups, and guarantees at least its widespread comprehensibility among young people. Using questionnaires based on words found in *Bravo*, Walter (1978) confirms its fairly uniform accessibility to a cross-section of 14–15-year-olds. There have been vocabularies of youth register (Müller-Thurau 1983) as well as 'translations into it' of the Old Testament and the Nibelungenlied. A youth register with regional and general colloquial features is employed in sociopolitical critique in the form of comic books by Gerhard Seyfried such as *Flucht aus Berlin* (1990). Müller-Thurau (1983), Pörksen (1984) and Weber (1984) offer sympathetic treatments of youth register, stressing its expressiveness and effectiveness.

Neuland (1987) discusses the problems of eliciting data as an 'outsider' and of working with questionnaires, which cannot indicate frequency of use. Januschek (1989) notes that, of the three most likely methods – asking the speakers, a language-use study based on a cultural analysis, and a listing of marked features to assess the intention of the register – the last named is the one usually employed and the least satisfactory. Later, Schlobinski *et*

---

[1] Some of these words are declining in use.

al. (1993) question the validity of some assertions on *Jugendsprache* on the grounds of a shaky or unrevealed empirical basis. For instance, Henne (1986), a very extensive account, is based on information given by 536 secondary school students in response to a questionnaire eliciting names for certain things and introspective and attitudinal information, rather than examining actual language use. It is not clear which sections of Heinemann's (1990) huge East German corpus, which is described only in the most general way, were actually used.

Schlobinski *et al.* themselves, in a more ethnographic study, analyze the actual language use of two groups of young people in northern Germany – a Catholic youth group and a group of Year 9 pupils (approximately 15–16-year-olds) taking an option on German media. Schlobinski *et al.* conclude that there are as many *Jugendsprachen* as there are speakers or situations. They do, however, admit to a youth style (*Jugendton*). This register, as I would prefer to call it, is characterized, according to Schlobinski *et al.*'s corpus, by:

(i) quick topic shifts with short questions and answers
(ii) ironical usage distancing them from a position
(iii) question tags, e.g. *nä, hä, mh*
(iv) intensifiers, e.g. *total, echt*
(v) a range of distinctive expressions denoting 'good', 'bad' and 'indifferent', e.g. *affengeil* (ape + *geil*), *steincool* (stone-cool), *voll cool* (fully cool), *super, affenstark* (< ape + strong) for 'good', *öde* (desolate), *scheiße* (shit), *herb* (harsh, bitter), *shit, fucking* for 'bad', *scheißegal* (= shit + equal) for 'indifferent'
(vi) *ey*, perhaps the most common feature (also identified by Henne 1986: 149–50, Ehmann 1992: 59), acts as an intensifier, attention-getter, comment, or reassurance particle – in initial, medial or (especially) final position, e.g.:
  Ey da sitz' ich (Well, I'm here)
  Ehm kannst du mithelfen ey? (Hm, do you reckon you can give us a hand?)
  Ich muß so lachen ey, ich konnt nicht mehr . . . (Gee, I have to laugh, I just couldn't go on . . .)
  (Schlobinski *et al.* 1993: 134)
(vii) sexual aggression, e.g. *Wenn du überhaupt unten was hast nä?* (If you've really got anything down there)

Among youth group members, who had known each other for a long time, only keywords were necessary for effective communication to take place because of common experience and shared values; this was the case

only to a lesser extent with the school group. In spite of the authors' scepticism about *Jugendsprache*, their informants were able to express attitudes to it, which varied from positive, via positive and critical, to negative. School was indicated as a venue for its use (but not home where, in some cases, it was banned). It enables them to talk in a creative but informal way. However, they regard 'adult language' as the norm which they will aspire to.

There is anecdotal evidence that the youth register spreads from children to some parents who use it with their children. According to some of Schlobinski *et al.*'s informants, some teachers will use it to create an informal atmosphere in class.

There are, in fact, different groups of young people who can be characterized by their lexical usage, e.g. Yuppies, working class, skinheads, alternative life-stylers, rockers, punks (cf. Neuland 1987, Müller-Thurau 1983). In the Mannheim study (see above, 5.1.7), the *Gymnasium* pupils have developed a style to contrast their identity with that of both adults and the 'vulgar asocial' young people (Schwitalla 1994).

Many of Schlobinski *et al.*'s (1993) findings confirm a previous small-scale study (Schlobinski 1989) of a group of Osnabrück boys aged 19 to 21 who meet to make music, watch videos and play fantasy games. Wachau (1989) ascertains attitudes to youth register through an ethnographic study of a group of seven Grade 10 students (and two hangers-on) in Hagen. The school students find the register less formal and restrictive and more interesting than adult language – observing more directness, spontaneity, freedom and fun. On the last point, Wachau quotes the young people responding *Wal!* (whale) or *Goldfisch!* (goldfish) to the Americanized greeting *Hi!* (German *Hai* = shark). Of course the parents were not ordinarily addressed in a youth register, but occasionally the children do spontaneously use it at home. When questioned, most parents considered the register 'normal' with a few unusual words and were disturbed only by onomatopoeia derived from comics. Some saw it as primitive or an act of hostility towards adults. Teachers, on the other hand, described it as slang, some complaining about impoverishment of the language.

Generally it is believed that a youth register is part of young people's development, something that they 'grow out of'. But it is also blamed by some for a 'deterioration' of the German language. Bayer (1982), for instance, while acknowledging creative elements, also suggests that it is indicative of young people's failing relationship to the written medium.

6.2.1   Regional differences

Another argument against the notion of a fairly homogeneous *Jugendsprache* is major regional (as well as national) variation. On the basis of attitudinal interviews, linguistic analysis and questionnaires on language use and perceptions among young people in Bern, Vienna, Munich, rural Upper Bavaria, Leipzig, the Ruhr and Hamburg, Ehmann (1992) deduces some major differences in the nature and origins of youth register in different parts of the German-speaking area. North Germans and, to a much lesser extent, the others use youth register in response to group pressure and in protest against conventions. Upper Bavarians tend to do so for the fun of it. In the areas where dialect is strong (Switzerland, Austria, and Bavaria), it provides much of the basis for the in-group youth register, which is not as marked. In North Germany, youth register draws more on anglicisms and expressions from other sub-cultural registers (e.g. drug scene, disco, Spontis). The Upper Bavarians and the East Germans are those least affected by the media. Historical factors are obviously the reason why the East Germans' youth register is less influenced by English than that of the other young people. The influence of the language of comics and, to a lesser extent, youth magazines is much greater in the cities than on the land, where the young people consider their usage to be more creative and less derivative.

Music has had a crucial input into the registers of young people, especially since the New Wave of the 1980s has shaken both musical and linguistic conventions in depicting dissonance and monotony. This has included the Austrian groups Falco and DöF, the Swiss Grauzone, and the German groups Trio, Nena and Ideal (Ehmann 1992: 80). But there are also major differences between Austria/Bavaria, North Germany and Switzerland. There are different kinds of preferences for pop music. In Bavaria and Austria, the Austrian singers Georg Danzer and Rainhard Fenderich and Austro-Pop groups such as Erste Allgemeine Versicherung are the examples for youth register (although Danzer satirizes *Alternativsprache* which has become sterile with clichés such as *Kommunikationsebene, Problem, Selbsterfahrungsgruppe, Selbstverwirklichung*, in his song *Total* (Ehmann 1992: 83–6). Bands such as BAP in Cologne, using a mixture of dialect and *Jugendsprache*, also exist in the North, but Ehmann's survey suggests that in the northern part of Germany, English-language pop music is more significant than elsewhere. He also indicates that media influence on the youth register is strongest in the cities and that is where the 'group markers' are most pronounced.

Using interviews, Beneke (1993) shows that there are still differences

between the youth registers of East and West Berliners, although there is much overlap.

> **For 'good'**
> Grade 7 pupils in West Berlin gave as their words: *geil / echt geil, cool, stark, super, spitze.*
> Grade 7 pupils in East Berlin: *geil, schau, cool, scharf.*
> **For 'teacher'**
> Grade 7 pupils in West Berlin: *Arschloch, Besserwisser, Hurensohn, Scheißlehrer.* (Note the aggressiveness!)
> Grade 7 in East Berlin: *Pauker, Lehrer, Arschloch.*

Clichés and stereotypes persist in relation to the 'other part' of Berlin. Youth register use is tolerated by more East Berliners (50%) than West Berliners.

6.3   Variation and change in political discourse

The sections on political discourse are based on a corpus gathered from party policies, pamphlets and public statements and advertisements. The section was completed prior to the 1994 elections and does not include material from these elections in Germany and Austria.

6.3.1   'Established mainstream' German parties and general political discourse

The 'established mainstream' German parties are:

> Christlich-demokratische Union (CDU) $\Big\}$ (conservative)
> Christlich-soziale Union (CSU)[2]
> Freie Demokratische Partei (FDP) (liberal)
> Sozialdemokratische Partei Deutschlands (SPD) (Labour Party
>   in Britain, Australia and New Zealand)

Like languages, ideas, ideals and philosophies play a crucial role in the cultures of the German-language countries, and political discourse can serve as a political barometer.

A decade or two ago, it was possible to recognize the political persuasion of speakers or writers by their language usage. An instance was the word used for the barring of people holding 'extremist' political views of

---

[2] The CSU is the Bavarian sister-party of the CDU but is more conservative and nationalist.

the right, and especially the left, from public office (e.g. as academics, schoolteachers, hospital doctors, railway drivers, postal clerks). The official term, *Radikalenerlaß* (declaration on radicals), was employed by middle-of-the-road newspapers; conservatives referred to it as *Extremistenbeschluß* (resolution on extremists); and left-wingers as *Berufsverbot* (prohibition from following your calling or occupation). The strength of people's opposition to left-wing terrorism was indicated by their reference to the *Baader-Meinhof-Gruppe* (group) or the *Baader-Meinhof-Bande* (band of gangsters). In fact, every time West Germans referred to their country, they expressed a political opinion (see also Glück and Sauer 1990: 18–22). The official designations were *Bundesrepublik Deutschland* or *BR Deutschland*. The left-wing *BRD*, paralleling *DDR*, was not approved by the West German Government because it concealed the word *Deutschland*. However, *Deutschland* was frequently employed in everyday speech and writing and in the media to relate to the Federal Republic, ignoring the existence of the GDR. Many West Germans referred to their country as *Die Bundesrepublik*; *Westdeutschland* was not used as much as its English equivalent. Some right-wingers still used inverted commas for the '*DDR*', implying a denial of the sovereign and 'democratic' status due to the absence of Western-style democratic elections; and refugee groups from the former German provinces beyond the rivers Oder and Neiße but also some of the right within the CDU/CSU still insisted on calling the GDR *Mitteldeutschland* to keep alive the possibility of the return of those provinces which they referred to as *Ostdeutschland*.

As Dieckmann (1964) has demonstrated, political language circulated around catchwords. There are complex symbols – general symbols embracing different semantic components – which may solicit a favourable attitude towards one's own viewpoint and an unfavourable one towards that of one's opponents (Klaus 1971: 56–76). The German political discourse of the 1970s and 1980s was set against the background of the cold war and the division of Germany. The meanings of the catchwords *Frieden* (peace), *Freiheit* (freedom) and *Sicherheit* (security) in the policy statements of the different political parties differed markedly. The SPD emphasized the securing of peace as its achievement through successful and tolerant negotiations with the GDR and other East Bloc nations. *Frieden*, in SPD discourse, was frequently associated with *Entspannung* (détente) and to a lesser extent with *Kompromiß* (compromise), *Verständigung* (communication), *Gleichberechtigung* (equality), *Gleichgewicht* (balance) and *Unabhängigkeit* (independence – especially of Third World nations). *Freiheit* was linked with *Gerechtigkeit* (justice) and *Chancengleichheit* (equality of opportunity). The CDU/CSU meaning of

Frieden was closely linked with *Freiheit* and *Sicherheit*. *Freiheit* expressed [Western/capitalist] as opposed to [Eastern/communist] and *Sicherheit* denoted defence against potential outside aggression and protection from terrorism from within. The FDP, which presents itself as the party of the centre, took an intermediate position between the two larger parties, with an emphasis on the rights of individuals and policies that are *freiheitlich* (free).

While it is still possible to detect markers of political ideology in discourse, there has been, since the *Wende*, a general convergence among the three mainstream parties. This is due partly to the 'homogenization' of political discourse throughout Western Europe, with the German parties having representatives in the European Parliament and interacting with party colleagues from other countries. It is due partly to the widespread belief that political ideology has failed the people. On the other hand, much of the programmes of the protest movements (e.g. ecology) has been absorbed into the platforms of the mainstream parties.

There has also been a general reversal of political categories in many parts of the world. Whereas for most of the post-Second World War period, *Änderung* (change), *Reform, dynamisch* (dynamic), *and Fortschritt* (progress) were identified with change in favour of egalitarianism and social justice, it is the proponents of economic rationalism who have now gained control of these terms. *Änderung, Fortschritt, dynamisch* and *Reform* now tend to mean a change in direction to a more 'business-like' approach. Behrens, Dieckmann and Kehl (1982) have shown how the CDU succeeded in the mid to late 1970s in creating their own register to replace the previously dominant left-wing register, changing the meanings of some of the words (e.g. *Reform, Frieden*) and replacing *Chancengleichheit* by *Chancengerechtigkeit*. This makes it possible for the CDU and CSU to refer to their SPD opponents as *Ewiggestrige* (yesterday's people), a designation also applied to the CDU liberals. In the period from 1989, hard-line Communists in Eastern Europe have been termed by the media *rechts* (right-wing) and *Konservative* (Conservatives), and hard-line Nationalists have been designated as *Radikale* (radicals). This is a reversal of earlier descriptions. There are some lexicosemantic differences in the discourse of the mainstream parties although they are not nearly as obvious as they used to be.

Politicians are, on the whole, very conscious of the importance of language in their work, and some of them have been prominent in the critique of political language. This includes the 1994 SPD candidate for the chancellorship, Rudolf Scharping, who declared that 'die Sprache der Politik muß deutlicher werden' (the language of politics had to become

countries centred around the term *Menschenrechte* (human rights). *Freiheitlich* continues to be a word of the conservative parties, which also include the symbol of the *ungeborenes Leben* (unborn life, i.e. anti-abortion) in its discourse of freedom with responsibility.

6.3.2   'Mainstream' Austrian parties

For historical reasons, it is impossible to assume a one-to-one correspondence between the main Austrian parties and their approximate German counterparts:

> Österreichische Volkspartei (ÖVP) – CDU/CSU
> Freiheitliche Partei Österreichs (FPÖ)[3] – FDP
> Sozialdemokratische Partei Österreichs (SPÖ) – SPD

It should be remembered that the Roman Catholic Church, the state church of the former empire, maintains an important position in public life, and that there has been a traditional rivalry and proportionate distribution of public offices between Catholics and Socialists, represented by the ÖVP and SPÖ respectively. On some issues, the SPÖ and the ÖVP have a large measure of commonality, and these two large parties have formed a coalition since 1986. The FPÖ is to the right of the ÖVP. The pre-Second World War forerunner of the FPÖ was the German Nationalist Party. (The term *freiheitlich* is a rather conservative marker in both German and Austrian political discourse. This means independence from the system which allocates public offices proportionately to SPÖ and ÖVP members.) The ultra-right policies and especially the discourse of the FPÖ's populist leader Jörg Haider prompted the more genuine liberal element under Heide Schmidt to form their own party, the Liberales Forum, in 1993.

As in Germany, all the mainstream parties in Austria allude to *Freiheit*. The common features of this complex symbol are [human dignity] [self-determination] and [social responsibility]. Interestingly, the SPÖ associates *Freiheit* with the related concepts of *Gerechtigkeit* and *Solidarität* that the German CDU/CSU also now do. In the SPÖ discourse, *Freiheit* has the components [+ social and material preconditions] and [– privileges]. For the ÖVP it has the features [+ own decision], [+ power to act], [– welfare state] and [+ social and material preconditions]. The FPÖ, for whom the concept of *Freiheit* is central, constructs the complex symbol with the features [+ self-chosen development], [+ responsibility], [+ order], [+ author-

---

[3]   In January 1995, the FPÖ changed its name to *Die Freiheitlichen* (note the deletion of *Österreich*), declaring itself to be a movement, not a party.

ity], [+ diversity] and [– uniformity]. This makes the FPÖ's concept of *Freiheit* very different from that of the SPÖ. *Freiheitlich* (see above) 'liberal-conservative' stands in contrast to *katholisch* and *sozialistisch*. The FPÖ and, to a lesser extent, the ÖVP places much emphasis on individual initiative and achievement (*Leistung*) and a decrease in bureaucratization. To the SPÖ, as to the SPD, *Gerechtigkeit* (justice) entails *Gleichheit* (equality). But this also applies to the ÖVP, which, like the FPÖ and their German counterparts, includes in *Gerechtigkeit* [– uniforming measures]. The ÖVP's *Subisidarität* is projected as offering protection from overmuch state control. The SPÖ and the ÖVP share the symbol *Solidarität*, which the FPÖ does not use. The ÖVP employs *Solidarismus* in contrast to the FPÖ's *Individualismus* and the SPÖ's *Kollektivismus*. The ÖVP's social doctrine also features *Partnerschaft*, which involves the peaceful resolution of conflict in all spheres, including industry and the economy. The SPÖ has also used *sozial-partnerschaft(lich)*. All the parties use *Demokratie* in a way which includes a component of *Mitbestimmung* (co-determination) and *Mitentscheidung* (involvement in decision-making), e.g. in the workplace. All parties project themselves as being cosmopolitan, but while the SPÖ is concerned with the protection of minorities, the FPÖ (and occasionally some members of the ÖVP) seek to protect the majority from 'discrimination' in favour of minorities, such as migrant workers! All the mainstream parties balance *Fortschritt* with *Umweltschutz* or *umweltfreundliche Politik*. The FPÖ alone, until 1993, maintained a declaration of allegiance to the *deutsche Volks- und Kulturgemeinschaft* (German ethnic and cultural community). This was dropped from the party's programme in November 1993 (*Österreichbericht* 254, 3 November 1993). However, Bruckmüller (1994: 17) records a decreased allegiance to the Austrian nation on the part of the FPÖ voters.

Since 1987, the FPÖ has been led by Jörg Haider, who has broken taboos by taking a strongly nationalist right-wing position, reflected in his opposition to *Multikultur*, emphasis on *Volkstum* and the *kleine Leute*. He has broken discourse taboos by employing expressions such as Goebbels' *totaler Krieg* (total war) in the internal political context and praising the *ordentliche Beschäftigungspolitik* (orderly employment policy) of the Third Reich (Januschek 1992). He is 'the respectable politician' using racist discourse unashamedly but who uses evasive language in references to contemporary racism or Nazi atrocities, e.g. the use of *Vorgänge* (occurrences) for genocide (Bailer-Galanda n.d: 44). This came to the fore in his unsuccessful campaign (1993) *Österreichischer zuerst* (Austrians first) to curb immigration.

Haider has become a cult figure in some circles, dreaded by others. He is portrayed as an uncompromising anti-socialist, a person with a more open mind, someone sticking up for the average citizen against the big

parties. The *Großparteien*, the left, and migrants and minorities such as the Slovenians represent the groups depicted as the 'enemies'.

His fairly extreme position has split his party as well as gaining it additional popular support. The vocabulary of the new party, Liberales Forum, formed by Heide Schmidt from the more liberal elements of the FPÖ, is dominated by *liberal/Liberalismus*, *Vernunft* (reason) and *Aufklärung* (enlightenment), *Reform* and *demokratisch*, the last standing for a political culture with participation and feedback between citizens, electors, the party and the parliament. Like its German counterpart, it emphasizes and rewards *Leistung* (achievement) / *Leistungsprinzip, Spitzenleistung*. Liberales Forum's notion of *Freiheit* includes elements of *Verantwortung* (responsibility), *Gleichheit* (equality), and *Offenheit* (openness), as well as *individuale Existenz* (individual existence) and *Sicherheit* (security). Liberales Forum sees itself as the antithesis both of their former party colleagues in the FPÖ and of the grand coalition which they describe as the *Machtduopol* (power duopoly).

6.3.3   Die Grünen in Germany and Austria

This party in both countries is the parliamentary offspring of various extraparliamentary movements: conservation, anti-nuclear, peace and disarmament, feminist, human rights, world development, Christian activist, workers' independence – many of them new left, some quite conservative. This coalition of interests is reflected in the issues they embrace and the language they employ. They include utopian and more pragmatic elements. The Greens have found themselves forming coalitions with the SPD in the German state of Lower Saxony and in some local councils. In Germany they are the product of a merger of the West German Greens and the East German Bündnis 90. On the whole, they show a more 'critical' use of language. Their keyword *ökologisch* (ecological), which has found its way into the rhetoric of the mainstream parties, comprises the features: [– wastage], [– destruction], [– violence], [+ health], [+ wholesome], [– nuclear] and [+ equality]. The word is employed by the Greens in many areas, including the environment, medicine and social relations. Its antithesis is *unverzügelter Verbrauch* (unrestrained consumption) (e.g. *Energie-, Arzneimittel-, Nikotinverbrauch*, consumption of energy, medication, nicotine), *Verschwendung* (wastage), and *Wachstum* (growth), which are given negative connotations, connected with destruction.

Freiheit comprises the features: [– compulsion], [+ self-determination], [+ participation], [+ opportunities for the individual], [– suppression], [+ full information], [– bureaucratization], [– centralization], [+ local initiatives], [– atomic energy / pollution], [+ 'Back to Nature'], [– environ-

mental threats], [– privileges], [+ solidarity], [+ right to work in one's profession] and [+ right to demonstrate].

Demokratie, whether in national and state affairs, in the work situation or in the armed forces, is understood as direct, grassroots democracy, rather than a completely representational system. It has semantic components of [+ social justice] and [– police control]. The Austrian Greens, in particular, employ inclusive language (see above, 6.1) far more than the other parties.

6.3.4   Racist discourse in Germany and Austria

Since much of the far-right discourse in policy documents, election pamphlets and the Republicans' monthly, *Der Republikaner*, is nationalist and racist, it would be appropriate to discuss at this juncture some of the essential characteristics of recent German and Austrian racist discourse.

(i) There are a number of schemata associated with the complex symbol *Ausländer*, as Van Dijk (e.g. 1987) has ascertained in his international research: they have caused a housing shortage; they are causing unemployment; they are coming illegally (in the Republicans' literature, *unkontrolliertes Einströmen*, uncontrollable influx); they are competing with us; they have increased the criminality rate; their customs are different; they are too different; there are too many of them (in the Republicans' political literature, Germans are *Fremde im eigenen Lande* 'strangers in our own country'). (Most of these associations with *Ausländer* were prominent in 45-minute interviews which Jäger (1992) conducted with 37 Germans in cities in North Rhine-Westphalia.) Note the '*us–them*' dichotomy.

(ii) A threat to the existence of Germany and to Germans is presented, e.g. the Republicans' emphasis on the threat of *Überfremdung der deutschen Sprache und Kultur* (foreign infiltration of German language and culture, see 6.3.1) and on *deutsche Werte* (German values) and *deutsche Würde* (German esteem). *Überfremdung* was the '*Unwort*' (ugly word) of the year 1993.

(iii) Apparent disclaimers such as 'Ich habe nichts gegen Schwarze, aber. . .' (I don't have anything against blacks, but . . .) are often used (Van Dijk 1992).

(iv) Racism is denied, there is an implied reproach of anti-racists, and a claim of the reversal of the actual situation, i.e. a claim of anti-German racism (see Van Dijk 1992).

A team from the University of Vienna Department of Linguistics (Mitten, Wodak and De Cillia 1989, Projektteam 'Sprache und Vorurteil' 1989, Gruber and Wodak 1992 based on the mass-circulation Vienna daily *Neue Kronen-Zeitung*) have examined Austrian media examples of anti-Semitic and other racist discourse. They have found a number of facets of anti-Semitism: Jews as Christ-murderers, dishonest dealers, the Jewish conspiracy (controlling the world press, banks and political power), Jews as the privileged, denying the Holocaust (Mitten *et al.* 1989). Linguistically, this is manifested, for instance, in:

(i) The predication of particular personal qualities, e.g. *der grünschnäblige Generalsekretär Singer* (green-beak Secretary-General Singer).

(ii) Equations, e.g. *Waldheim = Österreich; extreme Nationalsozialisten = Antisemiten; Israel = Juden; amerikanische Massenmedien = jüdische Journalisten und Politiker; Amerikas Juden = israelische Regierung.*

(iii) Playing down facts, e.g. 'Nur verhältnismäßig wenige der jüdischen Opfer sind vergast worden. Die anderen sind verhungert oder erschlagen worden; durch Fleckfieber, Ruhr und Typhus umgekommen, weil man ihnen ärztliche Hilfe verweigert hat; erfroren oder an Entkräftung gestorben' (Only relatively few of the Jewish victims were gassed. The others died of hunger or were beaten to death; died of typhoid or dysentery because they were refused medical assistance; froze to death or died of weakness) (cited by Gruber and Wodak 1992: 28).

(iv) Impersonal or passive constructions, such as the use of *man* in (iii) above.

(v) Vagueness, such as 'verhältnismäßig wenige' in (iii) above.

(vi) Playing down and euphemisms; e.g. *Emigration = Vertreibung; Judenangelegenheit = Genozid.* (Emigration = expulsion; matter of the Jews = genocide.)

(vii) Hedgings, leading to mystification; e.g. 'Tatsächlich wird in so gut wie allem, was bis dato "enthüllt" worden ist, mit halben Wahrheiten, mit deutlichen oder unterschwelligen Unterstellungen gearbeitet . . .' (re Waldheim) (In fact, in virtually everything that has been 'revealed' so far, they are working with half-truths and hidden assumptions) (*Die Presse*, 6 March 1986, cited in Mitten *et al.* 1989: 9).

(viii) Allusions through language, e.g. *düstere Vergangenheit* (dim past), implying a repudiation of responsibility.

(ix) Equation of Jews and Nazis through the cliché of the 'Christ-murderers'. e.g. Gruber and Wodak 1992: 29.

(x) 'Uncommentated' ironical exaggeration, e.g. 'Österreich – ein Naziland! . . . ein Land, das sich einen Kriegsverbrecher zum Staatsoberhaupt erwählt hat! Ein Land, wo heutzutage die Juden ihres Lebens nicht mehr sicher sind . . .!' (Austria – a Nazi country! . . . a country that elected a war criminal as its head of state, a country where Jews' lives are no longer safe . . .!) (cited in Gruber and Wodak 1992: 87).

(xi) Justification strategy through quoting 'Jewish authorities' to support prejudices, e.g. a Jewish American professor who said that more Auschwitz inmates died of secondary causes than of direct ones (cited in Gruber and Wodak 1992: 77).

6.3.5   Other right-wing groups in Germany

Here we need to distinguish between the Republicans (Die Republikaner), who try to present themselves as a 'respectable' *deutschnational* (right-wing German nationalist) party, using a combination of right-wing and mainstream discourse in a particular way, the more overt far-right parties, the National Democratic Party (Nationaldemokratische Partei Deutschlands (NPD)) and the German People's Union (Deutsche Volksunion (DVU)), and the racist ultra-right fringe. The latter groups, of whom there are about a hundred (Jäger 1989), employ physical violence but offer little verbally expressed ideology.

The Republicans[4] have reintroduced nationalism based on the notion of *Volk* into mainstream German politics after it had been discredited since the Holocaust. Whereas the slogan of the East German revolution – *Wir sind das Volk* – had been a reaction to the usurping of the people's rights to speak for themselves, by 1992 the slogan was employed by the Republicans to express racist sentiments. *Volk* was used to outlaw the *Ausländer*, migrant workers and their descendants and asylum seekers (Gruner 1993). The Republicans have been described as 'ideologically highly complex' (Kellershohn 1992: 91). They present a contradiction of submissiveness and rebelliousness. Their discourse projects a petty-bourgeois ideal, the 'heroization' of the *anständiger Deutsche* (decent German) (Kellershohn 1992: 93), capitalism without classes and, at the same time, it is rebelliously anti-capitalist, with an ideology around *Volk*, *Vaterland* and *Nation*, all of which are very prevalent in their literature. One of their good-value adjectives is *patriotisch*. Like the CDU/CSU, they support a

---

[4]   They fared badly in the November 1994 general election, receiving too few votes to send any members to the Bundestag.

free market economy; unlike the CDU/CSU they want a strong state. Their policy has elements of Christian fundamentalism and conservative environmentaiism combined with a strong basis in German right-wing nationalism. The reader is reminded that there is no post-war tradition of left-wing or centre-left German nationalism; the left and centre have been strongly international in orientation. The Republicans project themselves as *fortschrittlich* (in the modern 'conservative' sense of trying to bring about a change to right-wing values, rather than in the former left-wing meaning of 'progressive'), *zukunftsweisend* (showing the direction of the future), and as speaking for *die schweigende Mehrheit* (the silent majority). They claim to want to renew Germany ('Wir erneuern Deutschland'), offering a *moderne und offene Demokratie*. Like the Greens, they function also as a protest party, attracting votes away from both the major parties, which they constantly attack. Like the Greens, they stress *Altparteienkorruption und -ämterpatronage* (the corruption and patronage for offices of the old parties). The *Altparteien* are projected as similar and sometimes referred to by the Republicans as the *Große Koalition* (grand coalition). They also stress *Bürgermündigkeit* (mature citizens), and the need for *Volksabstimmungen* (referendums). Their appeal to small farmers includes references to *Ökologie*. They are not very enthusiastic about European union, projecting instead the idea of an *Europa der Vaterländer*.

An important aspect of the Republicans' discourse is racist. It features the keywords *Volk* and *Vaterland* (including *Vaterlandsliebe*). It constantly suggests that Germany and Germans are under threat (see above), e.g.

> schleichende Auflösung des deutschen Volkes (creeping
>   dissolution of the German people)
> Die *DM* darf nicht sterben. (The *German* Mark must not die.)
> Keine EG auf Kosten der deutschen Steuerzahler. (No EC at
>   the expense of the German taxpayer.)

Multikultur (a pejorative term for *Multikulturismus*) is described as a *Zeitbombe*, and Islam is presented as a threat to 'Western Christian values' in Germany. There are blatant outbursts of anti-Semitism, e.g. the then leader of the Republicans, Franz Schönhuber, describing the President of the Central Council of Jews in Germany, Ignaz Bubis, as 'einer der schlimmsten Volksverhetzer in Deutschland', accusing him of being responsible for anti-Semitism, following synagogue arson in Lübeck (*Mannheimer Morgen*, 2/3 April 1994, p.4).

The Republicans present themselves as the party of *Ruhe und Ordnung* (law and order). The keyword *Sicherheit* has semantic components of [protection] [stopping crime, including drug crimes and prostitution]

[increasing penalties] [justice] [improving border controls]. Another emphasis is on traditional family values. The role of the woman is described as 'mütterlicher Mittelpunkt der intakten Familie' (maternal centre of the intact family). While the pulpit is rejected as a vehicle for the propagation of a social gospel (*politische Propaganda*), religion is encouraged as a way of rekindling *Nationalbewußtsein* (national consciousness).

The Republicans describe their opponents and critics as *Chaoten, Neurotiker, Assoziale* and *Radikalinskis* (*Der Spiegel*, February 1989), while their opponents use words such as *Entsetzen, erschüttert, Enttäuschung, alarmierend* and *erschreckend* to describe them and their policies and language. Because the Republicans wish to portray themselves as 'respectable' and trustworthy, they stress in their political literature their democratic and non-violent intents:

> Nicht mit Gewalt – Nur mit dem Stimmzettel (Not by
> violence – Only by ballot paper)

This contrasts with some of their simple slogans which appear to be indirect speech acts of incitements:

> Schluß mit dem Asylbetrug (An end to asylum betrayal)
> Weg mit . . . (Down with . . .)
> Das Boot ist voll (The boat is full)

In April 1994, the mainstream parties instigated public discussion on whether the Republicans should be banned for anti-constitutional activity.

The discourse of the NPD and DVU does not make any attempt to speak to the middle-of-the-road protest voter and addresses mainly the issues of German national identity and migration, using a more traditional ultra-right register. The election propaganda of the two parties, the NPD's weekly newspaper *Deutsche Nachrichten*, the *Deutsche Wochenzeitung* and the longer-established *National-Zeitung* (weekly circulation 10,000), which are close to the DVU, give some insights into their language. The assumption of a threat of a foreign takeover of Germany provides the basis of most of the discourse, e.g.:

> Deutschland muß deutsch bleiben! (Germany must stay
> German!)
> Deutschland bleibt unser Land! (Germany will remain our
> country!)

Quite violent implications of forced removal or 'ethnic cleansing' are inherent in the slogans:

> Das ganze Deutschland uns Deutschen! (The whole of
>   Germany for us Germans!)
> Ausländer- und Asylantenrückführung! (Send back foreigners
>   and asylum seekers!)

The myth of Germans being second-class citizens in Germany and the 1993 controversy over Germany's liberal asylum laws form the basis of the strongly worded:

> Kampf der Inländerfeindlichkeit! (Down with hostility towards
>   natives!) (Note the formation of a hardly necessary antonym
>   of *Ausländerfeindlichkeit* – hatred of foreigners – an attitude
>   which has included the burning down of migrant hostels.)
> Kampf dem Asylschwindel! (Fight asylum swindle!)

The NPD has also occasionally attempted to reverse the real situation with a slogan such as:

> Dem Haß keine Chance! (No chance of hatred!)

The far-right publications focus on the keyword *Volk* in the exclusive sense of 'the German people'. A major preoccupation is the migration/ multicultural debate. For instance, under the heading, 'Im Jahr . . . 2000?' in an NPD election pamphlet there appears a picture of a collection of 'foreign-looking' faces dominated by an Iman calling beside a mosque, with the inscription 'Unsere Gemeinde' (Our community). The ultra-right newspapers still employ *Mitteldeutschland* for the former GDR states, reserving *Ostdeutschland* for the former German provinces east of the Oder-Neiße Line, indicating an unwillingness to accept that they are now part of Poland or Russia. The policy of accepting this is designated *Verrat* (betrayal) and *Verzicht* (renunciation), an old-established keyword in right-wing self-pity. A new line is the 'co-opting' of a small number of Germans of Jewish background (all dead and some who died well before 1933) as allies of their cause, while maintaining a generally anti-Semitic line playing down the Holocaust. The terms given to the 'good Jews' are *jüdische Humanisten* (Jewish humanists) and *große jüdische Deutsche* (great Jewish Germans) (e.g. *National-Zeitung*, 2 April 1993). In the following comment on Victor Gollancz, a hedged in-group statement is implied:

> Nach 1933 bekämpfte er publizistisch den Nationalsozialismus, mahnte
> *jedoch* während des Krieges zur *Vernunft*. (Though he fought National
> Socialism through the media after 1933, he appealed for commonsense
> during the war.) (*National-Zeitung*, 2 April 1993, p.6.)

People tried for or suspected of Nazi crimes are sympathetically described as *sieche Greise* (sickly old men) and their accusers as *antideutsche Hetzer* (Anti-German slanderers). 'Left-wingers' are termed *Gangster, Radikalinski, Terroristen, linker Terror, die Terrorszene, Roter Terror,* and the bureaucrats *Bonner Bonzen* (in Germany) and *Brüsseler Bonzen* (in the European Union).

Jäger (1989) has demonstrated the stylistic diversity of the ultra-right periodicals, ranging from the religious and military metaphors of *elemente* and the friend–foe schemata of *Neue Zeit* to the simple language and lower sociolect combined with youth register in *Klartext*. They all attempt to attract different groups to their right-wing nationalist ideology.

The young people's right-wing monthly newspaper *Junge Freiheit*, originally established by a splinter group of the Republicans, combines nationalist-conservativism, Christian-conservativism, and other ideological directions. While the content of its articles includes general material to attract a wider readership, the emphasis is on countering *Antifaschismus* and the perpetuation of German *Schuldgefühl* (guilt feeling), and opposing *Überfremdung* and *Ethnopluralismus*, the catchword against multiculturalism (Stosch 1993).

A Christian right-wing group ironically called Christliche Mitte (Christian Centre) is spreading a discourse based on fundamentalist Christianity:

> Rückkehr zu Gott (Return to God)
> Vertrauen zu Jesus Christus (Trust in Jesus Christ)
> Für ein Deutschland nach Gottes Geboten (For Germany
>   according to God's Commandments)

with social implications such as:

> Schutz des ungeborenen Kindes (Protection of the unborn
>   child, i.e. anti-abortion)

with the argument;

> Jeder Mensch ist einmalig (Every person is unique)

Voluntary euthanasia in the Netherlands is described as 'gewaltsame Tötung nicht mehr arbeitsfähiger Individuen' (violent killing of individuals no longer capable of working) and identified with Nazi experiments with the mentally ill. The group expresses a fervent opposition to multiculturalism and especially to Islam. The party's monthly, *Kurier der Christlichen Mitte*, and its pamphlets present Islam as a major threat to Germany, e.g.:

Islam ist auf dem Vormarsch in Deutschland. (Islam is on the
advance in Germany.)
Islam kämpft um Anerkennung als Körperschaft öffentliche
Rechts. (Islam is fighting for recognition in public law.)

Thus, many of the right-wing groups are aiming at catering for the
concerns of the average German and introducing their programme of
prejudice into the discussion partly through linguistic devices.

6.3.6   Other left-wing groups in Germany

The left-wing political groups to the left of the SPD and the Greens are
in no way homogeneous. They represent a range of competing interests –
some grassroots protest groups such as the Statt-Partei (instead party) and
some still dating back to the various communist parties which developed
from West German student activism in the late 1960s and early 1970s.
Some of these groups go under the name of the Autonomen (Autonomous). By far the most important far-left political force is the Partei des
Demokratischen Sozialismus (Party of Democratic Socialism), the
'respectable' successor of the SED, the East German Communist Party,
which predictably has far more support in the eastern states than in the
western ones.

After a resounding rejection in the 1990 federal elections, the PDS has
made a comeback in some municipal elections in the East,[5] partly as a
protest against the major parties not understanding the problems of the
East. The PDS attracts pacifists, East German nostalgics and disillusioned
Social Democrats concerned about a shift to the right (*Wochenpost*, 16
December 1993, pp. 1, 4–5). It is championing the causes of feminist,
tenants', consumer and ecological groups. Its language represents an
attempt to avoid tainted ex-GDR or New Left jargon and, in fact, any
ideological vocabulary. (Among the few exceptions are *Demokratie-Abbau*
(in a pamphlet) and *Hitlerfaschismus*, the GDR word for National
Socialism (in an issue of the Berlin PDS parliamentary party's news-sheet
Bannmeiler Report, 20 April 1994).) As with other parties, *Freiheit, Frieden,
soziale Gerechtigkeit* and especially *Demokratie* are the catchwords. Like the
other smaller parties, the PDS attacks the larger parties and the *bevor-
mundende Bürokratie des Staates* (patronizing state bureaucracy). The PDS
pamphlets are steeped in the discourse of discontent (see 6.3.8), focusing
on the disadvantaged and those discriminated against (e.g. women,

---

[5]   And in the 1994 federal election.

elderly, unemployed, handicapped), the job situation, the environment, and the swing to the right throughout Germany. Inclusive language is employed throughout, e.g *ArbeiterInnen* (worker), *VerbraucherInnen* (consumer). Campaign advertisements present the party, in a discourse combining features of a creed and a curriculum vitae, as having been born in the days of reform at the end of the GDR, grown up at the round tables of the East, declared clinically dead in the media, revived in the Brandenburg elections, committed to the interests of the socially declassed, as an opposition from both East and West in Strasbourg and Bonn, before and after 1994 e.g.:

> Geboren im Wendeherbst '89, aufgewachsen an den Runden Tischen des Ostens, in die Schule der Demokratie gegangen im ersten frei gewählten Parlament der DDR . . . für klinisch tot erklärt in den Medien, seit den Brandenburger Wahlen jedoch lebendig wie nie . . . engagiert für die Belange der sozial Deklassierten . . . als Opposition aus dem Osten und dem Westen in Strasbourg und Bonn. Vor und nach 1994. (Advertisement in *Wochenpost*, 26 May 1994, p.37.)

The Deutsche Kommunistische Partei (DKP), the 'moderate' traditionally communist party in the old Federal Republic, publishes the daily newspaper *Unsere Zeit*. It uses a general vocabulary with a few traditional communist terms and attempts to appeal to the 'ordinary man and woman'. There is a disproportionately large number of colloquialisms, and capitalists are referred to with disdain, e.g. *Bosse, Konzernherren* (tycoons), *Millionäre*.

Unfortunately I have no data on the remaining far-left groups, except for the anti-nuclear lobby, which has avoided the euphemisms created by the protagonists of nuclear energy. Thus *Atomkraft*, with its associations with *Atombombe*, is employed instead of *Kernkraft*, which has connotations of wholesomeness and stability (*Kern* = nucleus, core, kernel). The anti-nuclear lobby has also used *Unfall* (accident) in preference to the euphemism *Störfall* (temporary disruption) and *Mülldeponie* (nuclear waste dump) instead of *Entsorgungspark* (*Park* being associated with recreation, relaxation and an area kept in its natural state for the public benefit, and *entsorgen* literally meaning 'taking away worries') (see Dahl 1977).

6.3.7   Anti-racist groups in Germany

The far-left groups are very active in the anti-racist debate. But it is by no means their province alone, and some of the anti-racist initiatives are being taken by broadly based citizens' groups and professional groups, e.g.

lawyers and judges for peace. Arson attacks against asylum hostels and syn-
agogues and violence against migrants has generated massive protest
demonstrations and anxiety and frustration on the part of large numbers
of Germans from many social and political backgrounds and many with
no political affiliations.

Most of the language of anti-racist groups is not characterized by a
specific register. Their slogans are direct, e.g. *Gegen den Fremdenhaß*
(Against hatred of foreigners), *Gegen die Ausländerhetze und Neonazis*
(Against agitation against foreigners and Neo-Nazis), *Nie wieder* (Never
again), *Kampf dem Faschismus* (Fight Facism), *Alle Menschen sind Ausländer*
(All people are foreigners, based on 'Alle Menschen werden Brüder', in
Schiller's 'Ode to Joy'), and *Es lebe die Geschwisterlichkeit der Völker* (Long
live the 'Geschwisterlichkeit' of the peoples – inclusive version of
Brüderlichkeit, fraternity). There is little if any suggestion that the
Ausländer should be regarded as *Deutsche.* However, much of the anti-
racist discourse tries to dispel the myth that migrants, refugees and
asylum seekers are responsible for Germany's economic ills, and turns
the argument around as a criticism of the government or even the
capitalist system, e.g.:

> Daß es in Deutschland Wohnungsnot, Arbeitslosigkeit usw. gibt, ist eine
> Folge der Fehler in der Politik und unseres Wirtschaftssystems. (The
> fact that there is a housing shortage, unemployment, etc. in Germany
> is the consequence of mistakes in policies and our economic system.)

> Wer kontrolliert den Wohnungsmarkt, Asylbewerber aus Kurdistan oder
> deutsche Makler? Wer nimmt Tausenden Stahl- und Bergarbeitern
> den Arbeitsplatz weg, ein türkischer Kumpel oder ein Deutscher in
> Bonn? Wer schließt Kindergärten, Jugendzentren und erhöht
> Steuern, Flüchtlinge aus Sri Lanka oder deutsche Politiker in
> Bundestag und Stadtrat? (Who is controlling the housing market,
> asylum seekers from Kurdistan or German estate agents? Who is
> taking away the jobs of thousands of steel workers and miners, a
> Turkish collier or a German in Bonn [i.e. the Chancellor]? Who is
> closing kindergartens, youth centres and raising taxes, refugees from
> Sri Lanka or German politicians in the Bundestag and the city
> council?)

The ultra-right-wing racist slogans *Ausländer 'raus* (Foreigners out) and
Türken 'raus (Turks out) are reversed in the anti-racist slogan *Nazis 'raus*
(Nazis out). In some of the posters, parallels between Auschwitz and the
burning down of asylum-seekers' hostels are presented semiotically.
Some of the anti-racist campaigns are taking place through music, with
rock groups counteracting the activities of racist pop groups and with

pop groups such as Sturmvogel opposing Neo-Nazism in Eastern Germany.

6.3.8   Discourse of discontent

There are common features of the discourse of discontent, but also divergences between the East and West German variants. We can identify particular schemata in spoken and written discourse – socially constructed patterns of communicative behaviour available to the speaker/hearer from their experience and knowledge (Rumelhart 1975, Van Dijk 1977). They include some of the following components:

West discourse	**East discourse**
(or referring to West)	(or referring to East)

      (1) Great expectations have not been fulfilled.

(2) Our taxes are used to help the East.	(2) No growth.
(3) The East does not do anything.	(3) It will take the East long to catch up.
(4) There is a worldwide recession.	(4) We are being exploited.
(5) Racism and nationalism are frightening us and harming our international reputation.	(5) The East is poorer and has more unemployed.

      (6) We are still divided.
      (7) No one can help us.
      (8) Politicians are not helping the situation.
      (9) Germans would rather have peace and security than this kind of unification.

The tendency towards a discourse of discontent has become universal. But it is more noticeable in Germany because of the previous polarization and the unfilled expectations. Rather than confrontation, there is now a lot of 'negative discourse'. Also, in Germany, there is a fear of uncertainty. Hofstede (1991), in his comparative study of cultural core values, points to the importance of uncertainty avoidance in German culture. (see also Schlosser 1993c on the yearning after security in East Germany.)

Aspects of the discourse of discontent are 'lexified' in the terms *Politikverdrossenheit*, (weariness of politics, also used in Austria, e.g. *Österreichbericht (ÖB)* 20 October 1993, 5 November 1993), *Parteiverdrossenheit* (weariness of political parties), *Parteimüdigkeit* (tiredness of parties), *Politikfrust* (frustration with politics).

In the light of some random examples collected from the weekly

Table 15 *Number of 'discontent' categories in each article*

	East	West
1	13	2
2	7	4
3	2	1
4 +	–	3

Note:
For 'discontent' categories, see above.

Table 16 *Actual 'discontent' categories represented*

	East German	West German
(1)	5	6
(2)	–	2 W, 1 E
(3)	3	3 W, 1 E
(4)	1	3
(5)	3	5 W, 1 E
(6)	9	2
(7)	3	2
(8)	1	–
(9)	1	–

newspapers, *Die Zeit* (West) and *Wochenpost* (East), 1992–4, and from the daily newspapers *Mannheimer Morgen* (West) and *Sächsische Zeitung* (East), the following observations could be made:

The foci that the Western newspapers were most likely to select are (1) and (5), while the Eastern newspapers are most likely to focus on (6) and (1), the latter often including a nostalgic reference to the GDR, e.g. in a letter to the editor on the situation of mothers:

> In der damaligen DDR hatte eine schwangere Frau und junge Mutter mehr soziale Zuwendungen. (In the then GDR a pregnant woman and young mother had more social benefits.) ('Das Kind ist Glück', *Sächsische Zeitung*, 22/23 January 1994, p.1.)

The number of categories included in a piece of discourse will vary according to whether it is entirely devoted to the question of German unity or is on the German economy in general, or some aspect of it, whether it is an article or a letter to the editor. The largest number of cat-

egories (up to five) is touched on in various articles in *Die Zeit* around the second anniversary of unification.

The key sections from just two articles show how these foci are combined. The first three extracts are from an article in *Die Zeit*, 'Wer sagt dem Volk die Wahrheit?' (Who is going to tell the people the truth?) (*Die Zeit*, 2 October 1992, p. 1):

> (1) Die Rede von den 'blühenden Landschaften', noch dazu in vier, fünf Jahren, war blühender Unsinn. Die Behauptung, im Osten werde es allen besser und im Westen keinem schlechter gehen, war töricht. Und die Vorstellung, wir Westdeutschen könnten die Einheit kurz und schmerzlos aus dem Zuwachs finanzieren, war nicht nur ökonomisch absurd, sondern vor allem mordisch fatal. (Talk of the 'blooming regions', particularly in four or five years, was blooming nonsense. The claim that everyone would be better off in the East and no one would be worse off in the West was mad. And the idea that West Germans could finance unification quickly and painlessly from growth was not only economically absurd but above all murderously fatal.)

> (5) Sind Aggressivität im Inneren und Auftrumpfen nach außen die Merkmale der neuen Identität? (Are internal aggressiveness and one-upmanship externally the features of the new identity?)

> (6) Doch dieser Irrglaube konnte keine Berge versetzen – er riß nur tiefe Gräben auf: zwischen Ost und West und innerhalb der beiden Gesellschaften Deutschlands. (Yet this misguided belief could not move mountains – it only tore open deep fissures; between East and West and within the two societies of Germany.)

In the next two extracts, from a letter entitled 'Schwindel mitgemacht' (Gone along with the swindle) (*Sächsische Zeitung*, 7/8 August 1993, p. 32), commenting on the claim that the collaborators are still in power and those in resistance still on the outside, categories 1 and 7 are thematized:

> (1) '. . . aber es ist schon bedrückend, immer mehr Hoffnungen schwinden zu sehen und Probleme auf 40 Jahre DDR und unsere miserabel Einstellung abzuwälzen. (. . . but it is already depressing to see more and more hopes disappear and offload problems onto 40 years of GDR and our lousy attitudes.)

> (7) Wenn es zu Wahlen geht, wird von den Politikern (auch die im Osten haben sehr schnell gelernt) versprochen, erzählt und gelogen, was das Zeug hält. (When it comes to elections, politicians (those in the East have learned very quickly too) will promise, talk and lie unscrupulously.)

Individual lexical items resound the general tone of stagnation, depression and false expectations, e.g.:

> Da saßen sie nämlich schon, oder vielmehr noch immer, all die...
> geflohenen, guten und schlechten Bekannten von früher, auf den
> *abgeschabten, wackligen* Barstühlchen, hinter den *gleichen angeschlagenen*
> Kaffeetassen, und sahen den seit Jahrhunderten in ein und derselben
> Kneipen *ausharrenden* ... verblüffend ähnlich [my emphasis]. (For there
> they were sitting already rather still, all the ... refugees, good and bad
> acquaintances (friends) from before, on the worn out, wobbly bar
> stools, behind the same chipped coffee cups, and looked astonishingly
> like those lingering in one and the same pub for decades.) ('Der Preis
> der neuen Freiheit' (The price of the new freedom), *Zeitmagazin*, 2
> October 1992, p.19.)

6.4   Brief summary

Women and young people are expressing their discontent with their position in society through language. As in many other countries, feminists in German-language countries have succeeded in drawing attention to the way in which they have been marginalized through language. Some recognition of this has been made in professional terminology, but the question of inclusive language has perhaps been addressed less seriously than in English-language countries.

Young people's registers are very diverse – according to social groups. They generally make use of anglicisms, onomatopoeia, particles and neologisms, and in South Germany, Austria, and Switzerland, features of local dialects. Agencies of distribution of youth registers include school, youth magazines and pop music.

World and national events have caused the discourse of mainstream political groups to converge. There is a general discourse of discontent, with East and West German variants. Covert and overt racist features have penetrated the discourse of the FPÖ and are prevalent in that of the Republicans.

6.5   Further reading

On language and gender, Hellinger (1985a) is a useful book of readings and Hellinger (1990) gives a comparative perspective. On youth registers, Schlobinski *et al.* (1993) gives a critical overview as well as a report on the authors' research. The sections on political discourse are based almost entirely on primary sources. On racist discourse, see Gruber and Wodak (1992) and the appropriate sections of Butterwegge and Jäger (1992).

7

Communication norms and communication barriers

This chapter deals with some ongoing issues concerning norms in the German language, including the international controversy on orthographic reform. It then addresses the nature of communication barriers within German and Austrian societies, including limited access to information.

7.1   Language norms and language planning in German

Language planning may be defined as policy formulation and implementation, by official and non-official bodies, on the creation, alphabetization, standardization and use of languages. Two types of language planning (treatment) are usually differentiated (Kloss 1967): *status planning*, which emphasizes questions concerning the language as a totality and in relation to other languages (e.g. the international spread of German, see Chapter 1, and when to use dialect and Standard, see Chapter 4), and *corpus planning*, which is preoccupied with normative questions such as correctness and efficiency of particular forms.

The German language does not possess central language planning authorities like the Académie Française, nor does the parliament of any German-language country pass laws concerning standard forms, as is the case in Norway (Haugen 1966). During the National Socialist régime, the Reichspresseamt (Reich Press Office) did possess and exercise planning powers, e.g. on 13 December 1937, it 'abolished' the word *Völkerbund* (League of Nations) and on 1 September 1939, it declared that *tapfer* (brave) could be collocated only with *deutsch*! (Berning 1964: 163–4).

There has been a 'purist' movement with a long tradition in Germany which has concerned itself with *Sprachpflege*, i.e. stylistics. What was previously the main body of 'purists' in West Germany, the Gesellschaft für deutsche Sprache (the Society for the German Language), has relaxed its policy on 'foreign words' , but it is still somewhat preoccupied with the defence of traditional norms in the interests of 'clear and effective

communication'. The society now has 2,000 individual members, including some in eastern Germany (where there are twelve branches). It offers advice on correct German through its periodical, *Der Sprachdienst*, and its enquiry office, which receives about 650 written and 15,000 personal and telephone queries on language use per year (Uwe Förster, personal communication). It also publishes a journal *Muttersprache* with articles on contemporary German. The Duden editorial staff, the German Department of the University of Aachen and the Department of German as a Foreign Language at the University of Düsseldorf also maintain language advice bureaux. In 1992 Aachen received 350 queries a week (*Süddeutsche Zeitung*, 24/25 October 1992). The 10,000 queries received by the Duden act as an indicator of difficulties. 88% of the calls received in Düsseldorf are from Germans. Like Aachen and Wiesbaden, they are mainly in the areas of spelling, punctuation and grammar. An analysis of the first 10,000 calls to the Düsseldorf bureau (Brons-Albert and Höhne 1991) shows a desire for stricter norms, many of the problems being with alternative forms. Orthographical questions were more prevalent among the Germans, while the non-native speakers, who were chiefly people who had learned German formally, had more queries of a lexicostylistic nature than the native speakers. In morphology, the 'foreigners' asked more about word formation, the Germans about inflections. 'Foreigners' wanted to know about the cases after particular verbs and the auxiliary to be used with a particular participle, while Germans asked about the declension of the adjective after certain quantifiers such as *alle, beide* and *einige*, cases after prepositions, and congruency with a subject such as *die Mehrheit der Abgeordneten* (the majority of the parliamentarians – singular or plural?). This type of survey gives some indications as to where there has been a weakening of or change in the norms.

In Austria, the conservative camp publicly manifested itself from 1950 until June 1978, through a fortnightly radio programme *Achtung, Sprachpolizei* (Attention, Language Police!), which kept thousands of listeners on guard against violations of the norms. The programme stimulated listeners' questions and had the effect of correcting some tendencies, such as the dropping of the genitive *-s* in some public notices (Hornung 1968). Over the years, however, the audiences decreased as the concept of the programme became outmoded[1] and there is now no programme of its

---

[1] 'Im Laufe der Jahre hat sich das Konzept von der Gestaltung der Sendung her überlebt' (Over the years the concept has become outdated in respect to the shaping of the programme) (letter from Gundomar Eibegger, Landesintendant des Studios Wien, 18 April 1980).

kind on Austrian radio or television. Some journalists see themselves as *Sprachpolizisten* on newspaper staffs (Elisabeth Welzig, personal communication). In keeping with reformist tendencies in the political and social life of Austria, the major language cultivation organization is now not the ultraconservative Verein Muttersprache (Mother Tongue Society), but the Österreichische Gesellschaft für Sprachpflege und Rechtschreiberneuerung (Austrian Society for Language Cultivation and Spelling Reform), which has advocated deviations from norms where appropriate to efficient communication.

In Switzerland, the Deutschschweizerische Sprachverein, founded in 1904, exists for the purpose of promoting 'besseres und reines Deutsch' (better and pure German). To this end, it runs a bimonthly, *Sprachspiegel*, and issues guidelines for business, proofreaders and others. It has succeeded in having a language advice bureau established. No such body exists in Luxembourg although its population, like the German-Swiss, use (Standard) German principally as a written language.

Language planning was more highly developed in the GDR, the notion of *Sprachkultur* (cultivation), devised by the Prague school of linguists, having been taken over in the 1960s to adapt the language to the demands of contemporary living, appropriate to the given situation. The more normative approach was inherent in the Leipzig Duden and the journal *Sprachpflege*, which gave advice on 'appropriate' German.

An important role in corpus planning is played by dictionaries, grammars and handbooks. Decisions for such authoritative reference books as *Duden-Rechtschreibung* for lexicon and spelling, *Duden-Grammatik* (Mannheim) for grammar, *Duden Aussprache-Wörterbuch* for pronunciation, *Duden-Fremdwörterbuch* for lexical transfers, and Wahrig's *Deutsches Wörterbuch* and the six-volume *Duden Universal-Wörterbuch* for lexicon and meanings are made by the staff of private enterprise firms and by committees of academics.[2] Though the Dudens have become increasingly flexible in recent editions, they are still conservatively directed somewhat more towards norm than towards usage. They are less normative than the dictionary of the Académie Française or the *Oxford English Dictionary*. The use of monolingual dictionaries in the wider (non-academic) community is probably not as developed as in English-language countries, perhaps because most spelling rules are not as difficult in German as in English. (Additional reasons may be that the authoritative *Duden-Rechtschreibung*

---

[2] A committee of the Ständige Konferenz der Kultusminister (Council of State Education Ministers) in West Germany has made recommendations on spelling conventions since 1956.

indicates meanings only for certain lexical transfers and 'internationalisms' and that Grimm's *Deutsches Wörterbuch*, the publication which spanned a century, has sixteen volumes and is hardly within the reach of the average native speaker.) On the other hand, English does not have an authoritative reference grammar corresponding to the Duden. The Mannheim Dudens are sold and used in Austria, Switzerland and Luxembourg (with the reservations expressed above in 2.4.3, 2.5.3).

As for status planning, the non-use of dialects in certain domains (e.g. public administration, education in Germany) is a piece of unwritten planning, with certain sanctions imposed (e.g. discrimination, ostracization, school failure; see 4.4). In corpus planning, on the other hand, the codices (grammars) and models (such as teachers) have long insisted on norms that are no longer generally accepted or adhered to. A number of non-standard rules are on the way to acceptance. These include the treatment of *brauchen* (to need) as a modal verb (i.e. without *zu*) (Grebe 1968: 39), the substitution of the present indicative for Subjunctive I in indirect speech *daß*-clauses, and the use of *trotz* (despite) with the dative as an alternative to the genitive (Süsskind 1968: 195), especially in the plural, where the dative noun, unlike the genitive, is marked (*trotz Unfällen*, cf. *trotz Unfälle*). These have received recognition in the *Duden-Grammatik*. There is also a growing tendency, in speech, to employ *weil* (because) as a co-ordinating (not subordinating) conjunction, e.g. *weil ich hab' ihn nicht gern* (Standard: *weil ich . . . habe*). This has previously been more common in Austria than in Germany. *Weil* as a co-ordinating conjunction is occurring increasingly in the written data corpus of the Duden, but, according to its editor (Günther Drosdowski, personal communication), this is perhaps because it now includes material from the 'alternative scene'. On the other hand, some inflectional endings are now being dropped in the written language. On the basis of a questionnaire of speakers' usage preferences on eleven sentences which normatively require the genitive (unfortunately she tells us nothing about the informants), Hentschel (1993) is able to present indications that:

(i) The genitive is most likely to stand in the plural, e.g.: *mit einem Stapel ausländischer Zeitungen* (with a pile of foreign newspapers).

(ii) In the case of parallel inflections in the singular, the genitive will more likely be replaced by the case of the other phrase, especially if it is in the accusative, e.g.: *Ich hätte gerne ein Glas kalten* (acc.) *Zitronentee* (I would like a glass (of) cold lemon tea). *Soll ich mir zwei Meter gelbe oder weiße* (acc.) *Seide kaufen?* (Should I buy (myself) two metres (of) yellow or white silk?)

To a lesser extent:

Könnte ich ihr mit einer Tasse heißem (dat.) *Tee eine Freude machen?*
(Could I give her some pleasure with a cup (of) hot tea?)

(iii) Genitive marking is disappearing where there is a preceding -*s*
(or -*z*), especially where there is already an indication of the
genitive, e.g.:

Florenz' Geschichte

Rowley (1988) observes that the 1984 Duden actually prescribes the
deletion of the -*s* as the ending on the noun in the following cases:

article + noun: *des heiligen Joseph*
measures: *eines Pfund Fleisch*
foreign proper nouns: *des Krim, Himalaya*
adjective + noun: *des modernen Deutsch*
months: *des Januar*

In oral German, the -*s* is omitted in *Jahrhundert* (century):

des 17. Jahrhundert

and there is fluctuation between:

wegen Umbau and *wegen Umbaus* (owing to removal)
wegen Urlaub and *wegen Urlaubs* (owing to leave)

We can also record differences between written and spoken Standard
German. For instance, in his study of the subjunctive in the comprehensive corpus of spoken Standard German collected by the now defunct
Freiburg branch of the Institut für deutsche Sprache, Bausch (1979) notes
the relatively rare occurrence of Subjunctive I, and that largely in the
public domains. He regards its use as interference from the written language (1979: 214). In Bausch's corpus only 0.73% of finite verbs are in
Subjunctive I as opposed to 5.99% in Subjunctive II. In Jäger's (1972)
corpus, the corresponding percentages are 2.79 and 3.95 respectively.
However, Subjunctive I is still in active use in Upper German dialects, as
Graf (1977) has shown. In many, especially Swabian, Alemannic, Baden
and Vorarlberg dialects, it predominates over Subjunctive II. In spoken
Swiss Standard German (e.g. on the radio), too, Subjunctive II is very
rarely used as a replacement for Subjunctive I (Rohrer 1973). According
to a newspaper study by Meier (1985), *würde* + infinitive is replacing
Subjunctive II, especially where there is a form that is not clearly subjunctive, e.g.:

Wenn er das kochte …

or where it is unusual or archaic, e.g. *hülfe, stürbe* (from *helfen, sterben*).

Gloy (1974: 239–71) has listed five criteria (or justifications) for norms: structural (systematic, e.g. *als* has to be contrasted with *wie*); historical (tradition dictates the norm); moral quality of varieties (what people are doing to the language by using lexical transfers, or by creating new words, e.g. in the GDR); comprehensibility; and actual use. He sees language norms partly as *social control* (Gloy 1978: 132). In fact, the norms are often an instrument for maintaining the power structure. Many of the arguments in favour of orthographical reform in German gravitate around this.

7.1.1   The spelling reform issue

Since the Second World War, there has been widespread discussion of a possible spelling reform in German. The long route to spelling reform shows the strong attitudinal allegiance to linguistic conventions and the problems of securing consensus on language planning, both within one society and particularly across nations using a pluricentric language.

The first phase of this discussion centred around the capitalization of nouns, which is complicated by a 'grey area' of nouns which are part of idiomatic expressions, and the use of adjectival nouns. This has led to anomalies such as:

> *mit **Bezug** auf / in **bezug** auf* (with reference to); *autofahren* (to drive); ***R**adfahren* (to cycle) (Moser 1968).

In 1954 and 1958, West German committees drafted recommendations in favour of:

(i) Moderate minusculization (*gemäßigte Kleinschreibung*), i.e. lower case in all words *except* the first word in a sentence, proper nouns (including names for God), pronouns of addresses (*Sie* and its derivatives; *Du/Ihr* and their derivatives in letters, appeals and declarations), and certain scientific and technical abbreviations (e.g, H_2O).

(ii) The restriction of comma use to cases where the sentence rhythm and grammatical structure correspond (at present, syntax is the sole criterion).

(iii) The graphemic integration of lexical transfers from other languages, including those of Greek origin (e.g. *Theater* → *Teater*, *Rhythmus* → *Ritmus*).

(iv) The separation of compounds that are, strictly speaking, verb and adverb, e.g. *auto fahren, rad fahren*.

These recommendations had supporters and opponents in the various German-language countries, according to political persuasion and attitudes to tradition and practicality (see Nerius and Scharnhorst 1977). The Federal Republic and GDR commissions voted in favour of the reforms, the Austrian commission deadlocked, and the Swiss voted outright against the proposals, so that they were taken back to the drawing board. (It should be noted that Switzerland had previously gone it alone in replacing *ß* by *ss*.) The Swiss in particular found the proposed rules for punctuation too vague and the recommended graphemic integration of transfers distasteful. The Swiss commission's main objection, however, was to the relaxation of capitalization, which had developed with the structure of German and was, they held, indispensable to effective communication. Fifty instances of ambiguity introduced by the proposed changes were cited, some of them highly emotive, e.g. *Jene schweizer, die den deutschen boden verkaufen* can be interpreted as *Jene Schweizer, die den deutschen Boden verkaufen,* (Those Swiss who are selling German land) *or as Jene Schweizer, die den Deutschen Boden verkaufen* (Those Swiss who are selling land to the Germans) (Studer 1963). By 1968, the Swiss *Nationalrat* (National Parliament) and a number of cantonal parliaments were discussing spelling reform, and some of the directors of education had recommended it (Bruderer 1973: 87).

Neither of the Germanies was prepared to threaten the unity of the German-language area by taking unilateral action. (It is suggested by Thierse (1993) that the GDR was discouraged by the Soviet Union from making its own changes to German orthography.) Wherever the proposals were discussed, the relationship to literary tradition, the technological costs and the problems of transition were seen as the main obstacles. Following the example of other languages was often cited as a motive for spelling reform (German being the only remaining European language with capitalization of all nouns). But by far the most powerful argument has been the educational one.

According to an article in *Die Zeit* (23 February 1973) cited by Zoller (1974: 93), three-quarters of all children who are kept down at school are not promoted because of their spelling, and 30% of all spelling errors are in capitalization. At primary school, there are twice as many failures in spelling as in arithmetic, and dictation is the main cause of non-promotion to secondary school. Spelling reform became an important issue in the educational debate which raged in the Federal Republic in the early 1970s. It was claimed that the present spelling rules (especially the capitalization rules) discriminate against working-class children, who have had less exposure to written German in the home than middle-class children.

A relaxation of spelling requirements was one of the guidelines proposed for German in the schools of Hessen (Christ *et al.* 1974: 103).

On the other hand, a survey among 1,244 schoolchildren (Pomm, Mewes and Schüttler 1974) suggested that there were no significant class differences in the distribution of pupils' spelling errors. The proposed reform would diminish the orthographical errors of *Hauptschüler* (pupils in schools offering the continuation of compulsory education from the primary school in Years 5 to 9 or 10) by 70% and those of pupils in the final year of the *Gymnasium* (the school leading to university) by 93% (Pomm, Mewes and Schüttler 1974: 75). In any case, the social sanctions of 'bad spelling' – non-admission into continuation schools and certain professions, mockery, rating as 'unintelligent' (Augst 1974, Zoller 1974), were increasingly recognized. So was the wastage of teachers' and pupils' time in schools due to the emphasis on capitalization (G. Bauer 1973: 109), corresponding to the time wasted in English-language countries due to the emphasis placed on the spelling of words.

In 1973, pressures for orthographical reform in the Federal Republic probably reached their climax. In that year, there were numerous citizens' action groups campaigning for change. A combined conference of the *Gewerkschaft Erziehung und Wissenschaft* (teachers' union), PEN and the *Schriftstellerverband* (authors' union) in 1973 supported spelling reform, as did a petition signed by fifty cultural personalities. The conference of secondary and tertiary German teachers (*Germanistentag*) in Trier in the same year emphatically advocated the need for *Kleinschreibung*, and declared itself opposed to using spelling marks as a criterion for promotion to a higher school grade and in favour of a boycott on marking spelling errors, which some teachers actually carried out. Some teachers misunderstood the reform movement as an indication that spelling was unimportant (B. Weisgerber 1985).

In 1973, public opinion polls found that 51% of West Germans were in favour of moderate minusculization and 32% against it, while 54% of Swiss were in favour of its immediate introduction, 25% of a gradual introduction, and only 17% against. Of the Germans, men favoured spelling reform more than did women, and young people more than the old (Zoller 1974: 116).

At the instigation of the *Bund für vereinfachte Rechtschreibung* (Association for Simplified Spelling), a new conference on spelling reform was held in Zürich. In Switzerland there were still powerful conservative forces holding back reform (Nerius and Scharnhorst 1977: 191). New spelling conferences in Austria and the GDR in 1973 set in motion research on the implementation of orthographical reform in both countries.

A new *Zeitschrift für germanistische Linguistik* (Journal of German Linguistics) was established in 1973: in its first few volumes, all its articles were printed in moderate minusculization. The magazine of the IG Druck und Papier (printers' union) also went over to *gemäßigte Kleinschreibung*. To an increasing extent, poetry was written in the new orthography;[3] so were private and business letters. But the education ministers could not be moved into reforms. In the pendulum swing to the right in matters social, educational and political in the subsequent years, the spelling debate gradually subsided. As in non-German-speaking countries, there is a frequent lament that standards are falling, although there is no evidence in that direction (Weisgerber 1985). Spelling reform continued to be an issue for discussion between the countries concerned. To an increasing extent, an alternative reform proposal, 'purified majusculization' in which rules are more clearly defined, became the object of consideration.

In 1988, the representatives of the national commissions of the four main German-language countries released new draft regulations for German orthography, to eliminate inconsistencies in phoneme–grapheme correspondencies. Thus, the reform proposals extended beyond the previous focus of *Groß- und Kleinschreibung*.

(i) Consistent representation of /aɪ/ by ⟨ei⟩ (currently ⟨ei⟩ or ⟨ai⟩), /ɔɪ/ by ⟨eu⟩ (currently ⟨eu⟩ or ⟨äu⟩), and /ɛː/ by ⟨e⟩ (currently ⟨e⟩ or ⟨ä⟩), e.g. *Keiser* (*instead of Kaiser*), *reuspern* (*instead of räuspern*), *hetscheln* (*instead of hätscheln*). (The exception would be *Seite* (side, page) / *Saite* (string of an instrument) – to avoid ambiguity.)

(ii) Consistent representation of long vowels by single vowels in a VCV sequence, e.g. *Al* (instead of *Aal*), *Bot* (instead of *Boot*), *Bet* (instead of *Beet*),

(iii) The consistent separation of idiomatic expressions in lower case, e.g. *auto fahren*.

(iv) *das* and *daß* to be written as *das*, and the /s/ to be represented by ⟨ss⟩ in final position (currently ⟨ß⟩), e.g. *Fluss* (cf. *Flüsse*).

(v) Loanwords would be integrated more fully, e.g. *Tron* (instead of *Thron*), *Grafem* (instead of *Graphem*), *Ritmus* (instead of *Rhythmus*), *Träner* (instead of *Trainer*), *fär* (instead of *fair*).

(vi) Words can be split consistently according to phonological criteria where current practice is based on derivational or historical/

---

[3] Some poets (e.g. members of the George circle) and philologists (e.g. Jakob Grimm) have turned to minusculization in past eras.

etymological considerations, e.g. *Pä-da-go-gik* (currently *Päd-ago-gik*), *wo-rauf* (currently *wor-auf*), *Inte-resse* (currently *Inter-esse*).

(vii) Contrary to present conventions, ⟨st⟩ and ⟨pf⟩ could be split, e.g. *Kis-te, imp-fen.*

(viii) It would not be necessary to separate clauses with commas, e.g. Er kam und sie empfing ihn wieder. (He came and she received him again.)
Sie hofft ihn wieder zu treffen (She hoped to meet him again.)
(Neuregelung 1989, Schader 1989)

These proposals, especially those under (i) and (ii), received a very bad press and had to be abandoned. This does give us some insights into the extent and effects of conservative attitudes in the media in Germany. In addition, the theoretical basis for change (i) was not strong enough and it would not lead to consistency (cf. *Seite/Saite*, the current spelling of *Mai* would remain).

After international deliberations (Mentrup 1989), a new set of proposals was released in October 1992 by the international group consisting of delegates from the three main German-language countries, Luxembourg, Liechtenstein, Belgium, France (Alsace), Italy (South Tyrol), Hungary and Romania (Internationaler Arbeitskreis für Orthographie 1992). Like previous recommendations, these aimed at consistency and simplification, and the needs of both readers and writers were taken into account, e.g.:

(i) Derivation would be the basis for some changes, e.g.
aufwändig (currently *aufwendig*) < *Aufwand*
nummerieren (currently *numerieren*) < *Nummer*
Packet (currently Paket) < *packen*
platzieren (currently *plazieren*) < *Platz*

(ii) Length of preceding vowel would determine the spelling of final /s/, e.g. *Fluss* after short vowel /U/, *Maß* after long vowel /a:/.

(iii) This recommendation does not give any real guidance but leaves open a choice in degree of integration of lexical transfers ('foreign words') spelt with a *ph, rh, th, gh* or *é* into the German graphemic system, e.g. *Asfalt* (currently *Asphalt*), *Diskotek* (currently *Diskothek*), *Haschee* (currently *Haché*). (More radical suggestions such as *fär, Träner* were not taken over from 1988.)

(iv) The comma can be omitted in the compound sentences described in the 1988 proposals, e.g. *Sie hatte geplant ins Kino zu gehen.*

(v) *st* and foreign words can be split according to normal conventions (see 1988 proposals).

(vi) Three options were outlined for *Groß- und Kleinschreibung*: The *status quo*, the modification of capitalization to correct inconsistencies, and the minusculization of nouns.

A modified *Großschreibung* together with the recommendations (i) to (v) were accepted at a meeting of linguists and official representatives of German-language countries in Vienna in November 1994 (Heller 1994).

7.2   Communication barriers

In Chapter 8, I shall outline how the spelling of lexical transfers can function as a communication barrier in West German society (8.7). The role of dialect (and the town–country dichotomy) and orthography in general in perpetuating class distinctions has already been considered (4.4 and 7.1.1 respectively). Sex-specific language barriers are discussed under 6.1. An important part in exacerbating communication barriers is played by the media, especially in the Federal Republic, largely through the implementation of the widespread use of lexical and semantic transfers and of *Fachsprache* (technical language).

Another important aspect of the problem is that the complexity of German syntactic rules for embedding offers potential for considerable syntactic differences between more 'learned' and more 'ordinary' registers. (In English, such differences are manifested mainly at the lexical level.) This applies to both participial and dependent clauses.

Compare the following:

> die *über drei Jahre durchgeführte* Untersuchung (the investigation conducted over three years)
> die Untersuchung, die drei Jahre dauert (the investigation which takes (will take) three years)

The former construction, in which the second sentence is embedded into the noun phrase, is more characteristic of the 'learned' register, as is the next example:

> daß diese Veröffentlichung, die erst jetzt, wo die Ergebnisse schon ohnehin bekannt *sind, erschienen ist,* (that the publication only appeared now that the results are known anyway)

In more ordinary register, the *erschienen ist* would follow *erst jetzt* directly, and the sentence would most likely be split.

German academic register is also marked by the following:

(i) Agentless passives, and impersonal and reflexive constructions (von Polenz 1981, Panther 1981), e.g. *Als allgemeiner Begriff **empfiehlt sich*** ... (As general concept ... *recommends itself*).

(ii) Hedged performatives using modals *kann, muß and darf* and passive infinitives (Panther 1981), e.g. *Wir können allgemeine Übereinstimmung **voraussagen.*** (We can *predict* general agreement.)

*Ein Kreis von Entscheidungen ist **zu kennzeichnen** als Aggression.* (A group of decisions is *to be characterized* as aggression.)

(iii) A large number of nominalizations and compound nouns (von Polenz 1963).

7.2.1   Media and the German language

The people of the German-language countries tend to be keenly interested in current affairs, local and international. The language of the mass media is therefore of real significance to them. As Burger (1984) has argued, the importance of TV and radio has not led to a decline of the newspaper but the language of the electronic media has influenced that of the press. The imminence of TV and the simultaneity of the presentation of events have been reflected in the tendency of some newspaper reports to incorporate some aspects of the spoken language, as Burger (1984: 50) has shown. We have to distinguish between the quality newspapers, which are concerned about objectivity, the naming of sources, and differentiating between information and commentary, and the mass-circulation press, which wishes to attract attention rather than to legitimate. The syntactic features of newspaper German, indicated by Burger (1984: 108–9) are still followed by the quality press:

(i) parataxis (i.e. dependent clauses)

(ii) nominalization (e.g. *Abschluß des südkoreanischen Passagierflugzeuges durch sowjetische Abfangjäger*, Shooting down of South Korean passenger plane by Soviet interceptors)

(iii) indirect speech (e.g. *Ein Regierungssprecher hatte angeküdigt, Kohl werde ... zum Ausdruck bringen*, A government speaker had announced Kohl would express ...)

(iv) the use of 'official vocabulary' (Burger 1984: 108)

The media have functioned as a distributor of *Fachsprache* vocabulary (see 7.2.2) into 'ordinary' German, e.g. *Gentechnologie* (gene technology), *Bruttosozialprodukt* (gross national product), *statistische Wahrscheinlichkeit* (statistical probability), *HIV-positiv*, to name just a few items. Space does

not allow me to give a detailed presentation of the specific techniques of using language in the various media in German-speaking countries. (These are discussed in Burger 1984, Holly, Kühn and Püschel 1986.)

There are few English-speaking countries where the distinction between high-quality national dailies and mass-circulation newspapers is as marked as it is in Germany. This is manifested in the layout, content, sentence lengths, syntactic structures and lexical choices. The two newspapers that are often contrasted are the quality daily the *Frankfurter Allgemeine*, and the *Bild-Zeitung*. *Bild* has a circulation many times greater than the quality dailies – 5 million in 1993 (*DAAD Letter*, June 1993, pp. 22–5), in contrast with the 390,000 copies of the *Süddeutsche Zeitung* sold daily, 380,000 of the *Frankfurter Allgemeine* and 220,000 of *Die Welt*. In *Bild*, headlines and pictures play an important part, while the print and columns are quite even in the *Frankfurter Allgemeine*, which lacks illustrations on the front page. According to Eggers (1969: 15), the typical sentence in the *Frankfurter Allgemeine* has 13 words, while *Bild*'s typical sentence is 5 words long. Braun (1979: 38) found that only 13% of the sentences in *Bild* comprised 21 words or more, as compared with 34.6% in the *Westdeutsche Allgemeine Zeitung* (a regional newspaper) and 46.3% in the *Frankfurter Allgemeine*. In Mittelberg's (1967: 244–5) corpus of twelve topically selected articles from each 1964 issue, 19.5% of *Bild* sentences and 40% of sentences in the *Frankfurter Allgemeine* had subordinate clauses. If we count only logically dependent clauses (i.e. not subordinate clauses used as independent sentences), the *Frankfurter Allgemeine* had 250% more subordination than *Bild*. On the other hand, exclamations, requests/ demands and rhetorical questions abound in *Bild* (Mittelberg 1967: 195), and the subjunctives (Mittelberg 1967: 293) and other more complicated formations are avoided. Syntax and lexicon are kept to the comprehension level of the less discerning reader. Because of the predominance of co-ordination, i.e. the relative absence of logical relations, and the limited space afforded to political news, the *Bild* reader is told what to believe, without very much evidence being given. *Bild* is the newspaper of the masses who read it on public transport. Since *Bild* gives its readers an ultra-conservative view of the world, German syntax plays a part in the manipulation of newspaper readers.[4] On the other hand, the *Frankfurter Allgemeine* (a moderately conservative newspaper) employs a lexicon (including lexical and semantic transfers and technical terms) and a syntax (with participial constructions and multiple embeddings) which

---

[4]   On the manipulation of readers by the West German press in general, as exemplified by reports of parliamentary debates, see Hoppenkamps (1977).

only the linguistically more able and the highly motivated can cope with.

In between the quality newspapers and *Bild* are the many regional and local dailies, most of which belong to a small number of media chains and derive their news from common sources. Examples of regional dailies are the *Mannheimer Morgen*, the *Bonner Rundschau*, the *Sächsische Zeitung* and the *Leipziger Volkszeitung*.

Seven sets of German daily newspaper articles on the same topics from the same days were analysed to compare the number of complex sentences, the number of participial clauses, and sentence lengths.[5] The newspapers selected were from 10 November 1988, 21 September 1990, 2/3 October 1990, 19 March 1992, 9 October 1992, 3 April 1993 and 7/8 August 1993. The newspapers were:

Quality daily newspapers
1. *Frankfurter Allgemeine Zeitung* (moderately conservative)
2. *Süddeutsche Zeitung* (liberal)
3. *Die Welt* (right-wing)

Regional/local (West)
4. *Bonner Rundschau*
5. *Mannheimer Morgen*
6. *Rhein-Neckar-Zeitung* (Heidelberg)
7. *Wiesbadener Kurier*

Regional/local (East)
8. *Berliner Zeitung*
9. *Leipziger Volkszeitung*
10. *Sächsische Zeitung*

Left-wing alternative
11. *Tageszeitung*

Left-wing (national, from East)
12. *Neues Deutschland*

Mass-circulation
13. *Bild*

It was not possible to select the same regional newspapers each time. Only one issue each was examined of newspapers 4, 6, 7, 8, and 9. *National-Zeitung* (ultra-right-wing nationalist) was not used because there was no overlap in content between its articles and those of the other newspapers.

In some cases, a particular topic was not reported in one or more of the newspapers. All in all, twenty-eight sets of articles were compared. The

---

[5] I am grateful to Theresa Wallner for carrying out the analysis.

Table 17 *Some syntactic characteristics of a number of German newspapers*

	Complex sentences (%)	Participial clauses (%)	Sentences > 21 words (%)	Average sentence length (words)
Frankfurter Allgemeine Zeitung	47.7	11.6	35.2	19.2
Süddeutsche Zeitung	46.2	9.6	35.3	19.1
Die Welt	41.8	13.2	29.7	17.5
Bonner Rundschau	45.8	4.2	33.3	16.3
Mannheimer Morgen	49.0	12.2	38.8	19.2
Rhein-Neckar-Zeitung	53.3	6.7	33.3	17.7
Wiesbadener Kurier	33.3	19.0	42.9	19.5
Berliner Zeitung	27.3	18.2	18.2	15.6
Leipziger Volkszeitung	40.0	20.0	30.0	18.8
Sächsische Zeitung	41.7	25.0	33.3	18.8
Tageszeitung	40.4	10.5	29.8	17.7
Neues Deutschland	27.5	15.0	30.0	16.7
Bild	20.5	2.3	2.3	9.8

topics range from a NATO ban on air traffic over Bosnia and a meeting between Clinton and Yeltzin, to the winner of the Nobel Prize for literature 1992, and unemployment.

From Table 17, it appears that there is not a substantial variation between the quality and regional newspapers in the literacy and syntactic demands on the reader. The striking difference is between *Bild* and all the other newspapers. Sometimes important events are disposed of in *Bild* through a headline and one or two sentences of text, although some of the 'reports' on prominent people can be relatively lengthy. Sentences are generally only slightly more than half as long as in the other dailies. About half as many complex sentences and participial clauses are employed as in the other newspapers. Long sentences are nearly absent. *Berliner Zeitung* has developed a tradition of catering for the general populace due to its position as an East Berlin newspaper which was not the organ of a political paper. *Neues Deutschland*, on the other hand, has changed its dry image from the days when it was the official organ of the SED. It has changed its syntax accordingly, and is attempting to appeal to the left wing (but, unlike the *TaZ*, not necessarily the intellectuals) throughout Germany, and to disgruntled East Germans in particular.

A similar situation obtains in Austria, although the two extremes do not have equivalents. Table 18 is based on four articles on the same topics,

Table 18 *Some syntactic characteristics of a number of Austrian newspapers*

	Complex sentences (%)	Participial clauses (%)	Sentences >21 words (%)	Average sentence length (words)
Kleine Zeitung	42.9	—	14.3	16.8
Kurier	23.5	5.9	11.8	16.0
Neue Kronen Zeitung	35.0	—	15.0	15.9
Die Presse	42.4	6.1	15.2	15.3
Salzburger Nachrichten	41.2	17.6	17.6	14.9
Der Standard	69.2	7.7	38.5	15.3

one in each of six Austrian newspapers, on 16 October 1992.[6] The topics are: a suggested referendum on immigration, Austrian troops for Somalia, a child lost in the forest and a football match.

The *Neue Kronen Zeitung* does not occupy the 'extreme' position in syntax that *Bild* does in Germany. In fact, *Kurier* has a lower percentage of complex sentences and of long sentences. *Der Standard*, founded in 1988, the newspaper of the intellectual liberals, requires the highest standard of literacy, while the older quality dailies, *Die Presse* and *Salzburger Nachrichten*, are also syntactically demanding. In *Die Presse*, long sentences are balanced by short sentences which are quotations. *Neue Kronen Zeitung* tends to trivialize important issues by publishing short articles with a few long sentences on them. *Der Standard* trivializes the trivial by publishing brief articles with a few short sentences on such topics.

The circulation figures for these newspapers in 1994 were as follows (Elisabeth Welzig, personal communication):

Neue Kronen Zeitung	1,066,670
Kurier	440,869
Kleine Zeitung (Graz)	272,430
Der Standard	96,760
Salzburger Nachrichten	95,938
Die Presse	76,920

Böhm *et al.* (1972) found that the syntactic complexity of West and East German radio news broadcasts was greater than that of urban every-day speech. This is particularly so in news about conferences, treaties, visits and debates, while the coverage of accidents, crime and weather is syntac-

---

[6]   I am grateful to Theresa Wallner for carrying out the analysis.

tically simpler. The average sentence length varied from 12.4 words on the Südwestfunk (Baden Baden) to 16.1 on the Norddeutscher Rundfunk (Hamburg). Cloze tests based on news broadcasts demonstrated the comprehension difficulties of (15-year-old) German pupils from working-class backgrounds who were attending *Hauptschulen*, in comparison with middle-class informants and those attending a 'higher' secondary school, a *Gymnasium* or *Realschule*. They could understand the sensational parts but not the political sections (Böhm *et al.* 1972: 168). Knowledge of, interest in and/ or relevance of the content must also have played a part. In about 50% of the news items, information and opinions are combined in a way that is confusing to the uncritical hearer (1972: 170). In a more recent Austrian study, Wodak, Menz and Laluschek (1989) found that 70% of those surveyed encountered problems understanding the radio news, which averaged 13–16 words per sentence. A retelling test indicated that middle-class girls understood the news better than other school students. Among the sources of comprehension problems in radio and TV news broadcasts are lexical transfers from English and other languages, and complex syntax. Even the separation of prefixes from verbs can be very taxing on the temporary memory where there are several phrases or embedded clauses (as is demonstrated by Yngve's (1960) hypothesis).

There is considerable situational variability in syntactic usage. In her study of the passive, based on a large corpus of spoken Standard German collected by the *Institut für deutsche Sprache* (former Freiburg branch), Schoenthal (1976) found passive constructions far more prevalent in the public domains (6% of utterances) than in private discourse (0.9%). They also occurred less in reportages (e.g. sport) than, say, in non-topical interviews or reports (e.g. of the visit of a foreign celebrity). Similarly, the average length of German sentences was higher in the public sphere (15.2 words) than in private domains (12 words).

7.2.2 Fachsprache

The use of *Fachsprache* (technical language) has been attributed, by Ammon (1973a: 76–81), to the division of labour between and within industries. Schönfeld and Donath (1978) conclude that, within factories in the GDR, technical terms can cause a communication barrier. They cite an incident (1978: 23) where workers could not name a machine that was disturbing them. They show that occupation, educational level (general and job training), years of service, the nature of employment and the reading of professional and trade literature are criteria for the mastery

of *Fachsprache*. In the factories they studied, the foremen were best able to understand and use *Fachsprache*. Abbreviations, which may be seen as part of *Fachsprache*, also make for in-group communication that may exclude those outside the group. Much *Fachsprache*, especially from the fields of politics and economics, has found its way into the everyday speech of individuals and groups in all German-language countries as well as into the mass media. This is a way in which all but people with a wide general knowledge and diverse interests can suffer some communication breakdown (Mentrup 1978). There are also problems in communication between 'experts' and lay people (Lippert 1978 and other papers in Mentrup 1978). Such problems are, of course, not restricted to German-language countries, but at the syntactic level, register differences tend to exacerbate them.

7.3   Social variation and communication barriers

Questions of social variation have been discussed in Chapter 4 in relation to regional variation. Barbour and Stevenson (1990: 191) rightly attribute the linguistic disadvantage of working-class Germans to attitudes and social conventions. In the following section, I would like to discuss some class-based linguistic differences discovered in research prompted by an issue in some English-speaking countries. In the 1970s, a number of German studies examined the 'deficit hypothesis' (Bernstein 1962) – that working-class children are conditioned by family class membership to use a less complex syntax and restricted strategies of verbal planning ('restricted code') than middle-class children (who use an 'elaborated code') and that the working-class children's cognitive development is thereby impaired. Kleinschmidt (1972), for instance, tried to replicate Bernstein's research, and concluded that the connection between 'restricted code' and working-class children and between 'elaborated code' and middle-class children could not be upheld. Kleinschmidt found that it was the level of authoritarianism in the family that was crucial in determining the 'elaborateness' of speech. Klann (1975), Neuland (1975) and Jäger (1978) all found class differences in samples of children's speech, but not the ones described by Bernstein and his followers. Neuland's corpus of 32,000 words is derived from descriptions of five pictures and the retelling of three stories by forty preschool children, whose age, sex and socioeconomic status are taken into account. Intelligence and creativity tests ensured that the middle- and lower-class children were comparable. Lower-class children used more nouns and prepositions, middle-class children more pronouns, verbs, articles, numerals and interjections. The

class predominance of nouns and pronouns was actually the reverse of that in Bernstein and Oevermann. Lower-class children did tend to employ more imperatives and interrogatives, while statement sentences and relative clauses were more common among the middle-class informants. But there appears to be a common repertoire of sentence patterns, with no differences in the incidence of subordination. More importantly, there were particular words which were class-specific, e.g. *sich einigen* (to agree), *Einladung* (invitation), *Eigentum* (property): middle class; colloquial words *Butters* (for *Butterbrote*, sandwiches), *Buxe* (for *Hose*, trousers), *Polente* (for *Polizei*, police): lower class. The middle-class children employed more specific lexemes, such as *Gummistiefel* (gum boots) and *Strickjacke* (cardigan), whereas more general ones predominated among the lower class, e.g. *Arbeitszeug* (work stuff), *Geburtstagssachen* (birthday things). Owing to their divergent social experiences, the two groups associated different items with the words *Arbeiter* (worker) and *Polizei* (police). From Neuland's work it can be concluded that any deficit (rather than difference) is only a later phenomenon caused by the school situation which is oriented towards the middle class.

Klann's conclusions are based on fifty-six 4th grade (*c.* 9-year-old) pupils retelling two stories to an unfamiliar adult. Klann's detailed comparisons indicate great difficulty in establishing class-specific language styles. Not only do class and sex differences sometimes polarize tendencies in the use of syntactic rules in different directions, but parental language support and the child's intelligence have a differing impact on the syntax in the two socioeconomic groups. However, Klann is able to conclude that the middle-class children produced speech that was, in fact, less complex and more 'ornamental' than that of the lower-class children. The latter's speech was, on the whole, structurally and cognitively more complex in their attempts to relate those parts of the stories relevant to them. Complex embedding was more common in the lower class, while middle-class children tended more towards simple embedding. While the working-class pupils kept to the original text, the middle-class informants simplified its syntax. However, pro-forms (e.g. pronouns) were to be found most in the speech of the lower-class children. Klann calls for research into class-specific speech to be directed towards a pragmatic approach to verbal planning strategies within the framework of a theory of action which can be substantiated by social psychology.

Jäger's (1978) 160 ten-year-olds and 80 fourteen-year-olds (matched for class and sex) related a cartoon entitled 'Warum weint die Giraffe?' (Why is the giraffe crying?) to a member of their peer-group they themselves had selected. The lower-class children tended to comment less than

the middle-class children and were less able to pass on concepts to others. They had more difficulty in structuring the plot, their formulations were more involved, and their language contained more deviations from the norms. The middle-class children's texts were longer, more abstract and more plastic.

The discussion on communication barriers sparked off by the debate on the Bernstein codes added a dimension to the study of dialects (e.g. Ammon 1972). In spite of the cooling down of the heat of the educational reform debate in recent years, the problems of working-class monodialectal speakers in the education system are still under discussion, as I have shown (see above, 4.4).

7.4   Guest worker German, German foreigner talk and the problems of *Aussiedler*

The greatest communication barrier of all is that experienced by the 1.6 million guest workers[7] and their families in Germany (together totalling 4.1 million) and by similar individuals and groups in Austria, Switzerland and Luxembourg. Those in Germany come mostly from Turkey, the former Yugoslavia, Italy, Greece or Spain, but there are also Kurds, Sri Lankans, Iranians and others who have been granted asylum. Migrants tend to lead a marginal existence due to the policy assumptions that they are only *temporary* members of the German workforce and that Germany is not an immigration country. Most of the guest workers have lived there for more than twenty years but many of them are not proficient in German. The guest workers have brought many of their dependants to Germany. There are also others, mainly from Asian countries, who have been granted asylum in Germany in recent years. There are now about a million 'foreign' children in Germany, most of whom were born there. (German nationality law makes it difficult for them to become German citizens while people who can claim German ancestry can obtain German nationality without any trouble.)

Some ethnic groups tend to concentrate in certain cities or regions (e.g. Turks in West Berlin, Yugoslavs in Stuttgart, Greeks in Munich). Many companies prefer to employ only guest workers of a particular nationality. This may result in large school populations of ethnic minority children in particular districts, e.g. some primary schools in the Berlin suburb of Kreuzberg draw over 50% of their enrolment from children of

---

[7]   To an increasing extent, *Migrant, Immigrant, Arbeitsmigrant* and *ausländischer Arbeiter* are used in the German literature in preference to the more popular but less appropriate *Gastarbeiter*.

Turkish background. Most of the 'foreign children' do not gain admission to the more advanced kinds of secondary schools, the *Gymnasium* or *Realschule*, and many do not complete the *Hauptschule*, whose certification is required for vocational training such as that required for skilled trades. A concern among some educationists for the problems of guest workers has highlighted the unsatisfactory nature of schooling arrangements, regardless of whether the children are likely to return to the country of origin or, as is more probable, to stay in Germany. The two main models followed are: (i) *Nationalklassen* – 'classes for particular nationalities' – for up to two years as a preparation for joining ordinary German classes (general model); (ii) *Nationalklassen* in primary schools and *Hauptschulen* (in Bavaria since 1973, in North Rhine-Westphalia since 1976), with an optional transfer to German classes (in North Rhine-Westphalia compulsory after Grade 6). Bilingual classes of type (ii) are on the increase and particularly prevalent in Bavaria, but, in the interests of future repatriation, they tend to isolate the children from migrant backgrounds and keep them at a lower level of education (see Skutnabb-Kangas 1980). A variation on these models is offered by 'international' preparatory classes consisting of different groups of 'foreigners' (Stölting 1978). But the 'general model' is still the most widespread after children have attended preparatory classes. 'Migrant' children are generally offered about five hours per week of 'mother tongue' instruction in the national language of their country of origin. This is usually given outside compulsory school hours, but it is now possible to take the 'mother tongue' as a school subject instead of a 'second foreign language'. However, a second foreign language is taught only in those schools which are not usually attended by 'migrant children'. There is support, among some educationists (e.g. Luchtenberg forthcoming, Reid and Reich 1992), for bilingual education to maintain and develop both languages, but implementation of such programmes has not proceeded very far.

'Migrant worker German' shows some commonalities, regardless of the speaker's base language. The speech of those whose German has not developed beyond a very restricted stage is marked by the deletion of articles, prepositions, subject-pronouns, copula and auxiliaries; the overgeneralization of a particular verbal form (either infinitive or stem); a tendency towards the deletion of bound morphemes; co-ordination (not subordination); and the generalized use of *du*, and of *nix* for *nicht*, *nichts*, *nie* and *kein*. But of course there is considerable variation. At the second cut-off point on the continuum, there are indications of the generalization of *die* as a definite article, as well as the extended use of *müssen* as an auxiliary (perhaps a reflection of their low status!), and some progression in

grammatical development, e.g. adverb-fronting with SVO order: *Morgen ich fahre nach Italien* (Heidelberger Forschungsprojekt 1975, 1976, 1978, Dittmar 1979, Gilbert and Orlović 1975, Meisel 1975, Clahsen, Meisel and Pienemann 1983, Clyne 1968b). Lattey and Müller (1976) suggest that many guest workers use a stable, rigid, formulaic variety in the workplace and a more innovative interlanguage in expanded communication situations.

Through interviews and participant observation, the Heidelberger Forschungsprojekt (1975, 1976, Dittmar 1978, Klein and Dittmar 1979) ranked Italian and Spanish adult learners according to their German proficiency and postulated an order for the acquisition of grammatical rules, e.g. '(preposition+) subject and nominal complex' is an early rule, as is 'simple verb'. Then follow 'simple verb modified by modal', then 'simple and copulative verb modified by modal or auxiliary' and finally 'simple and copulative verb modified by modal and auxiliary' (Dittmar 1978: 139). Meisel and his project team in Hamburg studied the acquisition of German by Italians, Spaniards and Portuguese through a longitudinal study, following their cross-sectional research (Clahsen, Meisel and Pienemann 1983). Often the basilectal features of the migrants' German gradually give way to first-language interference as the functions of the first and second languages become more similar. Not only syntactic but also discourse development have been examined comparatively among migrant workers across base and target languages in five European countries in a European Science Foundation project (e.g. Klein and Perdue 1992, Perdue 1994). By now, German has largely become the dominant language of the second generation and the source of interference in the first language. However, the situation varies between ethnic groups, language maintenance and problems of German acquisition being much greater among the Turks. Code-switching patterns between, say, Italian and German are similar to those between Italian and English in North America and Australia, with the 'other language' used for commentary, quotations or change of interlocutor. The younger generation identifies increasingly with the German language and regards Italian as the outgroup language (e.g. Auer 1980, Auer and di Luzio 1983).

The Heidelberger Forschungsprojekt (1976: 308–28) has isolated factors which appear to correlate with a higher level of syntax: (in order of importance) contact with Germans in leisure (applies mainly to those married to German speakers); age on arrival; contact with Germans at work; qualifications in home country; years of schooling; period of residence in Germany. Three factors of lesser significance were sex, base language and living conditions (the last being closely connected with

'contact with Germans in leisure'). A study by Bodemann and Ostow (1975) on communication between guest workers and Germans in the domains of work, the law and administration contributes the following points to the discussion, which are still valid today:

(i) The *Weisen* (wise people) – guest workers selected by the company to act as interpreters – control communication, monopolize both the German language and advancement in the factory, and assist in the exploitation of fellow-countrymen. This demonstrates the hierarchical significance of competence in German and the role of German as an instrument of exclusion.

(ii) The court interpreter controls communication between Germans and foreigners.

(iii) The employment of a homogeneous group of guest workers (i.e. of one nationality) by a company reduces the power of *Weisen* and facilitates an improvement both in conditions and in communications.

(iv) *Du* is used by German work superiors to guest workers as a symbol of power.

The majority of migrant workers have never attended German classes. They are not *supposed* to integrate into German society. They are frequently addressed in foreigner talk. In an early publication, the Heidelberger Forschungsprojekt (1975) postulates four stages along a continuum in the migrants' development of German:

(i) Deficient knowledge of German, better comprehension than production.

(ii) Contact with Germans and other guest workers, but they are not part of the main communication network and the subjects' German is insufficient for their communication needs.

(iii) Relatively stable; migrant worker German is integrated with their social and communicative needs; no motivation for further language acquisition.

(iv) Completely integrated; speech gravitates towards regional dialect.

Most of the subjects were at stage (ii) or (iii). On the basis of comparable American data, Schumann (1978) has demonstrated that pidginization is a universal of early natural second language acquisition.

Even though the Bloomfieldian (1933: 473) principle of foreigners and native speakers imitating one another is now generally not acceptable, there is widespread evidence of foreigners' language competence

influencing the way they are addressed (e.g. Clyne 1977b, Snow, van Eeden and Muysken 1981, Mühlhäusler 1981). Also, the use of foreigner talk reduces (or eliminates) the foreigners' access to the target language.

There is another category of immigrants who have come to Germany in recent years – the *Aussiedler*. About 850,000 came to Germany between 1990 and 1992. They are people from the Commonwealth of Independent States, Romania and Poland who can demonstrate some German descent. Some of those from the CIS – mainly people of Volga German background who had been resettled in the Kazakhstan – and some from Romania still speak a German variety, the Russian-Germans usually using an archaic dialect and understanding but not speaking Standard German (Berend 1991). They therefore encounter difficulties in areas of Germany where dialects are prevalent. the Russian-Germans generally have Russian as their dominant language, and this is the language they tend to speak at home in Germany (Berend 1991). In their initial period after migration, they experience problems with identity, having been permitted to migrate as Germans and having been discriminated against in their homeland as Germans but now not being felt altogether welcome. Their main contact with locals during this period is with professionals such as social workers and public servants. They continue to socialize within *Aussiedler* networks (Reitemeier 1994). All this applies even more to those from Poland, most of whom speak very little or no German. Their interlanguage shows features similar to those of guest workers.

7.5   A note on language in institutions

There is now a very extensive literature on language in institutions in German-language countries, covering classroom interaction (e.g. Goeppert 1977, Ehlich and Rehbein 1977), doctor–patient interaction (e.g. Bliesener 1980, Wodak, Menz and Laluschek 1989, Nothdurft 1992), psychotherapy (e.g. Sluga 1977, Flader 1978, Klann 1978a, Trömel-Plötz 1978b, Wodak-Leodolter 1980, Ehlich *et al.* 1989), court (e.g. Leodolter 1975, L. Hoffmann 1980, Wodak, Menz and Laluschek 1989) and restaurants (e.g. Ehlich and Rehbein 1972).

All these studies constitute in some measure research on communication barriers. To give another example, summarizing courtroom studies in Vienna, Dressler and Wodak (1982b) contrast the security of the middle-class defendants who use a single linguistic style with the insecurity of the working and lower middle classes manifested in style shifts. However, most studies contribute particularly to knowledge on the nature of interaction and the roles of language. It has not been possible, within this

monograph, to assess perhaps through comparisons with similar studies in English-language countries the specifically German character of institutional interaction.

7.6   Brief summary

German is not a language with strong centralized planning agencies. The role of conservative 'language societies' has declined over the years.

There is a social polarization of the German language due to variations in syntactic complexity, the use and integration of English transfers, and the use of technical language. The media (especially in Germany) play a role in exacerbating such barriers, and some people there and in Austria are denied access to objective information because of the sociolect used by most quality and even regional media.

Unsuccessful attempts at achieving orthographical reform have highlighted a problem of language planning in pluricentric languages maintaining unity. Demands for reform of capitalization rules have not been met despite some evidence that many people (especially schoolchildren) are discriminated against because of the confusing conventions. Resistance to change is strong in the German-language countries.

Examples of communication barriers may be found in various spheres of society. The greatest communication barriers, however, are those experienced by the guest workers and *Aussiedler*, due to their social marginality. Many have little opportunity or motivation to gain proficiency in German despite long-term residence in Germany. Foreigner talk employed by Germans to guest workers restricts the input of Standard German.

7.7   Further reading

The spelling reform issue is summarized in Neuregelung (1989) and Internationaler Arbeitskreis für Orthographie (1992). Normative issues are discussed in the periodicals *Der Sprachdienst* and the now defunct *Sprachpflege* (GDR). There is a flourishing German literature on *Fachsprache* in general. The papers in Mentrup (1978) are of special interest in the German context. The main results of the two large projects on guest worker German may be found in Klein and Dittmar (1979) and Clahsen, Meisel and Pienemann (1983). The results of the large-scale cross-European study are gradually being released (see e.g. Klein and Perdue 1992, Perdue 1994).

8

Recent Anglo-American influence

This chapter deals with the impact of English influence on German. The influence will be discussed first in relation to level of language, domain and national variety. Then the distribution of English transfers across the speech community will be discussed, and some attention will be paid to the possibility that they are contributing to communication barriers.

8.1   Anglo-American influence in a general context

A language can undergo renewal and enrichment through neologisms, semantic shift (especially extension of meanings) and transference from other languages. Transference of items and elements is the result of culture contact. Virtually all languages have had periods of large-scale language contact. Manifestations of this in the history of the German language have been the Latin influence on Old High German and sixteenth-century German, as well as the French influence on Middle High German and eighteenth-century German. There have been epochs of nationalistic purism (Nüssler 1979). One such period was the seventeenth century, when writers who saw themselves as language planners grouped themselves into *Sprachgesellschaften* (language societies), one of whose tasks was to develop a German free of foreign (especially Romance) elements. During the nineteenth century many words of 'non-Germanic' origin were replaced by 'pure Germanic' lexemes (see Townson 1992).

The present period of openness to internationalization and foreign influence in Germany may be seen partly as a reaction to the xenophobia of the National Socialist era. Moreover, it is a consequence of post-war political and cultural developments. By the end of the Second World War, the German language had lost most of its international status in the West to English (as had French) and some of its position in the East temporarily to Russian. To an increasing extent, political alignments concentrated around what were to become the two 'super-powers', the United States

and the Soviet Union. They were the super-powers in a technological and scientific as well as a political sense, and they provided German-language countries with new concepts as well as the new vocabulary of politics, economics, technology and many other fields. English influence is part of an 'internationalization' and facilitates the ready translatability of concepts and texts from language to language as well as a technologization of communication (computers, fax, e-mail). The use of English has contributed to the efficiency of press agencies and simultaneous translation. Particularly in the American occupational zone of the old Federal Republic, the period of intense language contact was initiated by the presence of American troops since four years before the foundation of the Federal Republic in 1949.[1] Parts of Austria, too, were occupied by armies from English-language countries until 1955.

In the western German-language countries, English influence on the German language is symptomatic of the internationalization of many domains. These domains include close economic, political and/or strategic alliances such as NATO, the European Union and the European Free Trade Association; scientific, technological and cultural co-operation; the mass media; multinational corporations; and supranational tendencies in the arts, student politics, terrorism, the pop and drug scenes and pornography. More people from more different language backgrounds are communicating than ever before (except perhaps in wartime), and, in Western Europe, their lingua franca tends to be English.

This has resulted in the replacement of national languages by English in some domains within one country (e.g. computer science and air travel in most Western European countries, academic publishing in the Netherlands and Scandinavia), between nations with related languages (e.g. as a conference language in Scandinavia, Hughes 1972), and, to a growing extent, sometimes even between the ethnic groups of one nation (e.g. in Belgium). Naturally 'specialized' vocabulary (*Fachwortschatz*) is then transferred from English into the vernaculars throughout Western Europe and beyond. (This has been discussed beyond German, e.g. by Fishman, Cooper and Conrad 1977; in the papers in Viereck and Bald 1986, for twenty-six languages in Europe, Asia, and Oceania.)

In almost all the schools of Germany and Austria, English is now the first foreign language,[2] a situation also common to the Netherlands, the

---

[1]   It is interesting to note, however, that French had little or no influence on the German of the French-occupied areas.

[2]   Except in the Saarland and some areas of Baden-Württemberg, where it is French, and in some other border areas, where 'languages of the neighbours' are taught in primary schools.

Scandinavian countries and other parts of Europe. Many countries are now teaching English in the primary school. Young children from, say, Germany, Sweden and the Netherlands will converse with each other in English when they meet on holidays. The majority of students entering university in Germany will have taken nine years of English at school.

Exposure to English is greater in the Netherlands, Belgium and Scandinavia than in the German-language countries, due at least in part to the predominance, in the former, of subtitled, rather than dubbed, English films on their television channels, which are seen even by children who cannot read their first language!

I will not attempt to distinguish here between American and British influence, but in most cases it is American culture that has been the source of English transference into German in the post-war period. In some cases it is impossible to differentiate between new developments due to English influence and those that have other causes. The lifespan of different transfers varies, as would be revealed by diachronic studies if they had been undertaken. English influence on contemporary German has not been examined extensively in Switzerland and Luxembourg. The remarks on these countries are therefore superficial, as are those on comic language, a promising area for future research. There is a need for macro-sociolinguistic studies on the use of functions of (spoken and written) English in the German-language countries, both internally and in communication with people from other countries.

8.2   Types of transference

There are a great many examples of elements and rules transferred from English into German and these include not only lexical but also semantic and syntactic transfers.

8.2.1   Lexical and semantic transfers

By far the most common type of transference from English has been at the *lexical* level – words such as *Beat*, *Cockpit*, *Marketing* and *Team*, which have been taken over from English in form and meaning. This lexical transference includes nouns (e.g. *der Appeal*, *die Blue Jeans*,[3] *das Comeback*), verbs (e.g. *babysitten*, *jobben*, *killen*), adjectives/adverbs (e.g. *fit*, *high*, *live*) and interjections (e.g. *bye bye*, *hi!*).

There are also *semantic* transfers, where the meaning of English words is

---

[3]   Usually feminine singular (Stephen Barbour, personal communication).

transferred to existing German ones with which they share some phonic correspondence, partial semantic correspondence, or both. Instances include the following:

> 'loan-translations' (each part translated) such as: *Beiprodukt* (by-product), *Datenverarbeitung* (data processing), *Drogenszene* (drug scene) and *Herzschrittmacher* (cardiac pace-maker)
>
> 'loan-renditions' (one part transferred, one created) such as: *Autodienststation* (service station; literally, 'car service station'); *Titelgeschichte* (cover story; literally, 'title story'); *Untertreibung* (understatement; cf. *Übertreibung*, overstatement)
>
> 'loan-meanings' (transference of meaning) such as *feuern* (to fire from job, original German meaning: to fire, to shoot), *sehen* (to see, to visit, original German meaning: to see with one's eyes)
>
> 'loan-idioms' (morpheme-for-morpheme transference of idiom) such as: *das Beste aus etwas machen* (to make the best of something), *Geben und Nehmen* (give and take), *grünes Licht geben* (to give the green light), *im gleichen Boot sein* (to be in the same boat)
>
> (Carstensen 1965, Carstensen and Galinsky 1967; and my own corpus from German newspapers, 1992–4; terminology based on Betz 1949.)

Some semantic transfers were originally lexical transfers from English or French, whose meaning or domain has been extended as a result of further language contact, e.g. *starten* (from the domain of sport and motoring to a more general usage), *realisieren* (from a transitive verb, 'to realize' a wish or ambition, to an intransitive one, 'to grasp', 'to understand') *resignieren* (from 'to resign oneself to one's fate' to 'to resign from a job'). Sometimes older transfers are revitalized through English influence, e.g. *Allergie* (allergy, extended beyond the medical field), *Generation* (as in *'dritte Computergeneration'*, third generation of computers). On the basis of Galinsky's (1980) comparative analysis of English and German dictionary entries, the time lag for the reception of semantic transfers from English is longer than that for lexical transfers.

8.2.2   Syntactic transfers

According to Carstensen (1965: 80), the transference of English syntactic rules has led to the transitivization of verbs in environments where this was unusual for German, e.g. *Ich fliege Lufthansa* (I fly Lufthansa; for *Ich*

*fliege **mit der** Lufthansa*), *4000 Tote befürchtet* (headline: 4000 feared dead) (Carstensen 1965: 80). Besides, English influence has prompted the early placement of the genitive in phrases such as *Hamburgs Bürgermeister* (Hamburg's mayor; for *Der Bürgermeister von Hamburg*), as well as the loose addition of the age designation in newspaper articles, e.g. *Johann Müller, 51, wurde gestern zum Bürgermeister gewählt* (Johann Müller, 51, was elected mayor yesterday, previous norm: *Der **51-jährige** Johann Müller* . . .).

8.2.3   'Pseudo-transfers' and German usage

Some new lexemes, which resemble English but do not exist in the language, have been created in Germany, often involving the compounding of English morphemes, e.g. *Herren-Slip* (fashionable word for *Unterhose*, underpants), *Layouter* (from 'layout'), *Showmaster* (quizmaster) and *Slipper* (slip-on shoe, *not* English slipper, which is *Pantoffel* or *Hausschuh*). Carstensen (1980b) coined the term *Scheinentlehnungen* (pseudo-transfers) for such words. There are also English transfers which are consistently used in a different sense in German, e.g. *Top-Preis*. All over Germany, you can buy *Bücher* (books), *Hemden* (shirts) and *Schuhe* (shoes) *zu Top-Preisen*, i.e. at low prices!

8.3   Domains of English transference

8.3.1   Germany

The main domains of English transference are:

> sport, e.g. *Clinch, Comeback, Handicap, Rally, Sprint, Basketball*
> technology and information science, e.g. *Know-how, microwaven, Pipeline, Plastik*
> travel and tourism, e.g. *Charter, checken, Countdown, Hosteß, Jet, Service, Ticket*
> advertising, e.g. *Bestseller, Designer, Image, Look, Pack* (e.g. *Jeder Pack DM 4-*, four marks a packet), *Trend*
> computer technology, e.g. *Byte, Drive, E-mail, hacken, Link-up, Software, Spreadsheet*
> journalism, e.g. *Facts, Front-page, Back-page, Layout*
> economics, e.g. *Boss, floaten* (to float a currency), *Franchise, Full-time-Job, Headhunter, Leasing, Manager, Publicity, PR, recyclet, Splitting* (income splitting), *Supermarkt, toppen*
> politics, e.g. *Establishment, Hearing, Sit-in*

armed forces, e.g. *By-pass, crashen, Control-box, Debriefing, Jeep, taxien*

cosmetics, e.g. *After-Shave, Beauty-box, Hair tint, Make-up, Spray*

entertainment (especially pop music), e.g. *Evergreens, Happening, Hitparade, in, Quiz, sampeln* (put together music for a record or social event), *sponsern, Talkshow*

medicine, e.g. *By-pass, Clearance, Tranquillizer, Stress* (in general everyday use)

(Carstensen 1965, Carstensen and Galinsky 1967; Hugo Moser 1964, Fink 1970; and my own corpus.)

Anglicisms are strong in special registers such as those of young pop and rock enthusiasts (Ortner 1982, see also 6.2) and nuclear technology (Schmitt 1985 and Townson 1984).

Some domains are relatively unrepresented, e.g. the law, obviously because there is very little German–English contact in this field due to the differences in the legal systems prevailing in the German- and most of the English-language countries.

In comics, which are widely read by German (and also Austrian, Swiss and Luxembourgian) children, many of the sounds are represented by transfers from an (American) English original or from (American) English 'comic language' in general. Comics are, after all, an American cultural influence. Frequently there is a conversion of grammatical category, based on English, e.g. from verb to interjection: *Beiß!* (bite!), *Brumm!* (growl!), *Hup!* (toot!, beep!), *Quietsch!* (squeak!), *Schluck!* (gulp!), *Kreisch kreisch!* (screech screech!), *Schnaub!* (gulp!), *Klirr!* (clatter!, rattle!), *Krächz krächz!* (splurt splurt! – of computer/machine). Another sound representation is the actual transfer, more or less integrated into the German phonotactic (and graphotactic) system (see below, 8.6): *Boing! Dring!* (Ring! – of telephone), *Juuppa!* (Yippee!), *Klick klick!* (click – of gun), *Kratsch!* (Crash!), *Päng!* (Bang!), *Rubbel!* (Rub!), *Schnip!* (Snip!), *Schnorch!* (Snort!). *Bing bong!* appears to be a contamination between English *Ding dong!* and German **Bimm bamm!** As has been mentioned under 6.2, many of these sound representations have not only found their way into a youth register in German but they are also employed generally for onomatopoeia.

The opening-up of the GDR to Western influence was accompanied by an immediate increase in the public use of anglicisms (see above, 3.1.1). While East German newspapers have been very ready to employ lexical transfers from English before and after unification to help express their new reality, their usage indicates some uncertainty as to their form or meaning and how they should be integrated, e.g.:

Der Minister ist müde und hat *den* Blues. (*die*; The minister is tired and has the blues.) (*Wochenpost*, 2 September 1993, p.6)

bei *den* Australien Open (bei *dem* Australian Open, or: der Australische Open) (*Sächsische Zeitung* 23/24 January 1993, p.15)

in der dritten Runde *der* Australian Open (same article)

feminale lutheran bishop (female) (*Sächsische Zeitung*, 21 April 1992, p.4)

As will be gathered from Chapter 3, there is still some persistent opposition to the use of anglicisms in the eastern part of Germany.

8.3.2   Austria

The situation in Austria differs historically from that of the Federal Republic of Germany in so far as Austria never had a period of indigenous intense purism, but also in that the influence of both French and the languages of some of the neighbouring countries far exceeded that of English up to the Second World War. In Germany the German-English language contact was greater. Viereck *et al.* (1975: 216), comparing the extent of English transfers in daily newspapers, find that in Austrian newspapers 'anglicisms' appear in the text rather than in advertising while the reverse trend is evident in the Munich-based *Süddeutsche Zeitung*. The percentage of English transfers in the sports section is far higher in the supraregional Viennese paper *Die Presse* and (especially) the Graz regional daily *Kleine Zeitung*, than in the *Süddeutsche*. Viereck *et al.* explain the discrepancy by the replacement of older English transfers (including many of those in the field of sport) by German neologisms in nineteenth-century Germany, a development which did not have a parallel in Austria. However, on the whole, the transference of English items into Austrian Standard German is very similar to the situation in Germany.

8.3.3   Switzerland

There are three factors that make the situation in Switzerland different from that of the two countries treated above: the diglossia (see above, 2.5), the long-standing extensive French influence on both Swiss Standard German and Swiss-German dialects, and the role and language policies of Swiss business companies. The Swiss tend to react against puristic neologisms, which are identified with Germany.

The domains of transference (e.g. entertainment, business, fashion, sport, technology) and many of the examples are the same as in Germany. There are some additional transfers, such as *Dancing* (dance, dance-hall) and

Parking (parking area), which have come via French. While German multi-national companies tend to propagate the use of German, the Swiss ones (perhaps because of the multilingualism of the Swiss nation) are far more prepared to use English as their language (Clyne 1977c). This strengthens the influence of American and British multinationals on the German language in Switzerland. There are also English lexical transfers that are widely used in Swiss-German dialects (some of them products of an earlier period of language contact), e.g. *Glôn* (and *Klaun*, clown) (Dalcher 1966: 15–17), as well as words that have been integrated into dialects in a manner different from that employed in Swiss Standard German, e.g. Pipe*linie*, Grep*frucht* (grapefruit), Kchi*nd*näper (kidnapper) (Dalcher 1965: 19).

Some lexical transfers from English are replacing ones from French that were general in Swiss Standard German well into the post-war period[4] e.g. in entertainment: *Dinner* (for *Dîner*), *Show* (for *Revue*), *Song* (for *Chanson*, sometimes with a change of meaning to cover the new musical style), *Star* (for *Vedette*); in economics: *Boom* (for *Hausse*), *Boss* (for *Chef*); in travel: *Ticket* (for *Billet*); general: *Baby* (for *Bébé*) (Dalcher 1966: 18). Often it is unclear whether a transfer is of English or French origin (Charleston 1959: 272).

8.3.4   Luxembourg

As we have seen (2.7.3), Luxembourg Standard German draws heavily on French for its lexical and idiomatic renewal and as a basis for semantic shift. Consequently many of the English transfers used in Luxembourg (Magenau 1964) may have come via French, e.g. *Dancing* (dance-hall), *Folklore, Match, Meeting, Weekend*. However, the presence of European Union officials, a large number of international banks and Europe's only state commercial radio station, broadcasting American English in word and song, has greatly increased Luxembourg's immediate exposure to English. This has contributed to the transference of English lexemes, especially in the domains of economics, politics and entertainment.

8.4   Media of transmission

8.4.1   Institutions

The main institutions promoting the spread of English transfers into German are the press, radio and TV, advertising agencies and dictionaries.

---

[4]   To a much lesser extent, the competition between old French and new English transfers exists in the West German press (Burger 1979).

Carstensen (1965: 22–5; 1971) has demonstrated the importance of the weekly news-magazine *Der Spiegel* (modelled on *Time* and *Newsweek*) in the introduction of new lexical, semantic and syntactic transfers from English into the German language. *Der Spiegel* is widely read, by people who regard themselves as liberals, discerning readers, with an above-average education (Grimminger 1972). Some of the transfers in any given issue of *Der Spiegel* are nonce forms; others have found their way into general German usage. It has been asserted that *Der Spiegel* is 'tonangebend für die Sprachregelung von drei Vierteln der deutschen Presse und für wesentliche Teile des deutschen Funks' (sets the tone for the language policy of three-quarters of the German press and substantial sections of German radio and TV) (*Deutsche Tagespost*, Würzburg 1962; cited in Carstensen (1965: 24), my translation). While this may be a little overstated, and applies to the creative register of *Der Spiegel* and not simply to transfers, it contains a large element of truth. Many transfers have come from *Der Spiegel* via weekly and regional daily newspapers or illustrated magazines such as *Stern* and *Brigitte* into the language as a whole. Another very influential intermediary of English influence is the weekly *Die Zeit*, also a popular newspaper among more educated people, for those who understand and use English lexical transfers.[5] Mass-circulation news–pictorials such as *Bild-Zeitung* also make extensive use of 'anglicisms'. The need for instant translation on the part of news-agencies makes for frequent semantic and lexical, and sometimes syntactic, transference in West German newspapers, as well as in news broadcasts and telecasts.

In other German-language countries, newspapers also disseminate lexical and other transfers from English, as Viereck *et al.*'s (1975) study based on the Austrian papers *Die Presse* and *Kleine Zeitung* has shown. It should also be mentioned that both *Der Spiegel* and *Die Zeit* are also read in Switzerland and Austria.

The electronic media are also important in the transmission of transfers from English. American pop music is now presented on German radio stations. Many young German and Austrian children are able to reproduce the hits even before they know the meanings of most of the words! Many lexical transfers are disseminated through radio and television news and documentaries (Clyne 1973: 177, Viereck *et al.* 1975).

---

[5] In an empirical study on the use and comprehension of English transfers (Clyne 1973: 167, see below, 8.4.2), *Die Zeit* was the most widely read newspaper among the younger, more educated group, those with the most English, who used and understood the most transfers.

Carstensen (1965: 25–7) describes advertising as an area where the number of English transfers is especially high (though many of them are part of the special language of economics – Römer 1968: 128). But Carstensen also points out that many of the English-sounding words and brand-names have originated on German desks (see also above, 8.2.3).

When in doubt as to the meaning or acceptability of transfers, people will generally consult a monolingual dictionary. This applies particularly to the more educated sections of the population (three-quarters of the more educated informants, compared with a quarter of the less educated, in Clyne 1973: 166). The most widely used and most authoritative dictionary in the German-language countries, *Duden-Rechtschreibung* (Mannheim edition), contains lexical transfers together with their pronunciation and meanings. More copies are sold of the *Duden-Fremdwörterbuch* (dictionary of foreign words, which covers more lexical transfers than the *Rechtschreibung*) than of any other Duden dictionary with the exception of *Rechtschreibung*. This speaks for the interest that German-language users have in 'loanwords'. The reception of English transfers in the Duden is conservative, though by no means purist. The same may be said for the extensive *Deutsches Wörterbuch* edited by Gerhard Wahrig (1st edition, 1968).

In recent years, there has been a change of approach to 'foreign words' in German. Instead of producing dictionaries translating 'foreign words' into 'German' synonyms, there is now a tendency to offer dictionaries giving 'foreign word' equivalents, such as Von Normann (1991), which is ordered alphabetically, and Laudel (1992), ordered thematically, e.g. biology, boats, linguistics, music. *Fremdwörter* are thus seen as a resource rather than an impediment to communication.

8.4.1.1 *Institutional policy*

In response to a series of questions concerning their attitudes to, and criteria for, the use of 'loanwords' (Clyne 1973), West German newspapers and magazines indicated that there were no guidelines and that every journalist could make his/her own decision as to lexical selection. Such a choice is qualified by a restriction to words that are generally understood (e.g. in *Stern, Bild-Zeitung*) and a tendency towards a *pseudo-moderne Sprache* (pseudo-modern language) through the use of anglicisms (e.g. in *Bild-Zeitung*). Similar answers were given by those working in the electronic media, who also claimed 'die Verständlichkeit für jeden Zuschauer (Zuhörer)', (comprehensibility for all viewers (listeners)) is their main goal (e.g. for Norddeutscher Rundfunk). Only words that have become

'Bestandteil der allgemeinen Umgangssprache' (part of everyday language) are used, except for technical language (*Fachsprache*), names and quotations. Decisions as to which transfers are part of the language are made in an *ad hoc* way by consulting reference books (Duden on lexicon, Siebs on pronunciation of transfers) (e.g. for Süddeutscher Rundfunk).

Advertising agencies similarly asserted that they used only words that were part of 'language usage', e.g.:

> Die Werbung selbst fühlt sich nicht berufen, englische Wörter in die deutsche Sprache einzuführen ... Doch weil dann mit der Werbung solche Begriffe oft eine große Publikation erfahren, wirkt es dann so, als sei es die Werbung, die diese Begriffe eingeführt hatte, oder einführen will. (Advertising does not see itself called to introduce English words into the German language. Yet since concepts then receive great publicity through advertising, it seems as if advertising had introduced or wants to introduce these concepts.) (LINTAS Werbeagentur Hamburg.)

There are contradictions to this in reality, with some transfers regarded by advertisers as 'part of German' not being identified by speakers as words they (or others) would use in their German (Clyne 1973: 174). The use of English brand-names is seen as promoting international communication or safeguarding copyright. The advertising agencies did not seek to promote a particular image for a product by the use of transfers, but at least one of them (Deutsche Bundesbahn, Werbe- und Auskunftsamt (German Railways, Advertising and Information Office)) regarded young people and the managerial sector as the main target groups when English transfers were employed.

The editorial staff of the Duden works with a large corpus derived from books and periodicals (but not spoken language). However, decisions on the inclusion of items are made through discussions among its members. In Wahrig, much leeway is left to the individual contributor, though semantic transfers in translated works and lexical transfers used only in advertising are excluded.

The above comments apply to a large degree also to Austria and Switzerland, despite the different conditions described in 2.4 and 2.5.

8.4.2   People

It is the younger and more educated people who have been agents of transmission of English transfers in Germany (Clyne 1973). Informants were questioned about a corpus of fifty-one contemporary lexical and semantic transfers derived from texts (other than advertising) in newspapers and periodicals (*Die Zeit, Die Welt, Stuttgarter Zeitung, Süddeutsche*

Zeitung, Stern). They were asked for the meanings of the words and expressions, whether they themselves would use them, whether they had heard or read them, and if they would not use them, who would. The younger, more educated group knew most of the transfers and, on the whole, used them most. Older and less educated people often have difficulty in understanding the transfers, let alone using them. In normal conversation, speakers who frequently transfer from English will tend to vary this according to interlocutor, employing transfers less to older people and/or those who do not know any English. However, the source of this information is research conducted a generation ago and the number of people in the western part of Germany without a knowledge of English is rapidly diminishing. The generational differences on this point are now much greater in East Germany.

In an Austrian survey about the same time, Viereck *et al.* (1975) found that age and knowledge of English were less important as criteria for the knowledge of anglicisms than were education and exposure to newspapers and TV. Men knew more transfers drawn from newspapers than did women.

In a more extensive study, W. Viereck (1980b) tested the use and comprehension of 42 transfers taken from *Die Presse, Kleine Zeitung* and the *Süddeutsche Zeitung*, selected from 17 areas of the newspapers (e.g. politics, radio/TV, Sunday supplement). The 297 informants, all from Styria, were sampled according to the Austrian census. Age, sex, education, knowledge of English, and media consumption were taken into account. Through questionnaires, passive and active comprehension and use were assessed. Passive knowledge was greatest for transfers in the subject areas of travel/holidays, radio/TV and jobs; active knowledge in travel/holidays, general advertising and radio/TV. Transfers were used by the informants most in the fields of radio/TV, general advertising and travel/holidays. Men used and understood more transfers than did women. The main variables correlating with use and knowledge of transfers are: English proficiency, level of education and age (or rather youth).

Lexical transfers also often occur in the everyday register of people whose *Fachsprache* (special language) at work contains a large incidence of transference and in that of young people preoccupied with the pop scene. However, on the basis of research undertaken by Pechtold, Dobaj (1980) found that Austrian salespeople had a fairly low command of the meaning of English transfers used widely in their own special fields. This applied most to those in the radio/TV field (52.5% active command) and least to those in the photography trade (65.5%), the other fields being clothing and cosmetics. Again men scored higher than women.

In a GDR study, Schönfeld and Donath (1978) surveyed foremen, workers and apprentices in two factories in the GDR on the knowledge and comprehension of 79 lexical transfers, not exclusively ones from English. Foremen had the best command of these items. Among workers, level of education influenced the knowledge of the transfers, as did (to a lesser extent) political education. Many of the words are employed in the fields of politics and economics. For apprentices, too, the main factor was educational level, followed by party function, consumption of mass media, and the reading of trade journals.

8.5   Reasons for transference

At the beginning of this chapter, I outlined the social, political and scientific developments that have led to the large-scale transferences from English into German. The puristic attitude which holds that some or most transfers are unnecessary is now uncommon in German-language countries. Such an attitude disregards the contribution made by language contact to language change all over the world since the start of history. In fact, all transfers are necessary either for semantic, stylistic or sociolinguistic reasons; otherwise they would not be employed.

Galinsky (Carstensen and Galinsky 1967: 71) lists the following stylistic functions of (lexical) transference from American English: providing 'American color', establishing precision, offering intentional disguise, brevity, vividness, tone (e.g. sneering parody), and variation of expression. This applies to all German-language countries.

Transfers can fill gaps in lexical fields, even by taking on meanings that those words do not convey in the source languages (see below, 8.6). Sometimes, too, transfers are part of an 'in-group' language or are intended to give the user status or prestige. They are the basis of in-group bilingual puns and jokes – a kind of 'linguistic one-upmanship' – at least in West Germany and in Austria. They are to be found in graffiti on walls and on school and university desks.

8.6   Integration of transfers

Lexical transfers can be integrated, to a greater or lesser extent, into the grammatical, phonological and graphemic systems of the German language. The degree of this integration, together with the stability of the transfers, reflects whether transfers are considered peripheral or central elements of the recipient language. Heller (1966) has shown that German speakers will regard some 'loanwords' (e.g. *Flöte*, flute; *Gummi*, rubber;

Sport) as far more integrated into (and less foreign to) the language than some less used lexemes of German origin (e.g. *Flechse*, sinew; *tosen*, to rage, to roar; *gastieren*, to appear as a guest, which uses the same bound morpheme -*ieren* as many transfers).

Lexical transfers can be placed on a continuum according to their degree of integration. At the bottom of the continuum (zero integration), we would find, for example, the verb in Hugo Moser's (1964) quotation from a member of the West German Army: 'Ein Tief *moves* heran' (a low (pressure zone) is moving close), where the lexeme is transferred, complete with English grammatical morpheme (a fully integrated transfer would be *muft). A partially integrated form would be *poolt* (from 'to pool', used by young Germans for 'to share', e.g. money or cars). Transfers that are combined with German morphemes (e.g. **superklug**, superclever; **Smartheit**, smartness; **Fixer**, **Rivalin**, female rival) or abbreviated (e.g. *Pulli*, pullover) can be considered more integrated than those that are not (e.g. *Fairness/Fairneß; Filmstar*, not *Filmstarin*), with fluctuating or double forms (e.g. *campen/Camping*) occupying an intermediate position. The use of the hyphen between a German and a transferred morpheme is often an indication of a lower degree of integration (e.g. *Trial-Fahren*, testdriving; *Mai-Meeting*; cf. *Bestsellerliste*, bestseller list; *Haarspray*, hairspray; *Trendwende*, change of direction). There is variation between higher and lower degrees of (phonological) integration: [dʒæːz]/[dʒes]/[jats] 'jazz';[6] [dʒɔp]/[tʃɔp] or [jɔp] 'job'; ['kʌmbɛk], [kʌm'bɛk][7] 'comeback'. We can attribute this variation to the speaker's and hearer's knowledge of the source language, their educational background, the communication situation, and the interlocutor's attitude to transfers (see 8.4.2; 8.5). Some speakers vacillate between the variants, depending on the formality of the situation and the knowledge of English of the speech partner. At the graphemic level, variation also occurs, e.g. *Hostess/Hosteß; Stop/Stopp; Cosmetik/Kosmetik* (Carstensen 1965: 34). W. Viereck (1986: 114) reports the use of occasional graphemic integration of words such as *Feedback/Fiedbäck*, *Countdown/Kauntdaun* in the Bamberg newspaper *Fränkischer Tag*. The ÖWB (1985), unlike the Duden, lists *Kautsch* and *Baudenzug* (bowden wire) as alternatives to *Couch* and *Bowdenzug*. Semantically, lexical transfers are integrated by changing the structure of the appropriate German lexical field. Transfers frequently occupy a broader or narrower range of meanings than in English. For instance, *Bestseller* (used in English only for books) is extended to refer to home appliances or ladies' clothing in German, while

---

[6]   Sometimes [jats] is restricted to signify older, classical jazz.

[7]   Such compounds tend to shift the stress to the second syllables or morpheme.

Ticket is usually restricted to air tickets, and *Job* is specialized to mean an additional or part-time position or non-career employment. Semantic transfers (e.g. *realisieren; kontrollieren* meaning 'beherrschen', to control; *lieben* meaning 'gern mögen', to love) could also be regarded as highly integrated lexical transfers, where an attempt is made to eliminate any formal marker of 'foreignness'.

In the course of time, some transfers become more integrated. Words originally spelt with a *c* are written with a *k*, e.g. *Klub, Kode, Kolumnist,* but not *Komputer!* Also, older transfers are more likely to be phonologically integrated.

Transferred nouns need to be given a gender. This is determined by factors such as: nearest semantic equivalent (e.g. *der Job* < *der Beruf, die Couch* < *die Liege, das Girl* < *das Mädchen*), morphological factors, especially suffix analogy (e.g. der *Entertainer* because German nouns ending in *-er* are generally masculine), natural gender, number of syllables – monosyllabic nouns being usually masculine (Arndt 1970, Carstensen 1980c, Gregor 1983). Sometimes there are several semantic equivalents, or there are a number of competing determinants of gender allocation. Hence some nouns can have two or three genders, e.g.:

> *der/das* Countdown, Poster, Spiritual, Spray
> *die/das* Dinner-Jacket, Folklore, Trademark
> *der/die* Couch, Glamour, Lobby, Speech
> *der/die/das* Dreß, Gospel, Juice

The indefinite article *ein,* which is used for both *der* and *das* nouns, creates some uncertainty as to the gender of many transfers and leads to the vacillation between masculine and neuter (Carstensen 1980c).

On the other hand, different genders can distinguish several meanings of a transfer, e.g. *der Single* (bachelor), *die Single* (single record), *das Single* (singles match in tennis). A change in gender away from the link with the semantic equivalent of the word in the source language may signal greater integration. This may have been the case with *Team,* whose gender was given as feminine (cf. *die Mannschaft*) in the 1952 Duden and in Mackensen's *Deutsches Wörterbuch* (1952) but neuter in the 1954 Duden and in subsequent dictionaries. On the other hand, Carstensen (1980c) and W. Viereck (1980b) both find that older transfers are best known and are therefore the ones used most with an English pronunciation. An alternative explanation is proposed by Gregor (1983: 168), namely that *die Team* was an earlier irregular gender assignment since *Mannschaft* at the time had a different meaning and could not act as a model while *das Team* was based on *Spielerpaar* (pair of players) or *Gespann* (team of draught animals).

Some adjectives (e.g. *fair*) tend to be inflected; others (e.g. *supersonic, up-to-date*) are not. Transferred verbs are generally assigned to the weak conjugation (e.g. *gemanaget*). Some verbs (e.g. *babysitten*) are employed only in the infinitive form. This may be related to problems in separating the prefix from the rest of the verb and the formation of the past (*ich babysittete? ich sat baby? ich sittete baby?*). Similar difficulties of separation occur in some verbs of German origin (e.g. *bausparen*, to invest in a building society).

8.6.1 Variation in integration between national varieties

Some nouns have been assigned to different genders in different varieties of Standard German, e.g.:

> *die* Cottage (Germany) / *das* Cottage (Austria) / *der* or *die*
> Cottage (Switzerland)
> *die* Couch (Germany, Austria) / *der* / *die* Couch (Switzerland)
> *der* / *das* Dreß (Germany, Switzerland) / *der* Dreß (Austria)
> *das* Match (Germany, Austria) / *der* Match (Switzerland)
> *der* / *das* Service (Germany) / *das* Service (Austria)

Swiss Standard German uses the more graphemically integrated forms *Rezital* (GSG *Recital*), *Skore, skoren*, and *Skorer* (GSG *Score, scoren, Scorer*), and the less graphemically integrated forms *Handicap* (GSG *Handikap*), and *Plastic* (GSG *Plastik*) (Meyer 1989, Kaiser 1969–70).

8.6.2 Dictionaries and integration

Both *Duden-Rechtschreibung* and *Duden-Aussprachewörterbuch* tend to choose a phonologically integrated form (e.g. [buŋgaloː]), or else give two variants (e.g. [pusl, pʌzl], [jats, dʒæs]), while Wahrig tends towards more unintegrated forms. The phonologically least integrated forms as well as the highly integrated ones are to be found in Neske and Neske (1972). Carstensen (1980c) has shown that the gender allocation of transfers in dictionaries does not always correspond to variations in usage.

8.6.3 Social aspects of integration

Forms that are more highly integrated (e.g. [putslə] *Puzzle*, [ʃaːtə] *Charter*, [jats] *Jazz*, [(t)ʃɔp] *Job*) tend to be employed by the older and less educated, while the younger, more educated and/or English-speaking informants either use unintegrated forms exclusively or fluctuate between higher and lower integration (depending on interlocutor and situation)

(Clyne 1973, also Dalcher 1986). But Fink's (1980: 179–80) research indicates that even 3–6-year-old preschool children use unintegrated forms of some transfers (e.g. *Jeans*).

8.7   Transference and communication barriers

Studies conducted in all German-language countries show that educational level / social background, knowledge of English, and age were factors in the use and comprehension of transfers from English. This is borne out in research based on interviews in Stuttgart (Clyne 1973), south-east Westphalia (Fink 1975), the then GDR (Koller 1978, Schönfeld and Donath 1978), and ten places in Switzerland (Dalcher 1986, an analysis of a Swiss–German dialect study conducted in 1964/65. Older people had a more negative attitude to transfers and some did not recognize them in their written form (Clyne 1973, Fink 1975); workers, farmers and housewives had a low level of comprehension of transfers (Fink 1975, Clyne 1973; workers and apprentices – Schönfeld and Donath 1978). Transfers occur more frequently in the Austrian quality newspaper *Die Presse* (especially in the advertisements) than in the Graz regional daily *Kleine Zeitung* (where the main use of transfers is in the sports section) (K. Viereck 1986, see also 7.3).

In examining the use of English transfers in German female Yuppie magazines, such as *Elle*, *Petra*, *Cosmopolitan* and *Vogue* (1990–1), Donalies (1992) shows the importance of transference in the social status of career women.

As we have already seen (3.3), there is a negative response in East Germany to the widespread use of English transfers in newspapers, largely due to limited comprehension.

Transference may be seen as one of a number of areas of education-based communication barriers in the German-language countries (see 7.2.) It seems that the widespread use of unintegrated transfers from English by the media (the result of international understanding) has contributed to internal communication barriers between young and old, English- and non-English-speaking Germans (Austrians or Swiss), more educated and less educated people. Transfers have indeed developed into sociolectal markers.

8.8   Brief summary

The Anglo-American influence on German may be attributed to internationalization, inter-cultural contact, and the widespread learning of

English as a second language. This applies particularly to the western part of Germany. In the East, English transference since the *Wende* has been partly a reaction to the earlier isolation from the West and to official GDR disapproval of 'foreign words'. English transfers are not as well established and therefore not as well understood as in the West. In Austria, there has been traditionally less contact with English-language countries; on the other hand, there has been little or no indigenous purism. While this is also true in Switzerland (whose multinational companies have not enforced the use of German), English transfers in Swiss Standard German have been competing with earlier ones from French. In Luxembourg, much English transference has come via French.

The English influence on German has come in the form of lexical, semantic and syntactic transfers. The degree of integration varies, and there are also pseudo-transfers coined in the Federal Republic. The main domains of use of lexical transfers are sport, technology and information science, travel and tourism, advertising, journalism, economics, politics, armed forces and entertainment – new developments originating from the US and Britain.

The English transfers are transmitted by the press, electronic media, advertising agencies and dictionaries, although these institutions only admit to registering or employing words that are already widely used. The characteristics found to mark people who use transfers most have been youth and education, education and exposure to newspapers and TV. There is evidence of lexical transfers, especially in their written form, causing communication barriers.

8.9   Further reading

The most complete book on the subject is still Carstensen (1965), which, however, has been updated by countless articles and treatments of specific issues. A collection of papers reflecting the state of research in the late 1970s in the Federal Republic and Austria is W. Viereck (1980a). Kristensson (1977) is the most substantial study of English influence on the German of the former GDR, while Gregor (1983) is devoted to the gender assignment of nouns transferred from English. Four of the chapters in Viereck and Bald's (1986) international collection of English transference are on German-language countries.

Closing remarks

It is hoped that the preceding eight chapters may offer some stimulus to reflection on, and research into, the German language in social context. Throughout the book the question of who owns the German language recurs, for there are numerous sets of power structures which determine language norms and language change – national, regional, social-class, gender, educational, generational, and so on (see also Townson 1992). Language change both mirrors and influences social change and there are some elements of the German language which can be understood only as traditional or historical indicators and not as contemporary social indicators. The German language is both a unifier and a separator of people. As I have tried to show, it reflects both cultural cohesion and socioeconomic and political division and represents an antithesis between national and international communication.

The very dramatic political and socioeconomic changes which have occurred in Europe in recent years may be followed in the study of the norms, functions and use of the German language in its several varieties. As changes are continuing, nothing in this book should be regarded as final.

For people in non-German-language countries, especially teachers of German, some of the issues raised in this book can cause dilemmas. How strictly does one impose norms that are being questioned in the 'heartland'? The use of *man* and unmarked masculine nouns and some of the orthographic norms are among the problem cases. Also, how much attention needs to be given to the pluricentricity of German, and to what extent should 'regional standards' be accepted in foreign language teaching?

There is a great deal of scope for further research. Even small-scale assignments can activate a better understanding of the relation between language, culture and society in the countries that are the object of the study, as well as a better consciousness of how language functions in society.

GLOSSARY OF LINGUISTIC TERMS USED

Cloze test Test involving a continuous text from which words have been deleted and which informants are required to complete.

Code-switching Switching from one language to another, often due to sociolinguistic variables (such as interlocutor, domain, type of interaction).

Collocation A particular combination of words.

Complex symbol Word that functions as a general symbol, encompassing diverse components which may solicit an attitude on the part of the hearer or reader.

Contrastive analysis Contrasting the phonology, grammar, and/or semantics of two languages; often involves emphasizing the differences rather than the similarities; used as a basis for teaching materials to combat interference, *one* of the sources of errors in second language acquisition.

Conversation opener Routine used formulaically to open a conversation.

Co-occurrence rules Rules about which routines can be used with which other ones.

Copula An overt connecting link between subject and complement (e.g. *is* in *He is an old man*).

Creole (Usually) a pidgin which has developed into a mother tongue.

Deficit hypothesis The hypothesis that some language varieties are cognitively inferior to others (see also *restricted code* and *elaborated code*).

Descriptive approach Describing a language as it is used (cf. *prescriptive approach*).

Dialect A local or regional variety of a language.

Difference hypothesis The hypothesis that no language variety is cognitively inferior or less logical than another.

Diglossia A language situation in which two different languages or varieties are functionally complementary, one (H, the 'High' variety) being used for written and more formal spoken purposes, the other (L, the 'Low' variety) for ordinary interaction (cf. *triglossia*). Adjective: diglossic.

Discourse Connected speech (including writing) extending beyond a single sentence.

Domain Institutionalized context, sphere of activity, totality of interaction (e.g. family, work, school).

Downgrader Modal particle or other means used to play down the impact of an utterance (cf. *upgrader*).

Elaborated code More complex strategies of verbal planning identified by Bernstein with middle-class values (cf. *restricted code*).

Elliptic sentence Sentence from which have been deleted parts generally considered to be essential for it to be grammatical and well-formed.

Embedding Putting one clause (the embedded or lower clause) inside another (the matrix or higher one) so that the lower clause functions as part of the higher clause (e.g. subordination).

Fachsprache The special (technical) language of a particular field, e.g. sociology, chemistry.

Feature The smallest element constituting larger ones such as phonemes, morphemes and segmemes. Features are of a binary nature: + or − indicates if a segment belongs to a particular class of elements or not, e.g. [− voice] voiceless, [+ male]. (See also *semantic features*.)

Foreigner talk Modified (often reduced) variety used to people with less than full competence in a language, or generally to people identified as 'foreigners'.

Grapheme Minimum unit of the writing system, or of the relation between the sound and writing systems, of a language.

Graphic interference Interference in the spoken language caused by the written language.

Graphotactic Referring to the rules for combining graphemes in a particular language.

Illocutionary force The communicative effect of an utterance, e.g. the promise made as a result of the utterance 'I promise to do it'.

Internationalism Word or expression used in many (or most) languages, e.g. *atom, radio, radium*.

Koiné Levelled ('compromise') language variety which spreads as a common form for inter-dialectal communication.

L1 First language.

Lexeme Word. Adjective: lexical.

Lexical field Area of vocabulary, indicating which words belong together semantically.

Lexical transfer Word taken over from another language in form and meaning.

Lexicon Vocabulary of a language.

Lexicosemantic Lexical and semantic at the same time (i.e. referring to both the form and meaning of words).

Loan-creation Word created in a language as an equivalent to one existing in another language (e.g. *Bahnsteig* (platform) for *perron*).

Loan-idiom Idiom transferred morpheme for morpheme.

Loan-meaning Semantic transfer in which a meaning is taken over from a word in one language to a word in the other language which sounds similar or has a similar meaning.

Loan-rendition Semantic transfer in which one element is transferred from another language, the other element created.

Loan-translation Semantic transfer in which each morpheme is translated from one language to the other.

'*Loanword*' Word transferred from one language to another; here referred to as 'lexical transfer'.

Macrosociolinguistic Concerned with broad aspects of the relation between language and society (e.g. *language use*) rather than the sociolinguistic variables (e.g. rounding of vowels) distinguishing between varieties.

Marked Displaying a particular distinctive feature (cf. *unmarked*).

Modality markers Markers strengthening or weakening the force of an utterance, e.g. *absolutely, terribly, indeed, bloody, you must understand that* (strengthening); *perhaps, a bit, would you mind if . . . ?* (weakening).

Morpheme The smallest significant unit of grammatical form that conveys a meaning.

Morphology The system of word structure or word formation in a language.

Neologism A new word.

Phoneme One of the set of speech units that distinguish one utterance or word from another.

Phonology (here) The sound system of a language. Adjective: phonological.

Phonotactic Referring to the rules for combining phonemes in a particular language.

Pidgin Reduced (simplified) variety which arises for restricted communication functions between speakers of different L1s but which is no one's L1.

Polysemy Term used when a word has two or more meanings.

Pragmatic(s) (Pertaining to) that area of linguistics concerned with the communicative function, intention and effects of utterances.

Prescriptive approach Laying down how a language *ought* to be used (cf. *descriptive*).

Proxemic Pertaining to how people position themselves (sit, stand) in relation to one another.

Pseudo-transfer New lexeme that appears to be a transfer from another language but is not; often the result of compounding of morphemes from that language.

Register A (stylistic) variety of a language chosen according to particular situational circumstances.

Restricted code Less complex strategies of verbal planning identified by Bernstein with lower-class varieties (cf. *elaborated code*).

Schema Socially constructed patterns of communicative behaviour available to the interlocutors from the experience and knowledge they bring to the encounter, e.g. how to make (and sequence) a complaint about their treatment.

Semantic(s) (Pertaining to) the meaning aspect of language.

Semantic features Components into which the meaning of a word can be broken up.

Sociolect Social variety of a language.

Sprachkultur (language cultivation) That aspect of language planning concerning normative questions such as correctness and efficiency of particular forms.

Sprechbund Societies sharing sets of non-grammatical (communication) rules.

Substratum The effects of a previously spoken language in an area or speech community on the language now spoken.

Syntax The part of grammar concerning rules for the arrangement of words in sentences, constructions, and for relations between sentences.

Tag-question A question which in English typically comprises an auxiliary verb plus a pronoun at the end of a statement to convey a positive or negative orientation. The German equivalent takes *nicht wahr?* or *gelt?* (*gel* or *gelle* in some South German dialects) or an interjection (e.g. *hm?*).

Transfer An instance of transference.

Transference The adoption of a rule or element from another language (lexical – word transferred; semantic – meaning transferred; syntactic – grammatical rule transferred).

Triglossia A language situation in which three different languages or varieties are functionally complementary (cf. *diglossia*). Adjective: triglossic.

Turn-taking The parts played by individual participants in verbal interaction.

Umgangssprache (colloquial language) In some German writings, the varieties between local dialect and standard language; unclear concept which defies definition.

Unmarked Not displaying a particular distinctive feature (cf. *marked*).

Upgrader Modal particle or other means used to intensify the impact of an utterance (cf. downgrader).

Variation The use of different varieties, the selection of which is determined by such variables as who are the interlocutors, their role relationship, where they are, their topics, domains and interaction.

Variety A national, regional or social variant of a language which can be distinguished at the national, regional or social level by grammatical, phonological and/or lexical features.

BIBLIOGRAPHY

Abbreviations of journals used below

DS	*Deutsche Sprache*
GraDaF	*Grazer Arbeiten zu Deutsch als Fremdsprache und Deutsch in Österreich*
IJSL	*International Journal of Sociology of Language*
JMMD	*Journal of Multilingual and Multicultural Development*
LB	*Linguistische Berichte*
LiLi	*Zeitschrift für Literaturwissenschaft und Linguistik*
LPLP	*Language Problems and Language Planning*
OBST	*Osnabrücker Beiträge zur Sprachtheorie*
WLG	*Wiener Linguistische Gazette*
ZDL	*Zeitschrift für Dialektologie und Linguistik*
ZGL	*Zeitschrift für germanistische Linguistik*
ZMF	*Zeitschrift für Mundartforschung*

List of newspapers used in corpus or referred to in text

Berliner Zeitung. Berlin.
Bild-Zeitung. Cologne/Esslingen/Frankfurt-on-Main.
Bonner Rundschau. Bonn.
Frankfurter Allgemeine. Frankfurt-on-Main
Leipziger Volkszeitung. Leipzig.
Mannheimer Morgen. Mannheim.
National-Zeitung. Munich.
Neue Kronen-Zeitung. Vienna.
Neue Zürcher Zeitung. Zurich.
Neues Deutschland. Berlin.
Die Presse. Vienna.
Rhein-Neckar-Kurier. Heidelberg.
Sächsische Zeitung. Dresden.
Salzburger Nachrichten. Salzburg.
Der Standard. Vienna.
Süddeutsche Zeitung. Munich.

Tagesanzeiger. Zurich.
Tageszeitung. Berlin.
The Age. Melbourne.
Unsere Zeit. Neuss.
Die Welt. Hamburg.
Westdeutsche Allgemeine Zeitung. Düsseldorf.
Wiener Morgen-Kurier. Vienna.
Wiesbadener Kurier. Wiesbaden.
Wochenpost. Berlin.
Die Zeit. Hamburg.

Albrecht, U. and S. Mathis. 1990a Die sprachlichen Verhältnisse in der Schweiz. In R. Watts and F. Andres (eds.), *Zweisprachig durch die Schule / Le bilinguisme travers l'école.* Berne; 71–80.

1990b Sprachpolitische und sprachplanerische Aspekte des Projekts 'Unterrichtssprache Französisch': Überlegungen aus der Sicht der Deutschschweiz. In R. Watts and F. Andres (eds.) *Zweisprachig durch die Schule / Le bilinguisme travers l'école.* Berne; 81–6.

Allensbach. 1981 Mundart wird hoffähig. *Allensbacher berichte* 14. Allensbach.

1993 Schneller per du. *Allensbacher berichte* 9. Institut für Demoskopie Allensbach.

Althaus, H.P., H. Henne and H.E. Wiegand 1980 (eds.). *Lexikon der germanistischen Linguistik.* Tübingen (2nd edition).

Ammon, U. 1972 *Dialekt, soziale Ungleichheit und Schule.* Weinheim.

1973a *Probleme der Soziolinguistik.* Tübingen.

1973b *Dialekt und Einheitssprache in ihrer sozialen Verflechtung.* Weinheim.

1975 Die Schwierigkeiten der Dialektsprecher in der Grundschule und das Bewußtsein davon bei den Lehrern. In H. Halbfas *et al.* (eds.), *Sprache, Umgang und Erziehung.* Stuttgart; 87–115.

1979 Regionaldialekte und Einheitssprache in der Bundesrepublik Deutschland. *IJSL* 21; 25–40.

1989 Towards a descriptive framework for the status/function/social position of a language within a country. In U. Ammon (ed.), *Status and function of languages and language varieties.* Berlin; 21–106.

1991 *Die internationale Stellung der deutschen Sprache.* Berlin.

1992 Comments during panel discussion 'Zur Zukunft der deutschen Sprache in Europa. Warum nicht gleich Englisch?'. Reproduced in Born and Stickel 1993; 188–9.

1994 Über ein fehlendes Wörterbuch 'Wie sagt man in Deutschland?' und den übersehenen Wörterbuchtyp 'Nationale Varianten einer Sprache'. *DS* 7.

Anderson, B. 1983 *Imagined communities.* London.

Angeli, T. 1992 A community of nine languages. Lizentiatsarbeit, University of Berne.

Appel, K.O. 1976 (ed.). *Sprachpragmatik und Philosophie.* Frankfurt-on-Main.

Arbeitskreis für Rechtschreiben der ständige Konferenz der Kultusminister. 1959. *Empfehlungen.* Mannheim.

Arndt, W.W. 1970 Non-random assignment of loanwords: German noun gender. *Word* 26; 1973; 244–54.

Auer, J.C.P. 1980 Konversationsanalytische Aspekte der Organisation von 'Code Switching' in einer Gruppe italienischer Gastarbeiterkinder. *Sonderforschungsbereich 99 Linguistik.* Constance.

Auer, J.C.P. and A. di Luzio. 1983 Structure and meaning of linguistic variation in Italian migrant children in Germany. In R. Bäuerle, C. Schwarze and A. van Stechow (eds.), *Meaning, use and interpretation of Language.* Berlin; 1–21.

Auer, P. *et al.* 1993 Dialektwandel und sprachliche Anpassung bei 'Übersiedlern' und 'Übersiedlerinnen' aus Sachsen. *DS* 1/93; 80–87.

Augst, G. 1974 (ed.). *Deutsche Rechtschreibung mangelhaft? Materialen und Meinungen zur Rechtschreibreform.* Heidelberg.

   1980 Internationales Kolloquium 'Die Zukunft der deutschen Rechtschreibung'. *DS* 3; 281–7.

Aunger, E. 1993 Regional, national and official languages in Belgium. *IJSL* 104; 31–48.

Bach, A. 1956 *Geschichte der deutschen Sprache.* Heidelberg (5th edition).

Bahlcke, J. 1992 Deutsch in der Tschechoslowakei. *Sprachreport* 2–3/92; 30.

Bailer-Galanda, B. n.d. *Alte und neue Rechte.* Vienna.

Banac, I. 1990 Political change and national diversity. *Daedallus* Winter 1990; 141–59.

Banzer, R. 1990 Pragmatik und Interferenzen der Mundarten des Fürstentums Liechtenstein des Sankt Gallener Rheintals und Vorarlbergs. *Germanistische Linguistik* 1990; 341–59.

Barbour, S. 1985 Review of M. Clyne, Language and society in the German-speaking countries. *Journal of Multilingual and Multicultural Development* 6; 524–8.

   1987 Dialects and the teaching of a standard language. *Language in Society* 16; 227–44.

Barbour, S. and P. Stevenson 1990 *Variation in German.* Cambridge.

Barkowski, H., U. Harnisch and S. Kumm 1976 Sprachhandlungstheorie Deutsch für Ausländer. *LB* 45; 103–10.

Bartholomes, H. 1956 *Tausend Worte Sowjetdeutsch.* Göteborg.

Bassola, P. 1992 Deutsche Sprache in Ungarn. *Sprachreport* 2/3/92, 29–30.

Bates, E. 1976 *Language and context: the acquisition of pragmatics.* New York.

Bauer, D. 1993 *Das sprachliche Ost-West-Problem.* Frankfurt.

Bauer, G. 1973 Einige Grundsätze im Kampf um die vereinfachte Rechtschreibung. *LB* 45; 42–54.

Baulch, H. 1979 An investigation of the language and the subject matter of the jokes of North German and Australian children. BA (Hons.) thesis, Monash University.

Bausch, K.H. 1979 *Modalität des Konjunktivgebrauchs in der gesprochenen deutschen Standardsprache.* Munich.

1981 (ed.) *Mehrsprachigkeit in der Stadtregion* (= *Sprache der Gegenwart* 56). Düsseldorf.

Bausch, K.H. and W. Davies. 1988 'Es is gar net so eifach de rischdische Ton zu finne'. *Sprachreport* 4/88; 5–7.

Bausinger, H. 1967 *Deutsch für Deutsche.* Frankfurt-am-Main.

Bayer, K. 1979 Die Anredepronomina Du and Sie. *DS* 3; 212–19.

1982 Jugendsprache und Sprachnorm. *ZGL* 10; 139–55.

Becker, K. 1948 *Der Sprachbund.* Leipzig.

1956 *Sieben Sprachbriefe zur Gegenwart.* Halle.

Beersmans, F. 1987 Variatie en norm in het Duitse taalgebied. In J. de Rooij (ed.), *Variatie en Norm in de Standaardtaal.* Amsterdam; 43–55.

Behrens, F., W. Dieckmann and E. Kehl 1982 Politik als Sprachkampf. In J. Heringer (ed.), *Holzfeuer im hölzernen Ofen.* Tübingen; 216–65.

Bellmann, G. 1986 *Beiträge zur Dialektologie am Niederrhein.* Stuttgart.

Beneke, J. 1993 Am Anfang wollten wir zu einander . . . Was wollen wir heute. In Reiher and Läzer 1993; 210–38

Berend, N. 1991 'Alles ist anders . . .' *Sprachreport* 3/91; 1–3.

Berg, G. 1993 *'Mir welle bleiwe, wat mir sin'. Soziolinguistische und sprachtypologische Betrachtungen zur luxemburgischen Mehrsprachigkeit.* Tübingen.

Bergmann, U., R. Dutschke and W. Lefèvre 1968 *Rebellion der Studenten oder Die Neue Opposition.* Reinbek.

Bern 1986 Nationale Varianten der deutschen Hochsprache. In *Ziele und Wege des Unterrichts in Deutsch als Fremdsprache. Tagungsbericht. 4–8 August 1986.* Berne.

Berning, C. 1964 *Vom 'Abstimmungsnachweis' zum 'Zuchtwart'. Vokabular zum Nationalsozialismus.* Berlin.

Bernstein, B.B. 1962 Social class, linguistic codes and grammatical elements. *Language and Speech* 5; 31–46.

1970 Der Unfug mit der 'Kompensatorischen Erziehung'. *betrifft: erziehung* 9; 15–19.

Berschin, H. 1978 Ein Geisterreich wie Utopia? *Der Spiegel* 32, 50; 11 December 1978; 68–74.

Bertaux, P. 1982 Quelques remarques sur les termes d'adresse en français et en allemand. *Contrastes* 4–5; 7–28.

Besch, W. 1975 Bericht über das Forschungsprojekt 'Sprachvariation und Sprachwandel in gesprochener Sprache'. *DS* 2; 173–84.

1983 Entstehung und Ausprägung der binnensprachlichen Diglossie im Deutschen. In Besch *et al.* (1982–3); 1399–1411.

1990 Schrifteinheit – Sprechvielfalt. Zur Diskussion um die nationalen Varianten der deutschen Schriftsprache. *German Life and Letters* 43; 91–102.

1994 Hierarchie und Höflichkeit in der deutschen Sprache. In J. Kohnen, H. J. Solms and K. P. Wegera (eds.), *Brückenschlagen . . . 'Weit draußen auf eigenen Füßen.' Festschrift für Fernand Hoffmann.* Frankfurt; 247–60.

Besch, W. and A. Lund 1987 (eds.) *Soziolinguistik und Empirie*. Wiesbaden.

Besch, W. and K. Mattheier 1977 Bericht über das Forschungsprojekt 'Sprachvariation und Sprachwandel in gesprochener Sprache'. In H.U. Bielefeld, E. Hess-Lüttich and A. Lund (eds.), *Soziolinguistik und Empirie*. Wiesbaden; 30–58.

Besch, W., H. Löffler and H.H. Reich 1977 *Dialekt/Hochsprache-Kontrastiv* (series). Düsseldorf.

Besch, W., U. Knopp, W. Putschke and H.E. Wiegand 1982–3 (eds.). *Dialektologie: ein Handbuch zur deutschen und allgemeinen Dialektforschung*. 2 vols. Berlin.

Betz, W. 1949 *Deutsch und Lateinisch*. Bonn.

1960 Der zweigeteilte Duden. *Der Deutschunterricht* 12, 5; 82–98.

1980 Die Opfer und die Täter – Rechtextremismus in der Bundesrepublik. *Aus Politik und Zeitgeschichte. Beilage zu Parlament*. 1327/80; 5 July 1980; 29–45.

Bichel, U. 1973 *Problem und Begriff der Umgangssprache in der germanistischen Forschung*. Tübingen.

1980 Umgangssprache. In Althaus, Henne and Wiegand 1980; 379–83.

Biedenkopf, K. 1980 Rede vor dem 28. Bundesparteitag der CDU. *Union in Deutschland* 19; 30–6.

Biermann, W. 1972 *Für meine Genossen*. Berlin.

Bigler, I. *et al.* 1987 *Unser Wortschatz: Schweizer Wörterbuch der deutschen Sprache*. Zurich.

Bister, H. and R. Willemyns 1988 Periferale woordenschat in woordenboeken van het Duitse, Franse en Nederlandse taalgebied. *De nieuwe taalgids* 81; 417–29.

Blackall, E. A. 1978 *The emergence of German as a literary language 1700–1755*. Cambridge (2nd edition).

Bliesener, T. 1980 Erzählen unerwünscht. Erzählversuche von Patienten in der Visite. In K. Ehlich (ed.), *Erzählen im Alltag*. Frankfurt-on-Main; 143–78.

Bloomfield, L. 1933 *Language*. New York.

Bluhme, H. 1980 Zur funktionalen konkurrenz von ostfälisch, nordniedersächsisch und hochdeutsch im südlichen Niedersachsen. *ZGL* 8; 314–27.

Blum-Kulka, S., J. House and G. Kasper 1989 (eds). *Cross-cultural pragmatics*. Norwood.

Bodemann, Y.M. and R. Ostow 1975 Lingua franca und Pseudo-pidgin in der Bundesrepublik: Fremdarbeiter und Einheimische im Sprachzusammenhang. *LiLi* 5, 18; 122–46.

Bodi, L. 1980 Österreichische Literatur – Deutsche Literatur. Zur Frage von Literatur und nationaler Identität. *Akten des 6. Internationalen Germanisten-Kongresses*. Basle; 486–92.

1992 Europe, Central Europe and the Austrian identity. In B. Nelson, D. Roberts and W. Veit (eds.), *The idea of Europe. Problems of national and trans-national identity*. New York/Oxford; 139–51.

1993 Intellectuals, writers and the Stasi files. *Meanjin* 52; 7–22.

Boesch, B. 1968 Sprachpflege in der Schweiz. In H. Moser *et al.* (eds.), *Sprachnorm, Sprachpflege, Sprachkritik*. Düsseldorf; 222–35.

Boesch, B. *et al.* 1957 (ed.). *Die Aussprache des Hochdeutschen in der Schweiz*. Zurich.

Böhm, S. *et al.* 1972 Rundfunknachrichten. Sozio- und psycholinguistische Aspekte. In Rucktäschel 1972; 153–94.

Borbé, T. 1977 Text und Bild bei Wahlplakaten. *Wiener Linguistische Gazette* 15; 69–78.

Born, J. 1992 Eurospeak + Eurotexte = Eurolinguistik? *Sprachreport* 2–3/92: 1–4.

1993 Podiumsdiskussion. In Born and Stickel 1993, 164–7.

Born, J. and S. Dieckgießer 1989 *Deutschsprachige Minderheiten*. Mannheim.

Born, J. and W. Schütte 1993 'Hotels, die wie Pilze aus dem Boden schießen'. *Sprachreport* 4/93; 11–14.

Born, J. and G. Stickel 1993 (ed.) *Deutsch als Verkehrssprache in Europa*. Berlin.

Braun, P. 1979 *Tendenzen in der deutschen Gegenwartssprache*. Urban-Taschenbücher, Stuttgart.

1981 Untersuchung zu deutsch–deutschen Wörterbüchern. *Muttersprache* 91; 157–68.

BRD-Report 1990 *Maskuline und feminine Personenbezeichnungen in der Rechtssprache*. Bericht der Arbeitsgruppe Rechtssprache (17. Januar 1990). Bonn: Deutscher Bundestag.

Brekle, H.E. 1972 *Semantik: eine Einführung in die Sprachwissenschaftliche Bedeutungslehre*. Munich.

Brettschneider, W. 1972 *Zwischen literarischer Autonomie und Staatsdienst: die Literatur in der DDR*. Berlin.

Brons-Albert, R. and S. Höhne 1991 Problems with the German language: questions posed by Germans and foreigners to the language service telephone of the Heinrich-Heine-Universität in Düsseldorf. *Deutsche Sprache* 19; 257–69.

Brown, P. and S. Levinson 1987 *Politeness*. Cambridge.

Brown, R. and A. Gilman 1960 The pronouns of power and solidarity. In T.A. Sebeok (ed.), *Style in Language*. Cambridge, MA; 253–76.

Bruch, R. 1953 *Grundlegung einer Geschichte des Luxemburgischen*. Luxembourg.

Bruckmüller, E. 1984 *Nation Österreich*. Vienna.

1994 *Österreichbewußtsein im Wandel*. Vienna.

Bruderer, H. 1973 Kommt die Kleinschreibung? *LB* 24; 87–102.

Buch, H.C. 1978 (ed.). *Deutschland, das Kind mit den zwei Köpfen* (=*Tintenfisch* 15). Berlin.

Bücherl, R.F.J. 1982 Regularitäten bei Dialektveränderung und Dialektvariation. *ZDL* 49; 1–27.

Buhofer, A. and H. Burger 1993. Hochdeutsch bei sechs- bis achtjährigen Kindern: Verstehen – Einstellungen. In V. Schupp (ed.), *Alemannisch in der Region. Beiträge zur 10. Arbeitstagung alemannischer Dialektologen in Freiburg i. Br. 1990*. Goeppingen; 11–23.

Bungarten, T. 1981 (ed.). *Wissenschaftssprache*. Munich.

Burckhardt-Seebass, C. 1993 'Brünig-Napf-Reuss-Linie' oder 'Röstigraben' – das Konzept des ASV und die kulturellen und sprachlichen Grenzen in der

gegenwärtigen Schweiz. Paper presented at symposium on 'Kulturgrenzen und Nationale Identität'. 5.–7.4.93.

Burger, H. 1979 Die Konkurrenz englischer und französischer Fremdwörter in der modernen deutschen Pressesprache. In P. Braun (ed.), *Fremdwort-Diskussion*, Munich; 246–72.

1984 *Sprache der Massenmedien*. Berlin.

Burkhardt, A. and P. Fritzsche 1992 (ed.) *Sprache im Umbruch*. Berlin.

Bürkle, M. 1993. Zur Aussprache des österreichischen Standards, österreichisch-Typisches in der Nebensilbe. In Muhr 1993a; 53–66.

Butterwegge, C. and S. Jäger 1992 *Rassismus in Europa*. Cologne.

Cajot, J. and H. Beckers 1979 Zur Diatopie der deutschen Dialekte in Belgien. In Nelde 1979; 151–218.

Carstensen, B. 1965 *Englische Einflüße auf die deutschen Sprache nach 1945*. Heidelberg.

1967 Amerikanische Einflüße auf die deutsche Sprache. In B. Carstensen and H. Galinsky 1967; 11–32.

1971 *Spiegel-Wörter, Spiegel-Worte, Zur Sprache eines deutschen Nachrichtenmagazins*. Munich.

1978 Wörter des Jähres 1977. *Der Sprachdienst* 22; 1–8.

1979a Wörter des Jahres 1978. *Der Sprachdienst* 23; 17–24.

1979b Evidente und latente Einflüße auf das Deutsche. In P. Braun (ed.), *Fremdwort-Diskussion*. Munich; 90–4.

1980a Wörter des Jahres 1979. *Der Sprachdienst* 24; 17–22.

1980b Semantische Scheinentlehnungen des Deutschen aus dem Englischen. In W. Viereck 1980a; 77–100.

1980c Das Genus englischer Fremd- und Lehnwörter im Deutschen. In W. Viereck (1980a); 37–75.

1982 Wörter des Jahres 1981. *Der Sprachdienst* 26, 1/2; 1–16.

Carstensen, B. and H. Galinsky 1967 *Amerikanismen der deutschen Gegenwartssprache: Entlehnunsvorgänge und ihre stilistische Aspekte*. Heidelberg (3rd edition, 1975).

Charleston, B.H. 1959 The English linguistic invasion of Switzerland. *English Studies* 40; 271–82.

Chini, M. 1992 Italien et suisse allemand dans des familles bilingues au Tession: contact pacifique ou conflit latent. *Multilingua* 11(1); 75–100.

Christ, H. *et al.* 1974 *Hessische Rahmenrichtlinien Deutsch. Analyse und Dokumentation eines bildungspolitischen Konflikts*. Düsseldorf.

Christen, H. 1992 Die dialektale Prägung schweizerdeutschen Umgangssprachen. *ZDL* 59; 275–92.

Christophory, J. 1974 *Mir schwätze lëtzebuergisch*. Luxembourg.

Clahsen, H., J. Meisel and M. Pienemann 1983 *Deutsch als Zweitsprache: der Spracherwerb ausländischer Arbeiter*. Tübingen.

Clyne, M.G. 1968a Ökonomie, Mehrdeutigkeit und Vagheit bei Komposita in der deutschen Gegenwartssprache. *Muttersprache* 78; 122–6.

1968b Zum Pidgin-Deutsch der Gastarbeiter. *ZMF* 34; 130–9.

1973 Kommunikation und kommunikationsbarriere bei englischen entlehnungen im heutigen deutsch. *ZGL* 1; 163–77.

1975 German and English working pidgins. In *Papers in Pidgin and Creole Linguistics (=Pacific Linguistics* A, 57). Canberra; 135–50.

1977a The speech of foreign workers in Germany (review article). *Language in Society* 6; 268–74.

1977b Multilingualism and pidginization in Australian industry. *Ethnic Studies* 1, 2; 40–55.

1977c European multinational companies in Australia and the exportation of languages. *ITL* 37; 83–91.

1979 Communicative competence in contact. *ITL* 43; 17–37.

1980 Writing, testing and culture. *The Secondary Teacher* 11; 13–16.

1981 Culture and discourse structure. *Journal of Pragmatics* 5, 1; 61–6.

1984 *Language and society in the German-speaking countries.* Cambridge.

1987 Cultural differences in the organization of academic texts. *Journal of Pragmatics* 11; 217–47.

1988 A *tendenzwende* in the codification of Austrian German? *Multilingua* 7, 335–41.

1992a (ed.) *Pluricentric languages.* Berlin.

1992b German as a pluricentric language. In Clyne 1992a, 117–47.

1994 *Inter-cultural communication at work.* Cambridge.

Clyne, M.G., J. Hoeks and H. Kreutz 1988 Cross-cultural responses to academic discourse. *Folia Linguistica* 22; 457–75.

Clyne, M.G. and S.I. Manton 1979 Routines for conducting meetings in Australia: an inter-ethnic study. *Ethnic Studies* 3, 1; 25–34.

Collinson, W.E. 1953 *The German language today.* London.

Cooper, P.L. 1969 Two contextualised measures of degree in bilingualism. *Modern Language Journal* 53, 3; 172–8.

Cordes, G. 1963 Zur Terminologie des Begriffs 'Umgangssprache'. In W. Simon, W. Bachofen, W. Dittmar (eds.), *Festgabe für Ulrich Pretzel.* Berlin; 338–54.

Coulmas, F. 1979 On the sociolinguistic relevance of routine formulae. *Journal of Pragmatics* 3; 239–66.

1988 *With forked tongues. What are national languages good for?* Ann Arbor.

1991 *A language policy for the European Community.* Berlin.

1992 *Die Wirtschaft mit der Sprache.* Frankfurt.

1993 Was ist die deutsche Sprache wert? In Born and Stickel 1993; 9–25.

Coulthard, M.C. 1969 A discussion of restricted and elaborated codes. *Educational Review* 22, 1; 38–50.

DAAD Letter 1993 Leute in Osten lesen mehr. *DAAD Letter* 4, December 1993; 8.

Dahl E.S. 1974 Interferenz und Alternanz – zwei Typen der Sprachschichtenmischung in der Deutschen Demokratischen Republik. In G. Ising (ed.), *Aktuelle Probleme der sprachlichen Kommunikation: soziolinguistische Studien zur sprachlichen Situation in der Deutschen Demokratischen Republik.* Berlin; 9–36.

Dahl, J. 1977 Kommt Zeit, Kommt Unrat. *Schneidewege* 7; 39–62.

Dahrendorf, R. 1979 *Lebenschancen. Anläufe zur sozialen und politischen Theorie.* Frankfurt-on-Main.

Dalcher, P. 1966 Der Einfluß des Englischen auf die Umgangssprache der deutschen Schweiz. *Schweizerdeutsches Wörterbuch Bericht des Jahr 1966.* Zurich; 11–12.

1986 Anglicisms in Swiss-German. In Viereck and Bald 1986; 179–206.

Davis, K.A. 1994 *Language planning in multilingual contexts. Policies, communities and schools in Luxembourg.* Amsterdam.

De Cillia, R. and A. Anzengruber 1993 *Fremdsprachenpolitik in Österreich, Mitteleuropa und Osteuropa. Schulheft 68.* Vienna.

Debus, F. 1962 Zwischen Mundart und Hochsprache. *ZMF* 29; 1–43.

Deprez, K. and G. de Schutter 1980 Honderd Antwerpenaars en honderd Rotterdammers over dertien Nederlandse taalvariëteiten: een attitude-onderzoek. *Leuvense Bijdragen* 69, 167–256.

Des Schweizers Deutsch. Beiträge zum Thema Mundart und Hochsprache. Berne.

Dieckmann, W. 1964 *Information oder Überredung?* Marburg.

1989 Die Untersuchung der deutsch–deutschen Sprachentwicklung als linguistisches Problem. *ZGL* 17; 162–81.

Dieth, E. 1938 *Schwyzertütschi Dialäktschrift.* Zurich.

Dittmar, N. 1973 *Soziolinguistik: exemplarische und kritische Darstellung ihrer Theorie, Empirie und Anwendung.* Frankfurt-on-Main.

1978 Ordering adult learners according to language abilities. In Dittmar *et al.* 1978; 119–54.

1979 Fremdsprachenerwerb im sozialen Kontext: das Erlernen von Modalverben. *LiLi* 33; 84–103.

Dittmar, N. and B. Schlieben-Lange 1981 Stadtsprache. In Bausch 1981; 9–86.

Dittmar, N., B. Schlieben-Lange and P. Schlobinski 1981 Teilkommentierte Bibliographie zur soziolinguistik von Stadtsprachen. In Bausch 1981; 391–423.

Dittmar, N., P. Schlobinski and I. Wachs 1986 *Berlinisch.* Berlin.

Dittmar, N., H. Haberland, T. Skuttnabb-Kangas and U. Teleman 1978 (eds.). *Papers from the first Scandinavian-German symposium on the language of immigrant workers and their children.* Roskilde.

Dobaj, M. 1980 Anglizismen in der Rundfunkwerbung und von Verständnis von Werbeanglezismen beim Branchenpersonal. In W. Viereck (1980a); 101–7.

Domaschnew, A. 1993a Deutsch in Osteuropa. In Born and Stickel 1993; 251–61.

1993b Zum Problem der terminologischen Interpretation des Deutschen in Österreich. In Muhr 1993a; 7–20.

Donalies, E. 1992 Hippies Hopping and Toughe Trendies. *DS* 20, 97–110.

Donath, J. 1977 Überlegungen zur semantischen Norm zentraler Termini in der materiellen Produktion. In Hartung *et al.* 1977a; 247–79.

1980 Zum Einfluß der Kommunikationssituation auf die sprachliche Variation

im Produktionsbetrieb. In *Linguistische Studien. Reihe T. Arbeitsberichte* 72, 1; 28–35.

Döpke, S. 1993 *One parent – one language.* Amsterdam.

Dresden, A. 1978 Emigranten im eigenen Land. In Buch 1978; 7–13.

Dressler, W. and R. Wodak 1982a Soziolinguistische Überlegungen zum 'Österreichischen Wörterbuch'. In M. Dardano, W. Dressler and G. Held (eds.), *Parallela (=Akten des 2. österreichischen-italienischen Linguistentreffens).* Tübingen; 247–60.

1982b Sociophonological methods in the study of sociolinguistic variation in Viennese German. *Language in Society* 11; 339–70.

Drosdowski, G. and H. Henne 1980 Tendenzen der deutschen Gegenwartssprache. In Althaus, Henne and Wiegand 1980; 619–52.

Duden. 1952 *Rechtschreibung.* Mannheim.

1954 *Rechtschreibung.* Mannheim.

1959 *Grammatik.* Mannheim.

1972 *Rechtschreibung.* Leipzig.

1973 *Rechtschreibung.* Mannheim.

1974 *Aussprachewörterbuch.* Mannheim.

1976 *Das große Wörterbuch der deutschen Sprache.* 6 vols. Mannheim.

1983 *Deutsches Universalwörterbuch.* Mannheim.

1984 *Grammatik.* Mannheim.

1985 *Grammatik.* Mannheim.

1989 *Der kleine Duden: Sprachtips.* Mannheim.

1991 *Rechtschreibung.* Mannheim.

Dürmüller, U. 1991 Swiss multilingualism and international communication. *Sociolinguistica* 5; 111–59.

1993 Comments during panel discussion 'Zur Zukunft der deutschen Sprache in Europa. Warum nicht gleich Englisch?'. Reproduced in Born and Stickel 1993; 164–94.

Durrell, M. 1989 Die 'Main-Linie' als sprachliche Grenze. In W. Putschke, W. Veith and P. Wiesinger (eds.), *Dialektgeografie und Dialektologie. Günter Bellmann zum 60. Geburtstag.* Stuttgart; 89–107.

1992 *Using German.* Cambridge.

Ebner, J. 1969 *Wie sagt man in Österreich?* Mannheim.

Egger, K. 1985 *Zweisprachige Familien in Südtirol, Sprachgebrauch und Spracherziehung.* Innsbruck (= *Innsbrucker Beiträge zur Kulturwissenschaft. Germanistische Reihe.* Bd. 27.)

1993 Die Vielfalt der sprachlichen Ausdrucksmittel in der Umgangssprache von Schülern in Bozen. In K. J. Mattheier *et al.* (eds.), *Vielfalt des Deutschen: Festschrift für Werner Besch.* Frankfurt-on-Main; 653–63.

Eggers, H. 1963 Contemporary German: a sociological point of view. *Te Reo* 6; 1–8.

1969 Deutsche Gegenwartssprache im Wandel der Gesellschaft. In H. Moser *et al.* (eds.), *Sprache – Gegenwart und Geschichte.* Düsseldorf; 9–29.

Ehlich, K. and J. Rehbein 1972 Zur Konstitution pragmatischer Einheiten in einer Institution: das Speiserestaurant. In D. Wunderlich (ed.), *Linguistische Pragmatik*. Frankfurt-on-Main; 209–54.

1977 Wissen, kommunikatives Handeln und die Schule. In Goeppert 1977; 36–113.

1980 Sprache in Institutionen. In Althaus, Henne and Wiegand 1980; 338–45.

Ehlich, K., A. Koerfer, A. Redder and R. Weingarten 1989 (eds). *Medizinische und therapeutische Kommunikation*. Opladen.

Ehmann, H. 1992 *Jugendsprache und Dialekt*. Opladen.

Ehnert, R. 1993 Regionale Varianten des deutschen Sprachraums im Fremdsprachenunterricht. In Földes, C. (ed.), *Germanistik und Deutschlehrerausbildung. Festschrift zum hundertsten Jahrestag der Gründung des Lehrstuhls für deutsche Sprache und Literatur an der Pädagogischen Hochschule Szeged*. Szeged/Vienna; 277–288.

Eichhoff, J. 1976 Bibliography of German dialect spoken in the United States and Canada, and problems of German–English language contact, especially in North America 1968–1976 with pre-1968 supplements. *Monatshefte* 68; 196–208.

1977–8 *Wortatlas der deutschen Umgangssprachen*. Marburg.

1980 Zu einigen im 20. Jahrhundert entstandenen geographischen Unterschieden des Wortgebrauchs in der deutschen Sprache. In R. Hildebrant and H. Friebertshäusen, *Sprache und Brauchtum. Bernhard Martin zum 90. Geburtstag*. Marburg; 154–78.

Eichholz, R. 1975 Geschrieben wie gesprochen. Mundart wiederentdeckt. *Wirkendes Wort* 25; 377–83.

Eisermann, G. and J. Zeh 1979 *Die deutsche Sprachgemeinschaft in Ostbelgien: Ergebnisse eines empirischen Untersuchungs* (= Minorität, Medien und Sprache Bd 1. Bonner Beiträge zur Soziologie Bd. 17). Stuttgart.

Engel, U. 1961 Die Auslösung der Mundart. *Muttersprache* 7; 129–35.

1962 Schwäbische Mundart und Umgangssprache. *Muttersprache* 72; 257–61.

Eppler, E. 1992 *Kavalleriepferde beim Hornsignal*. Frankfurt.

Erdmann, K. D. 1987 Die Spur Österreichs in der deutschen Geschichte. *Geschichte in Wissenschaft und Unterricht* 10; 597–626.

Erdmann, U. 1992 *Language maintenance versus assimilation* (*ZDL*-Beiheft 70) Stuttgart.

Ervin-Tripp, S.M. 1971 Sociolinguistics. In J.A. Fishman (ed.), *Advances in the sociology of Language*. Vol. 1. The Hague; 15–92.

Faulseit, D. 1965 Von Fremdwörtern und anderen Unarten des Zeitungsdeutsches. *Sprachpflege* 14; 98–100.

1971 Vom Sinn und Unsinn des Fremdwortgebrauchs. Überlegungen nach dem VIII. Parteitag der SED. *Sprachpflege* 20; 241–3.

Fenske, H. 1973 *Schweizerische und österreichische Besonderheiten in deutschen Wörterbuchern* (= Institut für deutschen Sprache *Forschungsberichte* 10). Mannheim.

Ferguson, C.A. 1959 Diglossia. *Word* 15; 325–44.

Filipović, R. 1974 A contribution to the methods of studying anglicisms in European languages. *Studia Romanica et Anglica Zagrabiensia* 37; 135–48.

Fink, H. 1970 *Amerikanismen im Wortschatz der deutschen Tagespresse, dargestellt am Beispiel dreier überregionaler Zeitungen (Süddeutsche Zeitung, Frankfurter Allgemeine Zeitung, Die Welt)* (= *Mainzer Amerikanische Beiträge* 11). Munich.

1975 'Know-How' und 'Hifi-Pionier'. Zum Verständnis englischer Ausdrücke in der deutschen Werbesprache. *Muttersprache* 85; 186–203.

1977 'Texaslook' und 'party-bluse': assoziative effekte von englischem im deutschen. *Wirkendes Wort* 27; 394–402.

1980 Zur Aussprache von Angloamerikanischem im Deutschen. In W. Viereck 1980a; 109–83.

Fishman, J.A. 1965 Who speaks what language to whom and when? *Linguistique* 2; 67–88.

1967 Bilingualism with and without diglossia; diglossia with and without bilingualism. *Journal of Social Issues* 23, 2; 29–38.

1971 The sociology of language. In J.A Fishman (ed.), *Advances in the sociology of language*. Vol. 1. The Hague 1971; 217–404.

1985 Macrosociolinguistics – the sociology of language in the early 80's. *Annual Review of Sociology* 11; 113–27.

1991 *Reversing language shift. Theoretical and empirical foundations of assistance to threatened languages* (= Multilingual Matters 76). Cleveland; Philadelphia.

Fishman, J.A. and E. Lueder 1972 What has the sociology of language to say to the teacher? In C.A. Cazden, V. John and D. Hymes (eds.), *Functions of language in the classroom*. New York; 67–83.

Fishman, J.A., R.L Cooper and A.W. Conrad 1977 *The Spread of English*. Rowley, MA.

Fishman, J.A. *et al.* 1985 *The rise and fall of the ethnic revival*. Berlin.

Fix, U. 1991 Sprache: Vermittler von Kultur und Mittel soziokulturellen Handelns. Gedanken zur Rolle der Sprache und der Sprachwissenschaft im interkulturellen Diskurs 'Deutsch als Fremdsprache'. *Informationen Deutsch als Fremdsprache* 18, 136–47.

1992a Noch breiter entfalten und noch wirksamer untermauern. In R. Grosse, G. Lerchner and M. Schröder (eds.), *Beiträge zur Phraseologie Wortbildung Lexikologie. Festschrift für Wolfgang Fleischer zum 70. Geburtstag*. Frankfurt-on-Main; 13–28.

1992b Rituelle Kommunikation im öffentlichen Sprachgebrauch der DDR und ihre Begleitumstände. Möglichkeiten und Grenzen der selbstbestimmten und mitbestimmenden Kommunikation in der DDR. In Lerchner 1992a; 3–99.

1993 Medientexte diesseits und jenseits der 'Wende'. Das Beispiel 'Leserbrief'. In B.U. Biere and H. Henne (eds.), *Sprache in den Medien nach 1945*. Tübingen.

Flader, D. 1978 Die Psychoanalytische Therapie als Gegenstand sprachwissenschaftlicher Forschung. *Studium Linguistik* 5; 37–51.

Fleischer, H. 1993 Von der DDR zu den fünf neuen Bundesländern – Entwicklungen im Sprachgebrauch an ausgewähltem lexikalischem Material. Cand.ling.merc. thesis, Handelshojskolen Århus.

Fleischer, W. 1983 *Die deutsche Sprache in der DDR*. Leipzig.

1987 (ed.) *Wortschatz der deutschen Sprache in der DDR*. Leipzig.

Fleischer, W., W. Hartung, J. Schildt and P. Suchsland 1983 *Kleine Enzyklopädie deutsche Sprache*. Leipzig.

Földes, C. 1992 Zur gegenwärtigen Situation des Deutschen als Fremdsprache in Ungarn. *Zielsprache Deutsch* 23; 30–40.

1993 Deutsch als Verkehrssprache in Ostmitteleuropa – am Beispiel Ungarns. In Born and Stickel 1993; 217–35.

Fónagy, I. 1963 *Die Metaphern in der Phonetik*. The Hague.

Fox, J.A. 1977 Implications of the jargon/pidgin dichotomy for social and linguistic analysis of the Gastarbeiter Pidgin German speech community. In C. Molony, H. Zobl, W. Stölting (eds.), *Deutsch in Kontakt mit anderen Sprachen*. Kronberg; 40–6.

Fraas, C. 1993 Verständnisschwierigkeiten der Deutschen. *Muttersprache* 103; 260–3.

Fraas, C. and K. Steyer 1992 Sprache der Wende – Wende der Sprache? *DS* 2/92, 172–84.

Frei, G. 1985 S'Köchu-Verzëichnis – der die Verdrängung der Hochsprache beim Radio. In *Des Schweizers Deutsch*; 24–9.

Friebertshäuser, H. 1987 *Das hessische Dialektbuch*. Munich.

Fuchs, J. 1977 *Gedächtnisprotokolle* (roro aktuell 480). Hamburg.

Fussy, H. 1990. Wohin steuert das österreichische Wörterbuch? *GraDaF* 1/90, 17–25.

Gal, S. 1979 *Language Shift*. New York.

1993 Diversity and contestation in linguistic ideologies: German speakers in Hungary. *Language in Society* 22; 337–60.

Galinsky, H. 1977 Amerikanisch-englische und gesamtenglische Interferenzen in dem Deutschen und anderen Sprachen der Gegenwart. In H. Kolb and H. Lauffer (eds.), *Sprachliche Interferenz. Festschrift für Werner Betz*. Tübingen; 463–517.

1980 American English Post 1960. Neologisms in contemporary German: reception-lag variables as a neglected aspect of linguistic interference. In W. Viereck 1980a; 213–35.

Garbe, B. 1978 *Die deutsche Rechtschreibung und ihre Reform. 1722–1974* (=*Germanistische Linguistik* 10). Tübingen.

Gardner-Chloros, P. 1992 *Code-switching and code adaptation in Elsace*. Clevedon.

Gärtner, D. 1992 Vom Sekretärsdeutsch zur Kommerzsprache. Sprachmanipulation gestern und heute. In Lerchner 1992a; 203–62.

Geerts. G., J. Nootens and J. Vandenbroeck 1977 Opinies van Vlamingen over Dialekt en Standaardtaal. *Taal en Tongval* 29; 98–141.

Geißler, H. 1980 *Unser Grundsatz-Programm = ein Dokument geistiger Erneuerung*

(Rede auf dem 26. Bundesparteitag der CDU. 23–25. Oktober 1978, Ludwigshafen). Cologne.

Germany 1992 Sonderprogramm zur Förderung der deutschen Sprache in Mittel- und Osteuropa (MS, Auswärtiges Amt, Bonn).

Gfirtner, F.X. 1972 *Experimentale Studie über den Schriftlichen und mündlichen Sprachgebrauch von Kindern unterschiedlicher sozialer Herkunft*. Munich (Zulassungsarbeit).

Gilbert, G.G. 1978 Review of Klein (ed.) *Sprache ausländischer Arbeiter*. In *Language* 54; 983–7.

Gilbert, G.G. and M. Orlović 1975 *Pidgin – German spoken by foreign workers in West Germany: the definite article*. Paper presented at the International Congress on Pidgins and Creoles, Honolulu.

Giles, H. 1977 Social psychology and applied linguistics: toward an integrative approach *ITL* 35; 27–42.

Gläser, R. 1992 Gestalt- und Stilwandel in der kommerziellen Werbung der neuen Bundesländer. In E. Hess-Lüttich (ed.), *Medienkultur. Kulturkonflikt. Massenmedien in der interkulturellen und internationalen Kommunikation.* Opladen; 189–211.

Glattauer, W. 1971 *Strukturelle Lautgeographie der Mundarten im Südöstlichen Niederösterreich und in den angrenzenden Gebieten des Burgenlandes und der Steiermark (=Schriften zur deutschen Sprache in Österreich)*. Vienna.

Glovacki-Bernardi, Z. 1993 Österreichische und süddeutsche Elemente in der Agramer Mundart. In Muhr 1993a; 76–8.

Gloy, K. 1974 *Sprachnormen: Probleme ihre Analyse und Legitimation*. Constance.

1978 Ökologische Aspekte der Dialekt-Verwendung. Ein Beitrag zur neuen Dialektwelle. In U. Ammon *et al.* (eds.), *Grundlagen einer diatekt-orientierten Sprachdidaktik: theoretische empirische Beiträge in einem vernachlässigten Schulproblem*. Weinheim; 73–91.

1980 Behördliche Sprachregelungen gegen und für eine sprachliche Gleichbehandlung von Frauen und Männern. *LB* 69; 22–36.

Glück, H. and W. W. Sauer 1990 *Gegenwartsdeutsch*. Stuttgart.

Goeppert, H.C. 1977 (ed.). *Sprachverhalten im Unterricht*. Munich.

Good, C. 1989 *Zeitungssprache im geteilten Deutschland: exemplarische Textanalysen (= Analysen zur deutschen Sprache und Literatur)*. Munich.

1991 Der Kampf geht weiter oder Die sprachlichen Selbstrettungsversuche des SED-Staates. *Sprache und Literatur* 67; 48–55.

1993a 'Kultur des Mißverständnisses' im vereinten Deutschland. *Muttersprache* 103, 249–59.

1993b Fragile voices, forgotten tongues. *The Times Higher Education Supplement*, 29 January 1993; 19–20.

Graf, R. 1977 *Der Konjunktiv in gesprochener Sprache*. Tübingen.

Grebe, P. 1968 Sprachnorm und Sprachwirklichkeit. In Hugo Moser 1968; 28–44.

Gregor, D. 1983 *Genuszuordnung*. Tübingen.

Greiner, U. 1982 Gezielte Flucht. *Die Zeit* 50; 17 December 1982; 50; 17–18.

Grimm, J. and W. 1854–1961 *Deutsches Wörterbuch*. 16 vols. Leipzig.

Grimminger, R. 1972 Kaum aufklärender Konsum. In Rucktäschel 1972; 15–68.

Gruber, H. and R. Wodak 1992. *Ein Fall für den Staatsanwalt?* (*WLG* Beiheft 11). Vienna.

Gruner, P.-H. 1993 'Rechte' Karriere eines 'linken' Wortes? In Reiher and Läzer 1993; 272–88.

Guentherodt, I. 1979 Berufsbezeichnungen für Frauen. Problematik der deutschen Sprachen im Vergleich mit Beispielen aus dem Englischen und Französischen. *OBST* Beihefte 3; 120–32.

Guentherodt, I., M. Hellinger, L.F. Pusch and S. Trömel-Plötz 1980 Richtlinien zur Vermeidung sexistischen Sprachgebrauchs. *LB* 69; 15–21.

Guggenberger, G. 1979 Die Kulturrevolution der Bürgerinitiativen. *Frankfurter Allgemeine Zeitung*, 29 September 1979; 1.

Gumperz, J. 1994 Sprachlicher Variabilität in interaktionsanalytischer Perspektive. In Kallmeyer 1994; 611–39.

Gustafsson, L. 1978 *Die Allemande*. In Buch 1978; 73–81.

Gutfleisch, I. and B.-O. Rieck 1981 Immigrant workers (Gastarbeiter) in West Germany: teaching programmes for adults and children. In J. Megarry, S. Nisbet and E. Hoyle (eds.), *Education of minorities*. London; 341–58.

Häcki Buhofer, A. and H. Burger 1993 Hochdeutsch bei sechs- bis achtjährigen Kindern: Verstehen – Einstellungen. In V. Schupp (ed.), *Alemannisch in der Region. Beiträge zur 10. Arbeitstagung alemannischer Dialektologen in Greiburg i. Br. 1990*. Goeppingen; 11–23.

Hain, M. 1951 *Sprichwort und Volkssprache*. Gießen.

Halliday, M.A.K. 1978 *Language as a social semiotic: the social interpretation of language and meaning*. Baltimore.

Hameyer, K. Determining the linguistic variables of interdialectal intelligibility. *Lingua* 49, 283–93.

Hammarberg, B. and A. Viberg 1977 The place-holder constraint, language typology and the teaching of Swedish to immigrants. *Studia Linguistica* 31, 2; 106–63.

Hard, G. 1966 *Zur Mundartgeographie*. Düsseldorf.

Hartung, W. and H. Schönfeld 1981 (eds.). *Kommunikation und Sprachvariation*. Berlin.

Hartung, W. *et al.* 1974 (eds.). *Sprachliche Kommunikation und Gesellschaft*. Berlin.

1977a (eds.) *Normen in der Sprachlichen Kommunikation*. Berlin.

1977b Zum Inhalt des Normbegriffs in der Linguistik. In Hartung (1977a); 9–69.

Hasselberg, J. 1972 Die Abhängigkeit des Schülererfolgs vom Einfluß des Dialekts. *Muttersprache* 82; 201–23.

1976a *Dialekt-Hochsprache Kontrastiv: Hessisch*. Düsseldorf.

1976b *Dialekt und Bildungschancen*. Weinheim.

1981 Mundart als Schulproblem. In R. Schanze (ed.), *Sprache in Hessen*. Gießen; 29–55.

Hauck, W. 1993 Die Amtssprachen der Schweiz – Anspruch und Wirklichkeit. In Born and Stickel 1993; 147–63.

Haugen, E. 1966 *Language conflict and language planning: the case of modern Norwegian*. Cambridge.

1967 Semi-communication: the language gap in Scandinavia. *International Journal of American Linguistics* 33 (4); 152–59.

Heidelberger Forschungsprojekt 1975 *Sprache und Kommunikation ausländischer Arbeiter*. Kronberg.

1976 *Untersuchung zur Erlernung des Deutschen durch ausländische Arbeiter*. Heidelberg.

1978 *Zur Erlernung des Deutschen durch ausländische Arbeiter: Wortstellung und ausgewählte lexikalisch-semantische Aspekte* (mimeo) Frankfurt-on-Main.

Hein, V. and P. 1980 Dialekt und Hochsprache im Deutschunterricht. *LB* 65; 37–50.

Heinemann, M. 1990 *Kleines Wörterbuch der Jugendsprache*. Leipzig.

Heller, K. 1966 *Das Fremdwort*. Leipzig.

1994 Rechtschreibung. *Sprachreport*. Extra Ausgabe, Dezember 1994, 1–8.

Hellinger, M. 1980 Zum Gebrauch weiblicher Berufsbezeichnungen im Deutschen – Variabilität als Ausdruck außersprachlicher Machtstrukturen. *LB* 69; 37–58.

1985a (ed.) *Sprachwandel und feministische Sprachpolitik*. Opladen.

1985b Reaktionen auf die 'Richtlinien zur Vermeidung sexistischen Sprachgebrauchs'. In Hellinger 1985a; 255–60.

1990 *Kontrastive Feministische Linguistik*. Munich.

1993 Guidelines for the equal treatment of the sexes in German. *Working papers on language, gender and sexism* 3(2); 31–42.

Hellmann, M. 1973 Wortschatzdifferenzen und Verständigungsprobleme. Fragen bei der Erforschung der sprachlichen Situation in Ost und West. In M. Hellman (ed.), *Zum öffentlichen Sprachgebrauch in der Bundesrepublik Deutschland und in der DDR*. Düsseldorf; 126–45.

1978 Sprache zwischen Ost und West – Überlegungen zur Wortschatzdifferenzierung zwischen BRD und DDR und ihren Folgen. In W. Kühlwein and G. Radden (eds.), *Sprache und Kultur: Studien zu Diglossie, Gastarbeiterproblematik und kulterelle Integration*. Tübingen; 15–54.

1989a 'Binnendeutsch' und 'Hauptvariante Bundesrepublik'. Zu Peter von Polenz' Kritik an Hugo Moser. *ZGL* 17; 84–93.

1989b Zwei Gesellschaften – Zwei Sprachschichten. *Forum für interdisziplinäre Forschung* 2; 27–38.

1990a DDR-Sprachgebrauch nach der Wende – eine erste Bestandaufnahme. *Muttersprache* 100; 266–86.

1990b Der Broiler hat Überlebenschancen. *Tageszeitung*, 21 March 1990.

1993 Die Leipziger Volkszeitung vom 27.10.1989 – Eine Zeitung im Umbruach. *Muttersprache* 103; 186–218.

Helmers, H. 1971 *Sprache und Humor des Kindes*. Stuttgart.

Henne, H. 1980 Jugendsprache und Jugendgespräche. In P. Schröder and H. Steger (eds.), *Dialogforschung (= Jahrbuch 1980 des Instituts für deutsche Sprache)*. Düsseldorf; 370–84.

1986 *Jugend und ihre Sprache*. Berlin.

Hentschel, E. 1993 Flexionsverfall im Deutschen? *ZGL* 21; 320–33.

Herrgen, J. and J.E. Schmidt 1985 Systemkontrast und Hörerurteil. *ZDL* 52; 20–42.

Herrmann-Winter, R. 1974 Auswirkungen der sozialistischen Produktionsweise in der Landwirtschaft auf der sprachlichen Kommunikation in den Nordbezirken der Deutschen Demokratischen Republik. In Ising 1974b; 135–90.

1977 Soziolinguistische Aspekte empirischer Erhebungen zum sprachlichen Varianz. In Hartung (1977a); 209–46.

1979 *Studien zur gesprochenen Sprache im Norden der DDR*. Berlin.

Heuberger, V. and A. Suppan 1993 Nationale Minderheiten in Mitteleuropa. In Holzer and Münz 1993; 305–16.

Heuwagen, M. 1974 Die Verbreitung des Dialekts in der Bundesrepublik Deutschland. Staatsexamenarbeit (unpublished). Bonn.

Heym, E. 1979 *Collin*. Gütersloh.

Hobsbawm, E. 1990. *Nations and nationalism since 1780: programme, myth, reality.* Cambridge.

Hoffmann, F. 1969 *Das Luxemburgische im Unterricht*. Luxembourg.

1979 *Sprachen in Luxemburg*. Wiesbaden and Luxembourg.

1981 *Zwischenland*. Hildesheim.

1984 Schreiben im dreisprachigen Land. Zeitschrift für Literaturwissenschaft und Linguistik. In A. Ritter (ed.), *Deutschsprachige Literatur im Ausland*. Göttingen; 69–86.

1988 Luxemburg. In U.Ammon, N.Dittmar and K.Mattheier (eds.), *Sociolinguistics. An International Handbook*. Vol. 2 Berlin; 1334–40.

1989 Sprachen in Luxemburg. *Jahrbuch für internationale Germanistik*. 20; 45–62.

Hoffmann, F., J.P. Hoffmann, C. Russ, H. Klees and G. Newton forthcoming. *Luxembourg at the crossroads – the Luxembourg experience*. Oxford.

Hoffmann, L. 1980 Zur Pragmatik von Erzählformen vor Gericht. In K. Ehlich (ed.), *Erzählen vom Alltag*. Frankfurt-on-Main; 28–63.

Hoffmeister, W. 1977 *Sprachwechsel in Ost-Lothringen*. Wiesbaden.

Hoffmansthal, Hugo von 1927. *Wert und Ehre der deutschen Sprache*.

Hofmann, E. 1963 Sprachsoziologische Untersuchung über den Einflüß der Stadtsprache auf mundartsprechende Arbeiter. *Marburger Universitätsbund*; 201–81.

Hofstede, G. 1991 *Culture and organizations*. London.

Holly, W., P. Kühn and V. Püschel 1986 *Politische Fernsehdiskussionen*. Tübingen.

Holzer, W. and R. Münz 1993 (eds.). *Trendwende? Sprache und Ethnizität in Burgenland*. Vienna.

Hoppenkamps, H. 1977 *Information oder Manipulation? Untersuchungen zur Zeitungsberichterstattung über eine Debatte des Deutschen Bundestages*. Tübingen.

Hornung, M. 1968 Sprachpflege in Österreich. In Hugo Moser 1968; 215–19.

House, J. 1979 lnteraktionsnormen in deutschen und englischen Alltagsdialogen. *LB* 59; 76–90.

House, J. and G. Kasper 1981 Politeness markers in English and German. In F. Coulmas (ed.) *Conventional routine.* The Hague; 157–86.

Houssa, L. 1993 Probleme des Fremdsprachenunterrichts in der CSFR. In De Cillia and Anzengruber 1993; 107–10.

Hufschmidt, J. 1983 Erfahrungen, Beobachtungen und Wertungen zum Mundartgebrauch. In Hufschmidt *et al.* (1983): 11–59.

Hufschmidt, J., E. Klein, K.J. Mattheier and H. Mickartz. 1983 *Sprachverhalten in ländlichen Gemeinden.* Berlin.

Hughes, E.C. 1972 The linguistic division of labour in industrial and urban societies. In J.A. Fishman (ed.), *Advances in the sociology of language.* Vol. 2. The Hague 1972; 296–309.

Humboldt, W. 1830–5 *Über die Verschiedenheit des menschlichen Sprachbaues und ihren Einfluß auf die geistige Entwicklung des Menschengeschlechtes.* Berlin.

Hundt, M. 1992 *Einstellungen gegenüber dialektal gefärbter Stadtsprache (ZDL-*Beiheft 78). Stuttgart.

Hutterer, C.J. 1978 Der Standarddialekt von Graz in Vergangenheit und Gegenwart. In W. Steinbock (ed.), *850 Jahre Graz.* Graz; 323–54.

Hyltenstam, K. 1977 Implicational patterns in interlanguage syntax variation. *Language Learning* 27; 383–411.

Hymes, D. 1974 *Foundations in sociolinguistics: an ethnographic approach.* Philadelphia.

Innerhofer, F. 1993. Österreichische Schriftsteller, österreichisches Deutsch und deutsche Verlagslektoren. In Muhr 1993a; 21–5.

Inter Nationes. 1979 Erster 'Sprachatlas' wurde fertiggestellt. *Bildung und Wissenschaft* 10, 11; 135.

1980 *Prozeduren Programme Profile: die Bundesrepublik Deutschland wählt am 5. October 1980 den Deutschen Bundestag.* Mainz.

Internationaler Arbeitskreis für Orthographie. 1992 *Deutsche Rechtschreibung. Vorschläge zu ihrer Neuregelung.* Tübingen.

Ising, G. 1974a Struktur und Funktion der Sprache in der gesamt gesellschaftlichen Entwicklung. In Ising 1974b; 9–35.

1974b (ed.) *Aktuelle Probleme der sprachlichen Kommunikation. Soziolinguistische Studien zur sprachlichen Situation in der Deutschen Demokratischen Republik.* Berlin.

1977 (ed.) *Sprachkultur – warum – wozu?* Berlin.

Jaene, H.D. 1981 Das gedachte Dach. Zwei Staatsbürgerschaften – eine deutsche Nation? *Die Zeit* 8; 20 February 1981; 5.

Jäger, G. 1992 'Mobelparadies' im Kulturpalast. *Sprachreport* 2–3/92; 8.

Jäger, S. 1972 Sprachbarrieren und kompensatorische Erziehung: ein bürgerliches Trauerspiel. *LB* 19; 80–99.

1978 *'Warum weint die Giraffe'.* Kronberg.

1989 Rechtsextreme Propaganda heute. In K. Ehlich (ed.), *Sprache im Faschismus.* Frankfurt; 289–322.

1992 Wie die Deutschen die 'Fremden' sehen: Rassismus im Alltagsdiskurs. In Butterwegge and Jäger 1992; 230–47.

Jakob, G. 1992 'Möbelparadis' im Kulturpalast. *Sprachreport* 2/3–92; 8–12.

Jakob, K.H. 1982 Sprachliches Handeln von Schülern. *Deutsche Sprache* 2, 82; 156–92.

1992 Prestige und Status deutscher Dialektlandschaften. *ZDL* 49; 167–82.

Jakob, N. 1981 Sprachplanung in einer komplexen Diglossiesituation. *Language Problems and Language Planning* 5; 153–71.

Januschek, F. 1989 Die Erfindung der Jugendsprache. In Januschek and Schlobinski 1989; 125–46.

1992 Jörg Haider und der Rechtspopulismus in Österreich. In Butterwegge and Jäger 1992; 161–77.

Januschek, F. and P. Schlobinski (eds). 1989 *Jugendsprache* (= *Osnabrücker Beiträge zur Sprachtheorie* 41).

Jespersen, O. 1922 *Language: its nature, development and origin*. London.

Johnson, S. 1989 Attitudes towards the Berlin dialect. *Grazer Linguistische Studien* 32; 21–37.

1992 On the status of female informants in Peter Schlobinski's 'Stadtsprache Berlin'. *LB* 140; 246–55.

Johnston, W.M. 1983 *The Austrian mind*. Berkeley.

Jungk, R. 1977 *Der Atom-Staat*. Munich.

Kachru, B.B. 1981 American English and other Englishes. In C.A. Ferguson and S.B. Heath (eds.), *Language in the USA* Cambridge; 21–43.

Kadan, A. and A. Pelinka 1979 *Die Grundsatzprogramme der österreichischen Parteien*. St Pölten.

Kaiser, S. 1969–70 *Die Besonderheiten der deutschen Schriftsprache in der Schweiz*. 2 vols. Mannheim.

Kallmeyer, W. 1994 (ed.) *Kommunikation in der Stadt. Teil 1 – Exemplarische Analysen des Sprachverhaltens in Mannheim*. Berlin.

Kalverkämpfer, H. 1979 Die Frauen und die Sprache: eine Erwiderung auf S. Trömel-Plötz 'Linguistik und Frauensprache'. *LB* 62; 55–71.

Kaplan, R.B. 1993 The hegemony of English in science and technology. *JMMD* 14; 151–72.

Keim, I. and J. Schwitalla. 1993. Formen der Höflichkeit – Merkmale sozialen Stils. Am Beispiel zweier Frauengruppen aus unterschiedlichen sozialen Welten. In J. Schwitalla (ed.), *Vielfalt der kulturellen Systeme und Stile*. Tübingen.

Keller, R.E. 1961 *German dialects*. Manchester.

1973 Diglossia in German-speaking Switzerland. *Manchester Library Bulletin*. 56; 1.

1978 *The German language*. London.

Keller, T. 1976 *The city dialect of Regensburg*. Hamburg.

Kellershohn, H. 1992. 'Unser Programm heißt Deutschland' – Der Beitrag der REPublikaner zur Renaissance völkischen Denkens in Deutschland. In Butterwegge and Jäger 1992; 86–104.

Kern, R. 1979 Schriftsprachliche Ausdrucksschwierigkeiten deutschsprachiger Belgier an der französischen Universität zu Löwen. In Nelde 1979; 101–22.

Key, M. 1975 *Male/Female language*. Metuchen.

Klann, G. 1975 *Aspekte und Probleme der linguistischen Analyse schichtenspezifischen Sprachgebrauchs*. Berlin.

1978a Sprache in der Psychoanalyse. *Stadium Linguistik* 5; 52–66.

1978b Weibliche Sprache – Identität, Sprache und Kommunikation von Frauen. *OBST* 8; 9–62.

Klappenbach, G. and W. Steinitz 1976 *Wörterbuch der deutschen Gegenwartssprache*. Berlin.

Klaus, G. 1971 *Sprache der Politik*. Berlin.

Klein, E. 1983 Situation und Sprachlage. In Hufschmidt *et al.* (1983); 117–99.

Klein, W. and N. Dittmar 1979 *Developing grammars*. Berlin.

Klein, W. and C. Perdue 1992 *Utterance structures: developing grammars again*. Amsterdam.

Klein, W. and D. Wunderlich 1971 (eds.). *Aspekte der Soziolinguistik*. Frankfurt-on-Main.

Kleinschmidt, G. 1972 Sprachvermögen und soziale Status. In *Sprache-Brücke und Hindernis*. Munich; 99–110.

Klemperer, V. 1947 *LTI: Notizbuch eines Philologen*. Berlin.

Klieme, R.B. 1976 Untersuchungen zum Verhältnis von Gesellschaftsformation, Nation und Sprache und seiner Behandlung in der Sprachwissenschaft der DDR (dissertation). Berlin.

Kloss, H. 1967 Abstand languages and ausbau languages. *Anthropological Linguistics* 9(7); 29–31.

1974 Die den internationalen Rang einer Sprache bestimmenden Faktoren. In U.Engel and I. Vogel (eds.), *Forschungsberichte des IdS* 20; 7–77

1978 *Die Entwicklung neuer germanischer Kultursprachen seit 1800*. Düsseldorf (2nd edition).

Koller, W. 1978 Angloamerikanismen in der DDR-Zeitungssprache. *DS* 4; 306–23.

1992 *Deutsche in der Deutschschweiz*. Aarau.

König, W. 1978 (ed.). *dtv-Atlas zur deutschen Sprache* Munich (2nd edition).

1989 (ed.) *dtv-Atlas der deutschen Sprache*. Munich (3rd edition).

Konrád, G. and I. Szélenyi 1978 *Die Intelligenz auf dem Weg zur Klassenmacht*. Frankfurt-on-Main.

Korlén, G. 1962 Zur Entwicklung der deutschen Sprache diesseits und jenseits des eisernen Vorhangs. *Sprache im technischen Zeitalter* 4; 259–80.

1964 *Das Aueler Protokoll – Deutsche Sprache im Spannungsfeld zwischen West und Ost*. Düsseldorf.

1973 Rezension zu: Duden Rechtschreibung der deutschen Sprache und der Fremdwörter, 17. Auflage, Mannheim. *Muttersprache* 67; 272–5.

Kotthof, H. 1984 Gewinnen oder verlieren? Beobachtungen zum Sprachverhalten von Frauen und Männern in argumentativen Dialogen an

der Universität. In S. Trömel-Plötz (ed.), *Gewalt durch Sprache*. Frankfurt; 90–113.

Kowar, G. 1992 Sprachpolitik und. . .? In De Cillia and Anzengruber 1992; 61–8.

Kozmová, R. 1993 Lehnwörter österreichischen und süddeutschen Ursprungs im Slowakischen. In Muhr 1993a; 94–8.

Kreutz, H. 1993 Pragmatic implications of the convergence between East and West Germany. *Working Papers in Linguistics* 13; 63–78.

Krier, F. 1990 Empirische Daten zu einer Typologie der Kodeumschaltungsphänomene. In P.H.Nelde (ed.), *Language conflict and minorities*. Bonn; 213–22.

Kristensson, G. 1977 *Angloamerikanische Einflüße in DDR-Zeitungstexten*. Stockholm.

Kropf, T. 1986 *Kommunikative Funktionen des Dialekts im Unterricht: Theorie und Praxis in der deutschen Schweiz* (= *Reihe germanistische Linguistik* 67) Tübingen.

Kufner, H.L. 1961 *Strukturelle Grammatik der Münchener Stadtmundart*. Munich.

Kuhn, E. 1982 *Geschlechtsspezifische Unterschiede in der Sprachverwendung* (= LAUT, Serie B74).Trier.

Kühn, P. 1980 Deutsche Sprache in der Schweiz. In Althaus, Henne and Wiegand 1980; 531–6.

Kunert, G. 1966 *Verkündigung des Wetters: Gedichte*. Munich.

Kunze, K. 1978 *Die wunderbaren Jahre. Lyrik, Prosa, Dokumente* (ed. K. Corino). Frankfurt-on-Main.

Küpper, H. 1977 Die deutsche Schülersprache. *Wirkendes Wort* 27; 318–30.

Küpper, W. 1993 Lingua Stasi: ein Wörterbuch, das geheime Verschlußsache war. *Wochenpost* 37; 9 September 1993; 8.

Labov, W. 1966 *The social stratification of English in New York City*. Washington.

1969 The logic of nonstandard English. *Georgetown Monographs on Language and Linguistics* 22; 1–22, 26–31.

1970 The study of language in its social context. In J.A. Fishman (ed.), *Advances in the Sociology of Language*. Vol.1.The Hague 1971; 447–72.

1972 *Sociolinguistic patterns*. Philadelphia.

Lakoff, R. 1975 *Language and woman's place*. New York.

Lambert, W.E. 1967 A social psychology of bilingualism. *Journal of Social Issues* 23; 91–109.

Larcher, D. 1988 Halbsprachigkeit in Kärnten. *Sprachreport* 4/88; 8–10.

Lattey, E.M. and B.D. Müller 1976 Temporary language acquisition: migrant workers' speech in Germany. *Proceedings of the 4th International Congress of Applied Linguistics*. Stuttgart; 213–27.

Latzel, S. 1975 Perfekt und Präteritum in der deutschen Zeitungssprache. *Muttersprache* 85; 38–49.

Laudel, H. 1992 *Wort und Fremdwort*. Hamburg.

Lee, D. 1991 The voices of Swiss television commercials. *Multilingua* 10; 295–323.

Lehmann, H. 1972 *Russisch–deutsche Lehnbeziehung im Wortschatz offizieller Wirtschaftstexte der DDR (bis 1968)*. Düsseldorf.

Lehnert, M. 1986 The Anglo-American influence on the language of the German Democratic Republic. In Viereck and Bald 1986; 129–57.

Lehrplan der Realschule. 1991. Vaduz.

Lehrplan für die Primärschulen im Fürstentum Liechtenstein. n.d. Vaduz.

Leirbukt, O. 1983 Über einen Genitiv besonderen Typus. *Muttersprache* 93; 104–19.

Leodolter, R. 1975 *Das Sprachverhalten von Angeklagten vor Gericht.* Kronberg.

Leopold, W.F. 1968 The decline of dialects. In J.A. Fishman (ed.), *Readings in the Sociology of Language.* The Hague; 340–64.

Lerchner, G. 1974 Zur Spezifik der Gebrauchsweise der deutschen Sprache in der DDR und ihrer gesellschaftlichen Determination. *Deutsch als Fremdsprache* 1; 259–65.

1983 Der 'neue Substandard' in den kulturell-kommunikativen Traditionen des Dialekts. In Putschke *et al.* 1989; 289–303.

1992a (ed.) *Sprachgebrauch im Wandel. Anmerkungen zur Kommunikationskultur* (= *Leipziger Arbeiten zur Sprach- und Kommunikationsgeschichte* Vol. 1). Frankfurt.

1992b Vorwort. In Lerchner 1992a; 1–2.

1992c Broiler, Plast(e) und Datsche machen noch nicht den Unterschied. Fremdheit und Toleranz in einer polyzentrischen deutschen Kommunikationskultur. In Lerchner 1992a; 297–332.

Lettau, R. 1978 Deutschland als Ausland. In Buch 1978; 116–22.

Lewandowski, T. 1980 *Linguistisches Wörterbuch.* 3 vols. Heidelberg (3rd edition).

Lipold, G. 1988 Die österreichische Variante der deutschen Standardaussprache. In Wiesinger 1988a; 31–54.

Lippert, H. 1978 Sprachliche Mittel in der Kommunikation im Bereich der Medizin. In Mentrup 1978; 84–99.

Loest, E. 1978 *Es geht seinen Gang oder Mühen in unserer Ebene.* Stuttgart.

Löffler, H. 1985 *Germanistische Soziolinguistik.* Berlin.

1986 (ed.) *Das Deutsch der Schweizer.* Aarau.

Löffler, H., K. Pestalozzi and M. Stern 1979 (eds) *Standard und Dialekt. Studien zur gesprochenen und geschriebenen Gegenwartssprache. Festschrift für Heinz Rupp zum 60. Geburtstag.* Berne/Munich.

Lohm, C. 1992 The use of Swiss German on Swiss German television. (MS, English Department, University of Berne).

LPLP 1991 News/Novajoj/Nachrichten/Nieuws. *LPLP* 15; 282–96.

1993 Deutsch im Elsaß offiziell. *LPLP* 17 (2); 188.

Luchtenberg, S. 1994a A friendly voice to help you vs. working thoroughly through your manual: pragmatic differences between American and German software manuals. *Journal of Pragmatics* 21; 315–19.

1994b Bilingual education for migrant children. *Journal of Intercultural Studies* 15(2).

Lüdi, G. 1992 Internal migrants in a multilingual city. *Multilingua* 11; 45–73.

Ludwig, K.D. 1977 Sportsprache und Sprachkultur. In Ising 1977; 49–90.

Macha, J. 1986 Dialekt und Standardsprache. Zur heutigen Situation im deutschen Grenzgebiet. *Rheinische Vierteljahrschrift* 50; 298–305.

1988 'Muß man einfach flexibel sein' – Zur Rolle der Sprache im Handwerk. *Rheinische Vierteljahrschrift* 52; 190–209.

1990 'Wat is hier jebacken?' Zur Sprache von Handwerksmeistern aus Siegburg, Eitorf und Windeck. *Heimatblätter des Rhein-Sieg-Kreises.* Jahrbuch 1990; 116–32.

1991 *Der flexible Sprecher.* Cologne.

1992 Dialekt und Standardsprache. Ausprägung und Gebrauch bei rheinisch-ripuarischen Sprechern. In J.A. van Leuvensteijn and J.B. Berns (eds.), *Dialect and Standard Language. Proceedings of the colloquium 'Dialect and Standard Language', Amsterdam, 15–18 October 1990;* 271–89.

1993a 'Wie die Alten sungen. . .?' In K. Mattheier, K.-P. Wegera, W. Hoffmann, J. Macha and H.-J. Solms (eds.), *Vielfalt des Deutschen. Festschrift für Werner Besch.* Frankfurt-on-Main, 601–18.

1993b Der flexible Sprecher. *ZDL* (1).

Macha, J. und T. Wegera 1983 Mundart im Bewußtsein der Sprecher. *Rheinische Vierteljahrschrift* 47; 265–301.

Mackensen, L. 1952 *Deutsches Wörterbuch.* Laupheim.

Magenau, D. 1964 *Die Besonderheiten der deutschen Schriftsprache in Luxembourg und in den deutschsprachigen Teilen Belgiens.* Mannheim.

Magocsi, P.R. 1993 Scholarly seminar on the codification of the Rusyn language. *IJSL* 104; 120–3.

Maroldt, E. 1979 Anpassung des Letzebuergischen an das Industriezeitalter. Außersprachliche Faktoren des Sprachwandels und der Sprachtreue. *Dialektologie Heute: Festschrift für Hélène Palgen.* Luxembourg.

Mattheier, K.J. 1980 *Pragmatik und Soziologie der Dialekte.* Heidelberg.

1983 (ed.) *Aspekte der Dialekttheorie.* Munich.

Medgyes, P. and R.B.Kaplan. 1993 Discourse in a foreign language: the example of Hungarian scholars. *IJSL* 98; 67–100.

Meier, H. 1985 Die Verwendung von 'würde' in der deutschen Sprache der Gegenwart. *Sprachpflege* 1985/5; 65–71.

Meili, E. 1985 Wort und Sprache in der reformierten Kirche. In *Des Schweizers Deutsch*; 104–10.

Meisel, J. 1975 Ausländerdeutsch und Deutsch ausländischer Arbeiter: zur möglichen Entstehung eines Pidgin in der BRD. *LiLi* 5, 18; 9–53.

1977 The language of foreign workers in Germany. In C. Molony, H. Zobl and W. Stölting (eds.), *Deutsch im Kontakt mit anderen Sprachen.* Kronberg; 184–212.

Mentrup, W. 1978 *Fachsprache und Gemeinsprache.* Düsseldorf.

1979 *Die gemäßigte Kleinschreibung: Diskussion einiger Vorschläge zu ihrer Regelung und Folgerungen.* Mannheim.

1980 Deutsche Sprache in Österreich. In Althaus, Henne and Wiegand 1980; 527–31.

1989 Bericht und Kommentar. Die Frühjahrstagung der Studiengruppe 'Geschriebene Sprache'. *DS* 17 (4), 371–82.

Meyer, K. 1989 *Wie sagt man in der Schweiz?* Mannheim.

Meyer-Ingwersen, J., R. Neumann and M. Kummer. 1977 *Zur Sprachentwicklung türkischer Schüler in der Bundesrepublik.* Kronberg.

Meyers Lexikon. 1973. Leipzig.

Mitchell, A.G. and A. Delbridge 1965 *The speech of Australian adolescents.* Sydney.

Mittelberg, E. 1967 *Wortschatz und Syntax bei Bild-Zeitung.* Marburg.

Mitten, R., R. Wodak and R. de Cillia 1989 Sprechen Sie antisemitisch? *Sprachreport* 3/89; 6–10.

Moosmüller, S. 1988 Dialekt ist nicht gleich Dialekt. Spracheinschätzung in Wien. *Wiener Linguistische Gazette* 40–1; 55–80.

1991 *Hochsprache und Dialekt in Österreich.* Vienna.

Moosmüller, S. and W. Dressler 1988 Hochlautung und soziophonologische Variation in Österreich. *Jahrbuch für Internationale Germanistik* 20; 82–90.

Morain, G. 1979 The Cultoon. *Canadian Modern Language Review* 35, 4; 676–96.

Morf, D. 1985 Macht aus der Sprache keine Schikane. In *Des Schweizers Deutsch*; 99–103.

Moser, Hans 1990 Deutsche Standardsprache: Anspruch und Wirklichkeit. In *IDV-Tagung.* Vienna; 17–30.

Moser, Hugo. 1961a *Deutsche Sprachgeschichte.* Stuttgart (4th edition).

1961b Umgangssprache: Überlegungen zu ihrer Formen und ihrer Stellung. *ZMF* 19; 215–32.

1962 *Sprachliche Folgen der politischen Teilung Deutschlands* (=*Wirkendes Wort*, 3. Beiheft). Düsseldorf.

1964 Sprachprobleme bei der Bundeswehr. *Muttersprache* 74; 129–33.

1967 Wohin steuert das heutige Deutsch? In Hugo Moser (ed.), *Satz und Wort im heutigen Deutsch* (=*Sprache der Gegenwart* 1). Düsseldorf.

1968 (ed.) *Sprachnorm, Sprachpflege, Sprachkritik.* Düsseldorf.

1972 (ed.). Sprachbarriere als linguistisches und soziales Problem. In Rucktäschel 1972; 195–222.

1979a (ed.). *Studien zu Raum- und Sozialformen der deutschen Sprache in Geschichte und Gegenwart.* Berlin.

1979b Umsiedlung und Sprachwandel. In Hugo Moser 1979a; 322–37.

1980 Sprachnorm und Sprachentwicklung: zur Rolle sprachökonomischer Tendenzen in der heutigen deutschen Standardsprache. In *Meyers enzyklopädisches Lexikon.* Mannheim; 333–7.

1985 Die Entwicklung der deutschen Sprache seit 1945. In W. Besch, O. Reichmann, S. Sonderegger (eds.), *Sprachgeschichte.* Berlin; 1678–707.

Moulton, W.G. 1962 What standard for diglossia? The case of German Switzerland. *Georgetown University Monograph Series on Language and Linguistics* 15; 133–44.

Mühlhäusler, P. 1981 Foreigner Talk: Tok Masta in New Guinea. *IJSL* 28; 93–114.

Muhr, R. 1981 *Sprachwandel als soziales Phänomen.* Vienna.

1982 Österreich. Anmerkungen zur Schizophrenie einer Nation. In *Klagenfurter Beiträge zur Sprachwissenschaft*;306–19.

1987a Deutsch in Österreich – Österreichisch: zur Begriffsbestimmung der Standardsprache in Österreich. *Grazer Arbeiten zu Deutsch als Fremdsprache und Deutsch in Österreich* 1; 1–18 (2nd edition, 1990).

1987b Regionale Unterschiede im Gebrauch von Beziehungsindikatoren zwischen der Bundesrepublik Deutschland und Österreich und ihre Auswirkungen in Deutsch als Fremdsprache – dargestellt am Beispiel der Modalpartikel. In L.Götze (ed.), *Deutsch als Fremdsprache: Situation eines Faches*. Bonn; 144–56.

1988 Regionale Unterschiede in der deutschen Standardsprache und ihre Auswirkungen auf den Unterricht in Deutsch als Fremdsprache: die Unterschiede zwischen BRD-Deutsch und österreichischem Deutsch. In H. Schröder and C. Sörensen (eds.), *Deutsch als Fremdsprache und Österreich. Beiträge der 'Nordischen Tagung für Deutschlehrer und Germanisten' 1.–4. Juni 1986* (= Reports from the Language Centre for Finnish Universities 32). Jyväskylä; 35–68.

1989 Deutsch und Österreich(isch): Gespaltene Sprache – gespaltenes Bewußtsein – gespaltene Identität. *Informationen zur Deutschdidaktik* 2/89. Klagenfurt; 74–87.

1993a (ed.) *Internationale Arbeiten zum österreichischen Deutsch und seinen nachbarsprachlichen Bezügen*. Vienna.

1993b Pragmatische Unterschiede in der deutschsprachigen Kommunikation. Österreich – Deutschland. In Muhr 1993a; 26–38.

1993c Österreich – Bundesdeutsch – Schweizerisch. Zur Didaktik des Deutschen als plurizentrische Sprache. In Muhr 1993a; 111–27.

1993d Österreichisches Deutsch und österreichische Literatur in ihren nachbarsprachlichen Bezügen. Paper presented at conference on language policy in Austria and Central Europe, November 1993.

forthcoming. Pragmatische Unterschiede im deutschsprachigen Raum: österreichisches Deutsch – deutsches Deutsch. Habilitationsschrift, University of Graz.

Müller-Marzohl, A. 1961 Das schweizerische Wortgut im Jubiläumsduden. *Sprachspiegel* 17, 4; 97–113.

Müller-Thurau, C.P. 1983 *Laß uns mal 'ne Schnecke angraben*. Düsseldorf.

Nagy, A. 1990 Nationale Varianten der deutschen Hochsprache und die Behandlung im Deutschunterricht des Auslandes. *Grazer Arbeiten zu DaF und Deutsch in Österreich* 1/90; 9–16.

Naumann, C.L. 1989 Gesprochenes Deutsch und Orthographie. Linguistische und didaktische Studien zur Rolle der gesprochenen Sprache in System und Erwerb der Rechtschreibung. Habilitationsschrift, Frankfurt-on-Main.

Nelde, P. 1979 (ed.) *Deutsch als Muttersprache in Belgien*. Wiesbaden.

Nerius, D. 1975 *Untersuchungen zu einer Reform der deutschen Orthographie*. Berlin.

Nerius, D. and J. Scharnhorst 1977 Sprachwissenschaftliche Grundlagen einer Reform der deutschen Rechtschreibung. In Ising 1977; 156–94.

Neske, F. and I. 1972 *Wörterbuch englischer und amerikanischer Ausdrücke in der deutschen Sprache.* Munich.

Neuland, E. 1975 *Sprachbarrieren oder Klassensprach? Untersuchungen zum Sprachverhalten im Vorschulalter.* Frankfurt-on-Main.

1987 Spiegelungen und Gegenspiegelungen. *ZGL* 15; 58–82.

Neuregelung 1989 *Zur Neuregelung der deutschen Rechtschreibung.* Mannheim.

Neustupný, J. 1968 Some general aspects of 'language' problems and 'language' policy in developing societies. In J.A. Fishman, C.A. Ferguson and J. Das Gupta (eds.), *Language Problems of Developing Nations.* New York; 285–94.

1978 *Post-structural approaches to language: language theory in a Japanese context.* Tokyo.

Newton, G. 1979 *Einige Gedanken über Sprache und Geschäft. Dialektologie Heute: Festschrift für Hélène Palgen.* Luxembourg; 49–64.

1993 Allophonic variation in Luxemburgish palatal and alveolar-palatal fricatives: discussion of an areal survey taken in 1979. In J. Flood, P. Salmon, O. Sayce and C. Wells (eds.), *'Das unsichtbare Band der Sprache'. Studies in German language and linguistic history in memory of Leslie Seiffert* (= *Stuttgarter Arbeiten zur Germanistik* Vol. 280). Stuttgart; 627–56.

Newton, G., F. Hoffmann, J.-P. Hoffmann, C. Russ and H. Klees (forthcoming) *Luxembourg and Letzebuergesch: Language and communication at the crossroads of Europe.* Oxford.

Noelle, E. and E.P. Neumann 1967 *Jahrbuch der öffentlichen Meinung.* Allensbach.

1974 *Jahrbuch der öffentlichen Meinung.* Allensbach.

Noelle-Neumann, E. 1977 *Allensbacher Jahrbuch der Demoskopie 1977.* Vienna.

Nothdurft, W. 1992 Medizinische Kommunikation: geschlossene Diskurssysteme. *DS* 3/92, 193–206.

Nüssler, O. 1979 Das Sprachreinigungsgesetz. In P. Braun (ed.), *Fremdwortdiskussion.* Munich; 186–9.

Oevermann, U. 1970 *Sprache und soziale Herkunft: eine Beitrag zur Analyse schichtenspezifischer Sozialisationsprozesse und ihrer Bedeutung für den Schulerfolg.* Frankfurt-on-Main.

Oksaar, E. 1976 *Berufsbezeichnungen im heutigen Deutsch* (=*Sprache der Gegenwart* 25). Düsseldorf.

Opie, I. and P. 1959/1967 *The lore and language of schoolchildren.* Oxford (1st and 2nd editions).

Ortner, L. 1982 *Wortschatz der Pop-/Rockmusik.* Düsseldorf.

Oschlies, W. 1981 Ich glaub', mich nammt ein Rotkehlchen. *Muttersprache* 91; 185–95.

1989 *Würgende und wirkende Wörter – Deutschsprechen in der DDR.* Berlin.

1990 *'Wir sind das Volk'.* Cologne.

1993 Business, Wodka stehlen, Beute verkaufen, Erlös versaufen . . . *Muttersprache* 103; 231–48.

Osgood, C., G. Suci and P. Tannenbaum 1957 *The measurement of meaning.* Urbana, Ill.

Österreichisches Wörterbuch 1979. Vienna (35th edition).

1985 Vienna 36th edition.

1990 Vienna 37th edition.

Ott, J. and M. Philipp 1993 Dialekt und Standardsprache im Elsaß und im germanophonen Lotheringen. *Deutsche Sprache* 21; 1–21.

Pädagogische Hochschule Zwickau. 1991 *Zum Sprachgebrauch unter dem Zeichen von Hammer, Zirkel und Ährenkranz.* Zwickau.

Panther, K.U. 1981 Einige typische indirekte sprachliche Handlungen im wissenschaftlichen Diskurs. In Bungarten (1981); 231–60.

Pauwels, A. 1987 Language in transition: a study of the title 'Ms' in contemporary Australian society. In A. Pauwels (ed.), *Women and language in Australian society.* Sydney; 129–54.

Pelster, T. 1966 *Die Politische Rede in Western und Osten Deutschland* (=*Wirkendes Wort*, 14. Beiheft). Düsseldorf.

1981 Deutsch im geteilten Deutschland. *Muttersprache* 91; 121–44.

Perdue, C. 1994 (ed.) *Adult language acquisition: crosslinguistic perspectives.* 2 vols. Cambridge.

Perdue, C. and W. Klein 1993 *Utterance structures.* Amsterdam.

Platt, J. and H. Weber 1980 *English in Malaysia and Singapore: status, features, functions.* Kuala Lumpur.

Plenzdorf, U. 1973 *Die neuen Leiden des jungen W.* Rostock/Frankfurt-on-Main.

Pollak, W. 1992 *Was halten die Österreicher von ihrem Deutsch?* Vienna: Institut für Sozio-Semiotische Studien.

Pomm, H. P., U. Mewes and H. Schüttler 1974 Die Entwicklung der Rechtschreibleistung von Schulkindern unter Berücksichtigung von Reform. In August 1974; 59–78.

Pörksen, U. 1984 'Abi Nadek' oder: Wer erfindet die Jugend? In Pörksen and Weber 1984, 11–54.

Pörksen, U. and H. Weber 1984 *Spricht die Jugend eine andere Sprache?* Heidelberg.

Porsch, P. 1992 Alltag – Alltagsbewußtsein – Sprache. In Lerchner 1992a; 189–202.

Posner, R. 1991 Der polyglotte Dialog. *Sprachreport* 3/91; 6–10.

Projektteam 'Sprache und Vorurteil'. 1989 Wir sind alle unschuldige Täter. *WLG* 44. *WLG* 44.

Pusch, L.F. 1980 Das Deutsche als Männersprache – Diagnose und Therapievorschläge. *LB* 69; 59–74.

1984 *Das Deutsche als Männersprache.* Frankfurt.

1985 Frauen entpatrifizieren die Sprache. In Hellinger 1985a; 23–47.

Pusch, L.F., M. Hellinger, S. Trömel-Plötz and I. Guentherodt 1980–1 Richtlinien zur Vermeidung sexistischen Sprachgebrauchs. *LB* 69; 15–21.

Putschke, W., W.H. Veith and P.O. Wiesinger 1989 (eds.) *Dialektgeographie und Dialektologie. Festschrift für Günter Bellmann.* Stuttgart.

Radtke, I. 1978 Drei Aspekte der Dialektdiskussion. In U. Ammon (ed.), *Grundlagen einer dialektorientierten Sprachdidaktik: theoretische und empirische Beiträge zu einem vernachlässigten Schulproblem*. Weinheim; 13–32.

Ratholb, U., G. Schmid and G. Heiß 1990 (eds.) *Österreich und Deutschlands Größe. Ein schlampiges Verhältnis*. Salzburg.

Räthzel, N. 1992 Zur Bedeutung von Asylpolitik und neuen Rassismen bei der Reorganisierung der Deutschland. In Butterwegge and Jäger 1992; 213–29.

Reich, H.H. 1968 *Sprache der Politik*. Munich.

Reichert, A. 1983 *Schweizer Wörterbuch für Primarschulen*. Zurich.

Reid, E. and H. Reich 1992 (eds). *Breaking the boundaries*. Clevedon.

Reiffenstein, I. 1973 Österreichisches Deutsch. In A. Haslinger (ed.), *Deutsch heute*. Munich.

1977 Sprachebene und Sprachwandel im österreichischen Deutsch der Gegenwart. In H. Kolb and H. Lauffer (eds.), *Sprachliche Interferenz: Festschrift für Werner Betz*. Tübingen; 159–74.

1983 Deutsch in Österreich. In Reiffenstein *et al.* 1983; 15–27.

Reiffenstein, I., *et al.* 1983 (eds.) *Tendenzen, Formen und Strukturen der deutschen Standardsprache nach 1945. Vier Beiträge zum Deutsch in Österreich, der Schweiz, der Bundesrepublik Deutschland und der Deutschen Demokratischen Republik*. Marburg.

Reiher, R. 1993 Das 'Zu-sich-selber-kommen des Menschen'. In Reiher and Läzer (1993), 147–60.

Reiher, R. and R. Läzer 1993 *Wer spricht das wahre Deutsch?* Berlin.

Rein, K.L. 1983 Bestimmende Faktoren für den variierenden Sprachgebrauch des Dialektsprechers. In Besch *et al.* 1982–3; 1443.

Rein, K.L. and M. Scheffelmann-Meyer 1975 Funktion und Motivation des Gebrauchs von Dialekt und Hochsprache im Bayerischen. *ZDL* 42, 3; 257–90.

Reitemeier, U. 1994 'Hat jeder zu wissen, wo die Heimat ist.' *Sprachreport* 1/94; 12–13.

Reitmajer, V. 1975 Schlechte Chancen ohne Hochdeutsch. *Muttersprache* 85; 310–24.

Resch, G. 1974 Soziolinguistisches zur Sprache von Pendlern. *Wiener Linguistische Gazette* 7; 38–47.

Reséndiz, J. Liebe 1991 Woran erkennen sich Ost- und Westdeutsche? In Welke, Sauer and Glück 1991; 127–40.

Rieck, B.O. and I. Senft 1978 Situation of foreign workers in the Federal Republic. In Dittmar *et al.* 1978; 85–98.

Riekhoff, H. von and H. Neuhold 1993 *Unequal partners*. Boulder.

Riemschneider, E. 1963 *Veränderungen in der deutschen Sprache in der sowjetischbesetzten Zone seit 1945 (= Wirkendes Wort*, 4. Beiheft). Düsseldorf.

Ris, R. 1979 Dialekte und Einheitssprache in der deutschen Schweiz. *IJSL* 21; 41–62.

Rittenhauer, G. 1980 Österreichische Lektoren in aller Welt tätig. *Rot Weiß Rot* 28, 1; 22.

Rizzo-Baur, H. 1962 *Die Besonderheiten der deutschen Schriftsprache in Österreich und Südtirol.* Mannheim.

Robinson, W.P. 1965 The elaborated code in working-class language. *Language and Speech* 8; 243–52.

Roche, R. 1973 Sprachliche Beobachtung bei der Lektüre der 'Prager Volkszeitung'. In M. Hellmann, *Zum öffentlichen Sprachgebrauch in der Bundesrepublik Deutschland und in der DDR.* Düsseldorf; 293–330.
1991 Nach Tische liest man's anders. *Muttersprache* 101; 297–307.

Rogerson, M. 1992 How well do the last 3 editions of the Österreichisches Wörterbuch reflect the nature of the Austrian variety of German? B.A. (Hons.) thesis, Monash University.

Rohrer, C. 1973 *Der Konjunktiv im gesprochenen Schweizer Hochdeutschen.* Frauenfeld.

Römer, R. 1968 *Die Sprache der Anzeigenwerbung* (= *Sprache der Gegenwart* 4). Düsseldorf.

Roth. K.H. 1978 *'Deutsch'. Prolegomena zur neueren Wortgeographie* (=*Münchner germanistischer Beiträge* 18). Munich.

Rowley, A. 1988 Zum Genitiv der ganz besonderen Typ. *Muttersprache* 98; 58–68.

Rucktäschel, A. 1972 *Sprache und Gesellschaft.* Munich.

Rumelhart, D.E. 1975 Notes on a schema for stories. In D.G. Bobrow and A. Collins (eds.), *Representation and understanding.* New York; 211–36.

Ruoff, A. 1973 *Grundlagen und Methoden der Untersuchung gesprochener Sprache.* Tübingen.

Russ, C. 1987 Language and society in German Switzerland. Multilingualism, diglossia and variation. In Russ and Volkmar 1987; 94–121.
1990 (ed.) *German dialects.* London.

Russ, C. and C. Volkmar 1987 (eds.) *Sprache und Gesellschaft in deutschsprachigen Ländern.* York.

Salinger, J. 1951 *Catcher in the rye.* London.

Sapir, E. 1927 *Language.* New York.

Saunders, G. 1988 *Bilingual children from birth to teens.* Clevedon.

SBZ von A bis Z 1966 Bonn.

Schader, B. 1989 Probleme der deutschen Rechtschreibung und ihre Neuregelung (Rostock 10–15.10.1988). *DS* 1/89, 87–94.

Schädlich, H.-J. 1992 (ed.) *Aktenkundig.* Berlin.

Schäffner, C. 1992 Sprache des Umbruchs und ihre Übersetzung. In Burckhardt and Fritzsche 1992; 135–53.

Schegloff, E.A., G. Jefferson and H. Sacks 1974 A simplest systematics for the organisation of turn-taking for conversation. *Language* 50; 696–735.

Scheidweiler, G. 1988 Glanz und Elend des Luxemburgischen. *Muttersprache* 98; 226–54.

Schenker, W. 1978 *Sprachliche Mannieren – eine sprachsoziologische Erhebung im Raum Trier und Eiffel.* Basel.

Scheuringer, H. 1988 Powidltatschkerl oder Die kakanische Sicht aufs Österreichische. *Jahrbuch für internationale Germanistik* 1988/1; 63–70.

1990 Bayerisches Bairisch und österreichisches Bairisch. *Germanistische Linguistik* 101–3; 361–81.

1992 Deutsches Volk und deutsche Sprache. *Muttersprache* 102; 218–29.

Schiffman, H.E. 1993 Language policy and power. *IJSL* 103; 115–48.

Schildt, J. 1976 *Abriß der Geschichte der deutschen Sprache.* Berlin.

Schiller, J.C. F. v. *Musenalmanach für 1797.* Leipzig.

Schirmer, H. 1993 Deutsche Kulturpolitik und Ziele der Sprachförderung. In Born and Stickel 1993; 127–36.

Schläpfer, R. 1979 Schweizerhochdeutsch und Binnendeutsch. Zur Problematik der Abgrenzung und Berücksichtigung schweizerischen und binnendeutschen Sprachgebrauchs in einem Wörterbuch für Schweizer Schüler. In A. Löffler, K. Pestalozzi and M. Stern (eds.), *Standard und Dialekt. Festschrift für Heinz Rupp.* Berne; 151–63.

Schläpfer, R., J.Gutzweiler and B. Schmid 1991 *Das Spannungsfeld zwischen Mundart und Standardsprache in der deutschen Schweiz.* Aarau.

Schlieben-Lange, B. and H. Weydt 1978 Für eine Pragmatisierung der Dialektologie. *ZGL* 63; 257–82.

Schlobinski, P. 1982 Divided city – divided language? *Sociolinguistic Newsletter* 13(2).

1985 *Stadtsprache Berlin.* Berlin.

1989 Frau Meier hat Aids, Herr Tropfmann hat Herpes, was wollen Sie einsetzen? In Januschek and Schlobinski 1989; 1–34.

Schlobinski. P. and U. Blank 1985 *Sprachbetrachtung: Berlinisch. Ein Arbeitsbuch für den Deutschunterricht ab der 10. Klasse.* Berlin.

Schlobinski, P., G. Kohl and I. Ludewigt 1993 *Jugendsprache.* Opladen.

Schlobinski, P. and I. Wachs 1983 Forschungsprojekt 'Stadtsprache Berlin'. Sprachsoziologische Fragestellungen in einer Großstadt. *Deutsche Sprache*, 3; 261–7.

Schlomann, F.W. 1980 Trotzkisten – Europäische Arbeiterpartei – 'Maoisten'! *Aus Politik und Zeitgeschichte: Beilage zu Parlament.* B27/80; 5 July 1980; 12–28.

Schlosser, H.D. 1981 Die Verwechslung der deutschen Nationalsprache mit einer lexikalischen Teilmenge. *Muttersprache* 91; 145–56.

1989 Die Sprachentwicklung der DDR im Vergleich zur Bundesrepublik Deustschland. In M. Hättich and P.D. Pfitzner (eds.), *Nationalsprachen und europäische Gemeinschaft. Probleme am Beispiel der deutschen, französischen und englischen Sprache.* Munich; 36–52.

1990 Das Ende der 'Zweisprachigkeit'. In G.Strunk (ed.), *Wiederbegegnungen. Herausforderung an die politische Bildung.* Bonn; 26–39.

1991a Perspektiven des sprachlichen Zusammenwachsens. In Pädagogische Hochschule Zwickau 1991; 133–51.

1991b *Deutsche Teilung, deutsche Einheit und die Sprache der Deutschen. Aus Politik und Zeitgeschichte, Beilage zur Wochenzeitung Das Parlament* B17/91; 13–21.

1992 *Kommunikationsbedingungen und Alltagssprache in der ehemaligen DDR.* Hamburg.

1993a Die Unwörter des Jahres 1992. *Der Sprachdienst* 37; 49–59

1993b Die ins Leere befreite Sprache. *Muttersprache* 103; 219–28.

1993c Sicherheit – made in DDR. *Sprachdienst* 37; 68.

Schloßmacher, M. forthcoming. Die Arbeitssprachen in den Organen der Europäischen Gemeinschaften.

Schluppenhauer, C. and I. Werlen 1983 Stand und Tendenzen in der Domänenverteilung zwischen Dialekt und deutscher Standardsprache. In Besch *et al.* (1982–3); 1411–22.

Schmid, G. 1990. . . . sagen die Deutschen. Annäherung an eine Geschichte des Sprachimperialismus. In Ratholb *et al.* 1990; 23–35.

Schmidt, W. 1972 Thesen zu dem Thema: 'Sprache und Nation'. *Zeitschrift für Phonetik, allgemeine Sprachwissenschaft und Kommunikationsforschung* 25; 448–50.

Schmitt, E.H. 1992 *Interdialektale Verstehbarkeit.* Stuttgart.

Schmitt, P.A. 1985 *Anglizismen in der Fachsprache. Eine pragmatische Studie am Beispiel der Kerntechnik.* Heidelberg.

Schoenthal, G. 1976 *Das Passiv in der deutschen Standardsprache.* Munich.

1985 Sprache und Geschlecht. *DS* 13 (2); 143–85.

Schönbohm, W., J.B. Runge and P. Radunski 1968 *Die herausgeforderte Demokratie.* Mainz.

Schönfeld, H. 1974 Sprachverhalten und Sozialstruktur in einem sozialistischen Dorf der Altmark. In Ising 1974b; 191–283.

1977 Zur Rolle der sprachlichen Existenzformen in der sprachlichen Kommunikation. In Hartung (1977a); 163–208.

1991 Die niederdeutsche Sprache in den Ländern Sachsen-Anhalt und Brandenburg. *Niederdeutsches Jahrbuch* 114; 175–201.

1993 Auch sprachlich beigetreten. In Reiher and Läzer 1993; 187–209.

Schönfeld, H. and J. Donath 1978 *Sprache im sozialistischen Industriebetrieb: Untersuchungen zum Wortschatz bei sozialen Gruppen.* Berlin.

Schönfeld, H. and R. Pape 1981 Existenzformen. In Hartung and Schönfeld 1981; 130–213.

Schräpel, B. 1985 Tendenzen feministischer Sprachpolitik und die Reaktion des Patriarchats. In Hellinger (1985a); 212–30.

Schröder, G. 1972 *Außenpolitik für Deutschland* (Rede auf dem Bundesparteitag der CDU, Wiesbaden, 10 Oktober 1972).

Schumann, J.H. 1978 *The pidginization process: a model of second language acquisition.* Rowley, MA.

Schwarzenbach, R. 1969 *Die Stellung der Mundart in der deutschsprachigen Schweiz.* Frauenfeld.

Schwitalla, J. 1992 Comments on: Margret Senting: Intonation as a contextualization device. In P. Auer and A. Di Luzio (eds.), *The contextualization of language* (= *Pragmatics and Beyond New Series* Vol. 22). Amsterdam/Philadelphia; 259–71.

1994 Die Vergegenwärtigung einer Gegenwelt. In Kallmeyer 1994; 467–509.

Seidel, E. and I. Seidel-Slotty 1961 *Sprachwandel im Dritten Reich: eine kritische Untersuchung faschistischer Einflüsse.* Halle.

Seidelmann, E. 1989 Der Hochrhein als Sprachgrenze. In Putschke *et al.* 1989; 57–88.

Senft, G. 1982 *Sprachliche Varietät und Variation im Sprachverhalten Kaiserslautener Metallarbeiter.* Berne.

Seyfried, G. 1990 *Flucht aus Berlin.* Berlin.

Siebenhaar, B. 1994 Regionale Varianten des Schweizerhochdeutschen. *ZDL* 61; 31–65.

Sieber, P. and H. Sitta 1986 *Mundart und Standardsprache als Problem der Schule.* Aarau. 1988 (ed.) *Mundart und Standardsprache im Unterricht.* Aarau.

Siebs, T. 1969 *Deutsche Aussprache.* Berlin.

Sieburg, H. 1992 *Geschlechtstypischer Dialektgebrauch.* Cologne.

Skudlik, S. 1990 *Sprachen in den Wissenschaften.* Tübingen.

Skutnabb-Kangas, T. 1980. *Languages in the process of cultural assimilation and structural incorporation of linguistic minorities.* Roslyn, VA.

Sluga, W. 1977 Sprachsituation in geschlossenen Anstalten. *Dialekt. Internationale Halbjahresschrift für Mundartdichtung* 1. Vienna; 19–39.

Snow, C.E., R. Van Eeden and P. Muysken 1981 The interactional origins of foreigner talk: municipal employees and foreign workers. *IJSL* 28; 81–92.

Spáčilová, L. 1993 Die österreichische Sprachvariante und der Deutschunterricht an tschechischen Schulen. In Muhr 1993a; 99–107.

Spangenberg, K. 1963 Tendenzen volkssprachlicher Entwicklung in Thüringen. In H. Rosenkranz and K. Spangenberg (eds.), *Sprachsoziologische Studien in Thüringen.* Berlin; 54–85.

Spangenberg, K. and J. Wiese 1974 Sprachwirklichkeit und Sprachverhalten sowie deren Auswirkungen auf Leistungen auf muttersprachlichen Unterricht der Allgemeinbildenden Polytechnischen Oberschule. In Ising 1974b; 285–337.

Spender, D. 1980 *Man-made language.* London.

Spiegel, Der 1978a 'Wer BRD sagt, richtet Unheil an.' *Der Spiegel* 32, 39; 13 November 1978; 36–44.

1978b Etwas anderes als sex. *Der Spiegel* 32, 50; 11 November 1978.

1980 Wieder auf Null. *Der Spiegel* 34, 8, 11 February 1980; 41–6.

1981 'Sagen Sie gerne du zu mir.' *Der Spiegel* 35, 53; 28 December 1981; 34–41.

Der Spiegel. 1989 Grammatischer Phallus. *Der Spiegel* 43, 7, February 1989; 80–5.

Steger, H. 1971 (ed.). Soziolinguistik. In *Sprache und Gesellschaft* (= *Sprache der Gegenwart* 13). Düsseldorf; 9–44.

Stellmacher, D. 1977 *Studien zur gesprochenen Sprache in Niedersachsen* (= *Deutsche Dialektographie* Vol. 82). Marburg.

1987 *Wer spricht Platt? Zur Lage des Niederdeutschen heute.* Leer.

Sternberger, D., G. Storz and W.E. Süsskind 1945 Aus dem Wörterbuch des Unmenschen 1945–8. In *Die Wandlung,* 1957. Hamburg.

Stevenson, P. 1990 Political culture and intergroup relations in pluricentric Switzerland. *JMMD* 11; 227–55.

1993 The German language and the construction of national identities. In J. L. Flood, P. Salmon, O. Sayce and C. Wells (eds.), *'Das unsichtbare Band der Sprache.' Studies in German language and linguistic history in memory of Leslie Seiffert.* Stuttgart; 333–56.

Stickel, G. 1988 Beantragte staatliche Regelung zur 'sprachlichen Gleichbehandlung'. *ZGL* 16; 330–55.

Stölting, W. 1975 Wie die Ausländer sprechen. Eine jugoslawische Familie. *LiLi* 5, 18; 54–67.

1978 Teaching German to immigrant children. In Dittmar *et al.* (1978); 99–109.

1980 *Die Zweisprachigkeit jugoslawischer Schüler in der Bundesrepublik.* Wiesbaden.

Stosch, S. von 1993 Mich interessiert nicht, wie viele es in Auschwitz waren. *Wochenpost* 49; 2 December 1993; 6.

Straßner. E. 1983 Rolle und Ausmaß dialektalen Sprachgebrauchs in den Massenmedien in der Werbung. In Besch *et al.* (1993); 1509–25.

Strauß, F.J. 1980 *Mit aller Kraft für Deutschland* (Rede vor dem CSU-Parteitag am 29. September 1979 in München). Cologne.

Stroh, F. 1952 *Handbuch der germanischen Philologie.* Berlin.

Stubkjær, F.T. 1993 Zur Reihenfolge von Verbformen des Schlußfeldes im österreichischen Deutsch. In Muhr 1993a; 39–52.

Studer, E. 1963 Zur schweizerischen Orthographiekonferenz. *Neue Zürcher Zeitung,* 26 October 1963; 4.

Süsskind, W.E. 1968 Gedanken zur Sprachpflege. In Hugo Moser 1968; 191–203.

Swiss Report 1991 *Sprachliche Gleichbehandlung von Frau und Mann in der Gesetzes- und Verwaltungssprache. Bericht einer interdepartmentalen Arbeitsgruppe der Bundesverwaltung.* Berne: Schweizerische Bundeskanzlei.

Taeschner, T. 1983 *The sun is feminine.* Berlin.

Tages-Anzeiger-Magazin. 1980 'Bio-logisch'. *Tages-Anzeiger-Magazin* 19; 10 May 1980; 6–14.

Tatzreiter, H. 1978 Norm und Varietät in Ortsmundarten, *ZDL* 44; 133–48.

Taylor, B. 1978 German as a source of American prestige forms entering Australian English. *Talanya* 5; 1–4.

'Thaddäus Troll' (= H. Bayer) 1970 *Deutschland deine Schwaben.* Reinbeck bei Hamburg.

Thierse, W. 1993 'Sprich, damit ich dich sehe'. In Born and Stickel 1993; 114–26.

Thomas, P. 1979 Der BRF – die Rundfunkstimme im Grenzland. In Nelde (1979); 259–62.

1992 Musterbeispiel für Europa. Belgiens Umgang mit seiner deutschsprachigen Minderheit. *Sprachreport* 4/92; 1–2.

Thorne, B. and N. Henley 1975 (eds.). *Language and sex: difference and dominance.* Rowley, MA.

Townson, M. 1984 Nuclear neologisms. In C.V. Russ (ed.), *Foreign influences on German.* Dundee; 88–108.

1992 *Mother tongue and fatherland.* Manchester.

Trömel-Plötz, S. 1978a Linguistik und Frauensprache. *LB* 57; 49–68.

1978b Zur Semantik psychoanalytischer Interventionen. *Studium Linguistik* 5; 52–66.

Trudgill, P. 1974 *The social differentiation of English in Norwich.* Cambridge.

Turner, I. 1969 *Cinderella dressed in Yella.* Melbourne.

Urbánova, A. 1966 Zum Einfluß des amerikanischen Englisch auf die deutsche Gegenwartssprache. *Muttersprache* 76; 91–114.

Van den Branden, L. 1956 *Het Streven naar Verheerlijking, Zuivering en Opbouw van het Nederlands in de 16de Eeuw.* Gent.

Van Dijk, T. 1977 *Text and Context.* London.

1987 *Communicating racism.* Newbury Park.

1992. Subtiler Rassismus in westlichen Parlamenten. In Butterwegge and Jäger 1992; 200–12

Vandermeeren, S. 1992 Dialektvitalität links und rechts der belgischen Sprachgrenze. *Language Problems and Language Planning* 17(3); 201–24.

Veith, W.H. 1983 Die Sprachvariation in der Stadt. *Muttersprache* 93; 82–91.

Verdoodt, A. 1968 *Zweisprachige Nachbarn.* Vienna/Stuttgart.

Viereck, K. 1986 The influence of English on Austrian German. In Viereck and Bald 1986; 159–77.

Viereck, W. 1980a (ed.). *Studien zum Einfluß der englischen Sprache auf das Deutsche.* Tübingen.

1980b Empirische Untersuchungen insbesondere zum Verständnis und Gebrauch von Anglizismen im Deutschen. In Viereck 1980a; 237–321.

1986 The influence of English on German in the past and in the Federal Republic of Germany. In Viereck and Bald 1986; 107–26.

Viereck, W. *et al.* 1975 Wie Englisch ist unsere Pressesprache? *Grazer Linguistische Studien* 2; 205–26.

Viereck, W. and W.-D. Bald 1986 *English in contact with other languages.* Budapest.

Von Donat, M. 1993 Der Kommunikationsstreß in den EG-Institutionen. In Born and Stickel 1993; 77–87.

Von Normann, R. 1991 *Das treffende Fremdwort.* Frankfurt.

Von Polenz P. 1954 *Die altenburgische Landschaft. Untersuchungen zur ostthüringischen Sprach- und Siedlungsgeschichte.* Tübingen.

1963 *Funktionsverben im heutigen Deutsch.* Düsseldorf.

1981 Über die Jargonisierung von Wissenschaftssprache und wider die Deagentivierung. In Bungarten 1981; 85–110.

1988 'Binnendeutsch' oder plurizentrische Sprachkultur? *ZGL* 16; 198–218.

1990 Nationale Varianten der deutschen Sprache. *IJSL* 83; 5–38.

1993 Die Sprachrevolte in der DDR im Herbst 1989. *ZGL* 21; 127–49.

Wachau, S. 1989 'nicht so verschlüsselt und verschleimt!' In Januschek and Schlobinski 1989; 69–96.

Wagner, G. 1992 Sprachpolitik in Österreich. In De Cillia and Anzengruber 1993; 45–60.

Wahrig, G. 1968 *Deutsches Wörterbuch.* Gütersloh.

Walter, M. 1978 Englische Wörter im Wortschatz deutscher Jugendlichen. Staatsexamensarbeit. University of Stuttgart.

Wardhaugh, R. 1986 *An introduction to sociolinguistics*. Oxford.

Watts, R. 1988 Language, dialect and national identity in Switzerland. *Multilingua* 7; 313–34.

1989 Relevance and relational work: linguistic politeness as politic behavior. *Multilingua* 8; 131–66.

1991 Linguistic minorities and language conflict in Europe: learning from the Swiss experience. In Coulmas 1991; 75–101.

Watts, R. and F. Andres 1993. English as a lingua franca in Switzerland: myth or reality? In I. Werlen (ed.), *Bulletin CILA 58, special issue on 'Schweizer Soziolinguistik – Soziolinguistik der Schweiz'*; 109–27.

Weber, H. 1984 Du hast keine Chance. In Pörksen and Weber 1984; 59–131.

Weigel, H. 1968 *O du mein Österreich*. Munich.

Weisgerber, L. 1962 *Grundzüge der inhaltbezogenen Grammatik*. Düsseldorf.

Weisgerber, B. 1985 Rechtschreiben in Grund- und Hauptschule. In R. Hoberg (ed.), *Rechtschreibung im Beruf*. Tübingen; 43–50.

Welke, K., W.W. Sauer and H.Glück 1991 (eds.) *Die deutsche Sprache nach der Wende* (= *Germanistische Linguistik* 110–11).

Werlen *et al.* 1992 *Zweisprachigkeit im Kanton Wallis*. Brig/Berne.

Whinnom, K. 1971 Linguistic hybridization and the 'special case' of pidgins and creoles. In D. H. Hymes (ed.), *Pidginization and creolization of languages*. Cambridge; 91–116.

Whorf, B.L. 1956 *Language, thought and reality*. Cambridge, MA.

Wiesinger, P. 1980a Zum Wortschatz im 'österreichischen Wörterbuch'. *Österreich in Geschichte und Literatur* 24; 367–97.

1980b 'Sprache', 'Dialekt' und 'Mundart' als sachliches und terminologisches Problem. *ZDL*-Beiheft 26; 177–98.

1988a (ed.) *Das österreichische Deutsch*. Vienna.

1988b Die deutsche Sprache in Österreich. In Wiesinger 1988a; 9–54.

1990 Standardsprache und Mundarten in Österreich. In G. Stickel (ed.), *Deutsche Gegenwartssprache. Tendenzen und Perspektiven* (= *Jahrbuch des Instituts für deutsche Sprache 1989*). Berlin/New York; 218–43.

1994 Das österreichische Deutsch – eine Varietät der deutschen Sprache. *Terminologie et Traduction* 1; 41–59.

Wodak, R., F. Menz and J. Laluschek 1989 *Sprachbarrieren*. Vienna.

Wodak-Leodolter, R. 1980 Problemdarstellungen in gruppentherapeutischen Situationen. In K. Ehlich (ed.), *Erzählen im Alltag*. Frankfurt-on-Main; 179–208.

Wodak-Leodolter, R. and W. Dressler 1978 Phonological variation in colloquial Viennese. *Michigan Germanic Studies* 4, 1; 30–66.

Wolf, N.R. 1994 Österreichisches zum Österreichischen Deutsch. *ZDL* 61; 66–76.

Wolfsberger, H. 1967 *Mundartwandel im 20. Jahrhundert, dargestellt an Ausschnitten aus dem Sprachleben der Gemeinde Stäfa*. Frauenfeld.

Wörner, M. 1972 *Friedenspolitik in Sicherheit und Freiheit* (Rede auf dem Bundesparteitag der CDU, Wiesbaden, 10. Oktober 1972).

Ylönen, S. 1992 Probleme deutsch–deutscher Kommunikation. *Sprachreport* 2–3/92; 17–20.

Yngve, V. 1960 A model and an hypothesis for language structure. *Proceedings of the American Philosophical Society* 104; 444–66.

Zandvoort, R.W. 1964 *English in the Netherlands: a study in linguistic infiltration.* Groningen.

ZDF-Politikbarometer 1985 Repräsentative Bevölkerungsumfrage, Mai 1985.

Zehetner, L. 1985 *Das bairische Dialektbuch.* Munich.

Zimmer, R. 1977 Vergleichende Betrachtungen zum deutsch–französischen Kontaktbereich in der Schweiz, im Elsaß und in Luxemburg. *ZDL* 44; 145–57.

Zoller, W. 1974 Meinungen zur Rechtschreibung und Rechtschreibreform: Ergebnisse einer Umfrage. In August 1974; 91–116.

SUBJECT INDEX

address system in German 112, 122, 126, 128, 130–7, 139–40, 197

age 12, 13, 14, 17, 18, 19, 39, 77
and attitudes to spelling reform 182
and communication rules 131, 132
and use of dialect 42, 96, 99, 101, 102, 103, 104, 105, 106, 107, 108, 109, 111, 112, 118
and use of English transference 72, 82, 205, 208, 210–11, 215–16, 217
youth register 72, 148–53, 205

Austria 3, 4, 6, 7, 8, 11, 15, 24, 29, 30, 31–41, 42, 49, 58, 61, 63, 64, 104, 105, 106, 109, 118, 122–5, 129, 136, 139, 146, 152, 158–60, 161–2, 194, 200, 206, 210, 211, 212, 215, 216, 217
Austrian Standard German 21, 23, 24, 25, 26, 30, 32–41, 47, 48, 49, 57, 62, 64, 67, 92, 95, 114, 118, 122–5, 136, 138, 139, 152, 206, 215
grammar 35, 39–41, 123, 178
lexicon 25, 26, 30, 33, 34, 35, 38–9, 62, 63, 65, 215
phonology 29, 37–8
transference 39
dialects 21, 28, 29, 33, 35, 40, 90, 91, 92, 93, 94, 95, 101, 102, 103, 105, 106, 108, 109, 113–14, 117, 118
education 33, 201
language planning 11, 24, 25, 34, 35, 64, 65, 176–7, 181, 182, 184, 185
literature 35, 62, 113, 125
media 24, 25, 30, 32, 62, 162, 189–90, 206, 208, 211, 216

national identity 4, 31–2, 35, 36, 41, 64, 114
political language 158–60, 161, 162, 163

Austrian Standard German *see* **Austria**
Aussiedler 198, 199

communication barriers
dialect 116, 117, 185, 194
Fachsprache 185, 191–2, 199
foreigner talk 197–8
media 186–92
of guest workers 194–8, 199
orthography 181, 182
social variation 187, 189, 191
syntax 187, 191
transference 80, 191, 216
communication patterns *see* Ch.5

deficit hypothesis 192–4
dialects 21, 23, 27, 28, 58, 89–119, 175
age and use of 42, 96, 99, 101, 102, 103, 104, 105, 106, 107, 108, 109, 111, 112, 118
as protest language 112, 113, 119
attitudes to 44, 45, 46, 100, 101, 104, 105, 107, 108, 109, 111, 112, 116, 117–18
categorisation of 27, 28
communication barriers 116, 117, 185, 194
decline of 'local' dialect 99, 104, 105–10, 112, 113, 118
domains of use 35, 43, 44, 45, 50, 60, 96, 97, 99, 100, 106, 110, 112, 114, 115–16, 118, 177

NAME INDEX